THE QUÉBEC ESTABLISHMENT

THE QUÉBEC ESTABLISHMENT

The Ruling Class
and
The State

by Pierre Fournier

BLACK ROSE BOOKS   Montréal

BLACK ROSE BOOKS NO. F. 30

Hardcover — ISBN: 0-919618-28-6
Paperback — ISBN: 0-919618-27-8

Canadian Cataloguing in Publication Data

Fournier, Pierre, 1944-
    The Québec establishment

    Bibliography: p.
    ISBN 0-919618-28-6 bd.
    ISBN 0-919618-27-8 pa.

1. Corporations — Québec (Province). 2. Industry and state — Québec. (Province). 3. Québec (Province) — Economic policy. I. Title.

HN110.Q8F68   338.7'4'09714   C77-000105-X

Cover Design: Michael Carter
Cover Photograph: Olivia Rovinesau

BLACK ROSE BOOKS LTD.
3934 rue St. Urbain
Montréal H2W 1V2, Québec

Printed and bound in Québec, Canada

CONTENTS

Appendices:

LIST OF TABLES

LIST OF CHARTS

FOREWORD

THOSE WHO PARTICIPATE actively in attempting to bring about political and social change know very well that forces other than the general will shape politics in this country. Most of those who are passive feel intuitively that some are more equal than others in our society. This book is an attempt to document some of the "suspicions" which I had about business-government relations in the idealistic and frustrating sixties. It is largely the result of the information and analysis contained in the PhD thesis which I wrote at the department of Political economy of the University of Toronto. The thesis dealt with the influence of business in Québec politics and was researched and written between 1971 and 1975.

The main shortcoming of this study is the lack of a strong theoretical framework. When this project was conceived, I was still under the influence of the pluralist orthodoxy of McGill University and was not well enough acquainted with the major marxist contributions to the study of power. My thesis was thus conceived from an "anti-pluralist" or elitist perspective, perhaps in the tradition of John Porter's *The Vertical Mosaic*. The principal strength of the final product, I believe, is that it provides substantial amounts of data on business-government relations in Québec in the 1960 to 1974 period. It illustrates one of the aspects of monopoly capitalism which has received relatively scant treatment — the increasing fusion of business and governmental elites. It also provides data on the ability of business to use the State to its advantage and at the expense of other social classes.

I wish to thank Professor Paul Fox, my thesis director and Professors F. W. Peers and W. K. Bryden, all of the department of political economy at the University of Toronto, for their invaluable advice in preparing this study.

Pierre Fournier
Montréal, 1976

INTRODUCTION

IN THE DECADE that brought us Watergate, the oil cartel, the illegal activities of multinational corporations and, closer to home, "the dredging scandal" and "the skyshops affair", no elaborate justification is needed to study a country's business and political establishment. In one way or the other, most of these events, the bribes, political contributions, kickbacks and corruption, have involved the relationship between business and government. In the late sixties, when this manuscript got off the ground, most claims that an establishment existed, let alone exercised enormous political and economic power, and that business-government relations were anything less than above board, would have been greeted with a degree of scepticism. In the cynical and fatalistic post-Watergate era, the benefit of the doubt has shifted. In a few short years, much has become believable, possible and even likely.

Unfortunately, the level of political analysis and consciousness which has evolved from these events has not gone much beyond understandable cynicism, and has, by and large, remained superficial. There has been a strong tendency, encouraged of course by the political and economic leadership, to place the blame on the Richard Nixon's of this world, and a few unscrupulous businessmen and government officials. Beyond the avalanche of scandals and the headlines, which are, to use a tired cliché, only the tip of the iceberg, there is a clearly identifiable system of power. An analysis of this system provides an explanation as to why these things happen and shows that they are an integral part of a permanent ongoing process rather than the result of the devious behaviour of particularly self-serving individuals.

It is well known that the role of the State has increased substantially under monopoly capitalism. As a result of economic necessity the State has had to intervene more and more actively to attempt to appease the crisis of capitalism and to insure the continued development and survival of private business. As a result, the relationship between the business establishment and the political directorate has become increasingly incestuous and has assumed a somewhat more frantic nature than in the years of the apogee of capitalism. The sheer size and economic clout of multinational corporations have also contributed to making their power more visible and tangible than ever before.

This book presents an analysis of the political power and influence of Québec's business establishment. It is not an attempt to catalogue the scandals which have plagued Québec politics in recent years, but rather an examination of the relationship between business and government. Nor is this book a Québec version of Peter Newman's *The Canadian Establishment*. Newman deals with the lives, habits, idiosyncrasies and tastes of the individuals who presently constitute the Canadian business elite. This study emphasizes business institutions rather than elites, and business is "personalized" only to the extent that it helps to better understand the mechanics of the exercise of power. There are also important differences in emphasis between this book and the two major studies of the Canadian power structure, John Porter's *The Vertical Mosaic* (1965) and Wallace Clement's *The Canadian Corporate Elite* (1975). The latter deal with the various elite groups in Canada in terms of structure, composition, social characteristics and power. Particular attention is devoted to the degree of economic concentration, the economic structure and the corporate elite. Although I deal with some of these aspects as they relate to the Québec situation, particularly in the first three chapters, the main focus is on the nature and importance of the links between business and government and on business involvement and influence in specific policy areas.

In general terms, I intend to challenge the widely held view that capitalist electoral democracies are composed of groups which compete with one another on relatively even terms and that the political sphere or the government acts as a broker or balancer between the various socio-economic groups. In his analysis of the State in western democracies, Ralph Miliband pointed out that this theory, known as "pluralism", still enjoys considerable support. "Most western students of politics", he claimed, "tend to start with the assumption that power, in Western societies, is competitive, fragmented and diffused[1].

More specifically, part I examines the various components which make up Québec's business system of power. It emphasizes the institutional and strategic advantages of the business establishment. Chapter I discusses briefly the political significance of the economic power of corporations. Chapters 2 and 3 examine business institutions and elites and in particular the degree of operational and ideological unity of business. Chapter 4 looks at the part played by business associations in the exercise of influence. Chapter 5 examines the mechanisms and degree of business access to government decision-making structures. It also stresses some of the elements which make up the structural dependence of government on business: party financing, the need for government to borrow on the financial markets and the personnel overlaps and interchanges between government and business. Finally, chapter 6 analyses the corporate elite's control over media and chapter 7 looks at the difficulties of labour groups in their attempts to "counterbalance" business power.

Part II deals with three areas of public policy, economic development, labour and social legislation, and language and education issues, and attempts to determine the extent of business influence in each. In addition to analysing various case studies of specific pieces of legislation, I attempt to measure the degree to which business is satisfied with government policy in each issue area and to determine whether governmental activity has challenged the power of business in these areas. The reader who is interested in a more elaborate discussion of the methodology used in this book should consult Appendix A. The reader will also find a summary and critique of some of the major studies dealing with power and influence.

The main focus of this study is "big business", which is defined as the 100 largest corporations and financial institutions operating in Québec[2]. I will attempt to demonstrate that these institutions, and the individuals who own and manage them, dominate the economic and political life of Québec. Mainly for comparative purposes, consideration is at times given to the smaller and medium-sized business units.

This analysis of business-government relations in Québec concentrates on the period from 1960 to 1974. The nineteen-sixties are significant because they are the starting point for a strong and active provincial government in Québec. As opposed to the largely laissez-faire and paternalistic policies of the Taschereau and Duplessis regimes which governed Québec from 1914 to 1959, the governments of the sixties intervened actively in all fields of public policy: education, labour, and economic development, among others. Since the period also witnessed three changes in government, it became possible to examine the degree of consistency and continuity in business-government relations.

One of the main problems which a study of business influence encounters is the secrecy which often surrounds governmental and business activity. However, since business itself is by far the best and most reliable source for a study of this kind, this study relies primarily on a questionnaire sent to businessmen[3], personal interviews with corporate leaders, and business publications. Sources from outside business include newspapers, government documents and reports, as well as various publications critical of business or representing interests opposed to business, such as union sponsored studies and publications[4].

NOTES

(1) Ralph Miliband: *The State in Capitalist Society*, London: Camelot Press, 1969, p. 2.

(2) Appendix B contains a list of the 100 corporations in question. Appendix D outlines the criteria used to determine the largest business units and also explains why special attention is placed on them.

(3) See Appendix C for a copy of the questionnaire.

(4) Appendix D provides details concerning the methodology and procedures used in the questionnaire and interviews as well as the specific written sources consulted.

PART I

COMPONENTS OF BUSINESS POWER

CHAPTER 1

ECONOMIC POWER
AND THE CORPORATION

ECONOMIC POWER is the major source of business power and, consequently, of business's ability to influence government. The importance of the economic arena in societal terms is widely recognized. Decisions concerning production, distribution of goods and services, the location and volume of investments, the closing, building, or development of plants, the employment structure and the wage level, have a key impact on all levels of society from an economic, political, and social point of view. In the capitalist system, decisions are made autonomously by the private sector. A firm makes decisions on the basis of profitability. It is easy to prove that many decisions made on the basis of an eventual profit are not optimum decisions from the point of view of the needs of the population and the public interest. If this was not the case, the businessmen would spend less effort in their attempt to convince us of their "social responsibility." When public interest coincides with that of the corporation, so much the better. When it does not, the interests of the corporation will supersede it.

One does not have to look too far to measure the impact of an economic system based on profit. Recently I read a book published by the American economist Robert Heilbroner, entitled *In the Name of Profits,* in which the author documents six cases of fraud and conspiracy against public interest by corporations as large as General Motors, B.F. Goodrich and Dow Chemical. It also looks at the recent scandals involving Gulf, Lockheed and ITT. Finally, what can we say about the evolution of the quality of products during the last twenty years. Notwithstanding substantial technological progress, consumers have never had so much difficulty in obtaining satisfaction. Automobiles which lasted seven or eight years in the fifties and sixties do not last more than three or four years.

One should not take seriously those who try to convince us that big business is democratic. The Conseil du Patronat suggested a few years ago that the Québec population owned its corporations through pension funds and insurance policies. Undoubtedly, Insurance companies and other financial intermediaries are an important source of capital

14

for the economy as a whole and they exert, by the same token, a determining influence on industrial development. But it would be absurd to suggest that economic power is in the hands of the small investors or policyholders. All key decisions concerning the utilization of these funds are made by the management of the financial institutions in question, and the latter are accountable to no one.

Another myth, kept alive by business, and which is the foundation for the democratic "pretensions" of private enterprise, is the law of supply and demand. The most modern economists, whatever their political tendencies are, do not believe in the supremacy of the market. A number of factors, internal and external, do influence supply and demand and, in fact paralyse the market economy. On the demand side, it becomes more and more evident that the autonomy and freedom of the consumer is illusory. On one hand, through advertising, business succeeds in manipulating, directing and creating demand. Billions of dollars are spent annually to simulate the unsatisfaction of the individual and to convince him that consumption is happiness. We must also bear in mind that the economic system has its own system of remuneration and that demand is only partially a function of the needs of the individual. Poor people, for example, do not have the necessary resources to satisfy elementary needs with the result that the demand for milk and meat will be lower than the real needs of the population for the goods. The more affluent on the other hand, may create a demand for Mercedes-Benz or electrical toothbrushes. On the supply side, concentration has allowed the most important firms to ignore the discipline of the market and in a large measure to control prices and production.

The decline of the market system created a power vacuum which favored the leaders of the large business concerns. Many observers argue, however, that the power of business is more potential than real. They claim that private economic power is held in check not only by the divisions within business, such as competition between industrial sectors, variety of size and wealth of companies themselves, and political divisions between the leaders of businesses, but also by the political and economic power of governments.[1] They argue that the business system of power is pluralist and for that reason cannot threaten the autonomy of the political system. They also contend that the government is capable of putting sufficient restraints on private economic power and of exercising a significant amount of economic power independent of the private sector.[2]

Despite important changes in the functioning of the economy, the goal of private economic activity has remained the same. Chapter 3 will show, with the support of questionnaire data, that profit-making is still the fundamental motivation of the modern manager and that the claims of business units that they are primarily oriented towards social goals are not supported by fact.

The economic, social, and political impact of the economic decisions made by corporations in the private sector will now be examined briefly. According to Andrew Hacker, the fulcrum of corporate power is the decision about investment:

The uses of capital for investment purposes are, in the final analysis, decided by small handfuls of corporate managers. They decide how much is to be spent: what products are to be made; where they are to be manufactured; and who is to participate in the processes of production. A single corporation can draw up an investment program calling for the expenditure of several billions of dollars on new plants and products. A decision such as this may well determine the quality of life for a substantial segment of society: men and materials will move across continents; old communities will decay and new ones will prosper; tastes and habits will alter; new skills will be demanded, and the education of a nation will adjust itself accordingly; even government will fall into line, providing public services that corporate developments make necessary.[3]

Epstein went a step further by claiming that corporations are, on the whole, largely autonomous in making decisions, and the latter involve minimal governmental interference:

Despite the seeming omnipresence of governmental constraints, corporate managers actually make most of their operating decisions outside the scope of public scrutiny. For example, decisions relating to capital investment, product development, employment, pricing and plant location are, in the main, made by businessmen without the necessity of obtaining any approval from a public agency.[4]

Thus, corporate managers can also wield substantial power over individuals in their capacity as workers and consumers. Epstein noted the "critical importance of the corporation to the life of the individual."[5] The corporation can offer rewards, withhold benefits, or put limits on people's options and opportunities. The impact of the corporation is felt particularly by the white-collar group for they have tended to make the corporation into "the primary focus of personal commitment and identification," and they are also inclined "to identify with the policies and goals of the firm, including its political policies and goals.[6] Hacker further argued that the dependence of the individual on the corporation has had a negative impact on political participation. His claim was based on an analysis of what he called the "propertyless middle class:"

. . . The middle class employee is in no position to be active in politics. He is dependent on his corporate employment; and independent political behavior, he is led to believe, might jeopardize his corporate career . . .[7]

The corporation also has considerable impact on consumption patterns; it no longer simply responds to consumer needs or preferences but also spends increasing amounts of money and energy to mold them. According to Broadbent, the profit motive of the corporation makes it necessary to have a "permanently discontented nation of consumers" and that, to this end, "billions of dollars are spent annually in North America to convince man that it is only by consuming that he will achieve happiness."[8]

Corporate control over investment capital as well as the impact of advertising and publicity on demand and tastes almost certainly reduces the autonomy of the consumer. One cannot but wonder, for example, whether there is a genuine choice between social goods (such as parks, recreation facilities, city malls) and consumer goods, and also between increased wealth and increased leisure. One of the arguments in Galbraith's *The New Industrial State* is that the modern business system has influenced societal values in favour of emphasizing the im-

16

portance of material possessions at the cost of aesthetic and social considerations such as the quality of products and their real contribution to human welfare, or the pollution, noise, and congestion which accompanies their production.

What, then, is the connection between the economic and social power of business and its attempts to exercise political power? The main point is that the political power of business is largely derived from its economic power and that the economic power of the corporation makes government dependent on it. Indeed, since business in a private enterprise economy is responsible for the larger part of industrial and economic activity, the government is often not inclined to espouse policies that are in opposition to the needs of the corporations. The prosperity of the nation, and indirectly the viability of the government, depends in a real sense on corporate decisions. Decisions to build, close, or expand plants, decisions regarding lay-offs and employment, and decisions to invest in research and technological development are made by business and so, in large part, determine the level of well-being in a society.

If business feels threatened by government, it can, at least in the long run, halt its production and distribution of goods and transfer its capital to another country.[9] That this would happen only in extreme circumstances does not alter the fact that a hostile business community could threaten the survival of a government. Miliband showed that the various social democratic or socialist parties that have been elected to power in Europe (like the Popular Front in France in 1936 and the Labour Party in Britain) have, on the whole, not been successful in implementing their policies of reform because of the need to restore "business confidence." Put another way, these governments were so dependent on the economic power of business for the prosperity of the country that they had little leeway to bring in reforms.[10]

Economic power can be a direct source of political power in that political parties depend on money and expertise and in that governments need to borrow substantial amounts of capital on the financial markets. In these and other ways, as chapter 5 will show, business can obtain some benefits from its economic power. Further, part II will make it clear that business is fully conscious of its economic power and does not hesitate to "remind" and sometimes even threaten the government that the prosperity of Québec depends on legislation and attitudes conducive to a sound business climate.

NOTES

(1) See, for example, Arnold Rose, Robert Dahl, *Pluralist Democracy in the United States: Conflict and Consent* (Chicago: Rand McNally and Company, 1967), and Richard Rose, *Politics in England* (Boston: Little, Brown and Company, 1964).

(2) The next two chapters will analyse the validity of these claims and also whether, in the case of Québec, business remains an essentially pluralist system of power. Chapter 10 will examine the role of the Québec government with respect to private economic power.

(3) Andrew Hacker, ed. *The Corporation Take-Over* (New York: Anchor Books, 1965), pp. 9-10.

(4) Edwin Epstein: *The Corporation in American Politics*, Englewood Cliffs, New Jersey, Prentice-Hall, 1969, p. 135.

(5) Epstein, p. 294.

(6) Ibid.

(7) Hacker, p. 23.

(8) Edward Broadbent: *The Liberal Rip-off*, Toronto: New Press, 1970, p. 23.

(9) Milton Mankoff ("Power in Advanced Capitalist Society" *Social Problems*, vol. 17, 1970) argued:

"The capitalist class through its ownership and control over industry, commerce and finance is able potentially to disprut the social fabric if its interests are threatened." He cited the case of Italy in 1920 "when workers seized factories and actually attempted to continue production." The attempt failed because "the industrialists made sure that the workers were unable to procure raw materials, dispose of finished products, or obtain credit" (p. 427).

(10) See Miliband, pp. 97-118.

CHAPTER 2

THE STRUCTURE OF BUSINESS
IN QUÉBEC

THIS CHAPTER and the next will examine how and to what extent the business elite is in a position to exercise economic power. Specifically, I will deal here with some of the elements in the Québec economic structure which are conducive to the operational unity of business. Later on, it will be shown that the structural unity of business is strengthened both by the pattern of interactions of the corporate elite and also by the degree of ideological unity within that elite. The intention is to determine the degree of pluralism within the business system of power. If business is in fact reasonably unified operationally and ideologically, then its power and potential influence are greatly strengthened.

The first point to be made concerns the level of industrial concentration in Québec. Miliband claimed:

> Nothing about the economic organization of advanced countries is more basically important than the increasing domination of key sectors of industrial, financial and commercial life by a relatively small number of giant firms, often interlinked . . .[1]

It is reasonable to assume that the smaller the number of units in the industrial and financial arena, and within industrial groups, the greater are the possibilities of coordination and unity.

As in other advanced countries,[2] Canada has a very high level of concentration. Porter showed, among other things, that the 54 largest companies controlled 44% of Canadian industrial production in 1956.[3] More recent figures[4] indicate that the overall level of concentration in the Canadian economy has been increasing.

The same is true in Québec. Sixty-two corporations control over 50% of industrial production. In each industrial sector, a handful of corporations — from two to 10 — completely dominate production and distribution. Concentration is especially great in heavy industry: chemical products, metals, transportation equipment, for example.[5] A senior executive of the Canadian Manufacturers' Association (Québec sector) estimated at 30 to 40 the number of large and important manufacturing concerns in Québec.[6]

The facts reveal that industrial activity in Québec is dominated by private corporations. Only two of the major companies in the industrial sector are controlled by the state.[7] Sidbec-Dosco, a steel producing company, is owned by the Québec government; Marine Industries, a shipbuilder, is controlled by the General Investment Corporation whose main shareholder is the government. Two more of the major companies are cooperatives distributing agricultural products: the Coopérative Fédérée and the Coopérative Agricole de Granby.

The cooperative sector remains marginal in the Québec economic structure but is developing rapidly. Most of its assets are located in financial institutions, mainly in a network of "caisses populaires," which perform essentially the same functions as banks.[8] Recently, the cooperative movement has entered food retailing through a small network of stores called Cooprix. These have run into some resistance from the private sector. According to the *Financial Post,* "Cooprix's unending crusades on behalf of its members have run into stiff opposition on occasion. Some domestic manufacturers, for example, refuse to service the stores because Cooprix refuses to respect their pre-pricing."[9]

The degree of concentration is only one element of the dominant position held by the larger firms. A few other structural characteristics of modern industry restrict the competitiveness of business and lead to a greater degree of operational unity than is suggested by concentration figures alone. These include the existence of holding corporations which allow a proprietary company to wield effective control over a large number of companies with relatively small amounts of capital; vertical and horizontal integration which characterizes many companies and industrial groups; parent-subsidiary relationships;[10] the ability of large corporations to effectively control the behaviour of small companies; the potentially coordinating role played by financial institutions; and, to some extent, the fact that many companies are foreign-owned. These characteristics will be examined in turn.

The pulp and paper industry is a good example of industrial concentration and also illustrates some of the main features of vertical and horizontal integration. Pulp and paper is a crucial industrial sector in Québec since it employs about 45,000 workers in manufacturing and 18,135 more at the primary level in the forest. The indirect employment generated by the industry approximates 100,000 jobs.[11] The industry accounts for 18% of Québec's total exports, and the value of its annual production in 1970 was $1.3 billion, which represents 40% of total Canadian production. At present, seven corporations control about 90% of Québec's annual pulp and paper production[12] and employ more than two-thirds of the workers in that sector.

Chart 1, which reconstructs ownership ties in the pulp and paper industry, shows how 60 Canadian companies linked with one another and also with 27 foreign companies and 36 corporations belonging to other firms, together own nearly 90% of Canada's newsprint and pulp and paper production. Six of the seven largest Québec companies are part of this closely-knit pulp and paper empire. Only E. B. Eddy, owned by the food conglomerate George Weston Ltd., does not appear on the chart and does not have any share holdings in other paper companies.

The Financial Post explained this development as follows:

The links will be mostly through subsidiaries created to own the giant mills that must now be built to produce pulp and paper economically and competitive-

20

CHART 1

OWNERSHIP TIES IN THE NORTH AMERICAN PULP AND PAPER INDUSTRY[a]

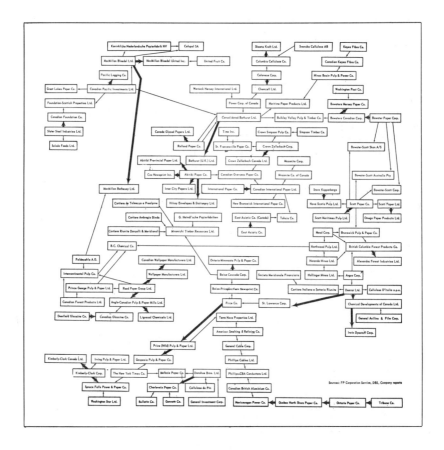

NOTE: Each arrow points to the companies whose shares are owned by the corporation at the tail of the arrow. The thick arrows represent control-holdings of more than 50%. The thin arrows represent holdings of less than 50% but do not necessarily exclude control or influence. The companies with darker perimeters (emphasis added) are the main Quebec producers.

[a] Philip Mathias, "Tighter Links May Alter World Paper Rivalry," *Financial Post*, 17 January 1970.

ly. . . . The growth of technology and marketing psychology make the trend towards communal subsidiaries relentless . . . Some of the advantages of the trend include captive markets which ensure that the mills product will be sold at a steady level.[13]

Pulp and paper companies are linked together in other ways. Domtar, for example, owns 97% of St. Lawrence Corporation which in turn owns 10% of the capital stock of Price Company. While 10% is not sufficient for control, it is safe to say that this pattern of ownership substantially reduces the competition between the two companies.[14] Also, Domtar is controlled by Argus Corporation which controls another large pulp and paper producer, British Columbia Forest Corporation.[15]

Domtar, one of the major pulp and paper producers, is a good example of horizontal and vertical integration. In 1970 it had annual sales of over $500 million and employed more than 18,000 people in some 270 locations in eight provinces. It comprised three divisions, each operating in a different industrial sector: pulp and paper, which was responsible for 67% of its sales, chemical products, and construction materials, representing respectively 14% and 19% of total sales.

This horizontal integration manifests itself at all levels of the company. Domtar Woodland, for example, is a source of raw materials for both the pulp and paper and construction materials divisions. Domtar Fine Paper buys the chemical products it requires for the production of fine paper from Chemical Developments of Canada. Domtar Chemicals and Domtar Pulp and Paper use the same distributor to sell their products.

Domtar is also integrated vertically. Its pulp and paper division, for example, controls the sources of its raw materials and primary transformation (Domtar Woodland for cutting wood and McFadden Lumber, a sawmill), its manufacturing plants (such as Domtar Newsprint, Domtar Packaging, and Domtar Fine Paper), as well as the companies needed for distribution and sales (Domtar Newsprint Sales for North America and Canadian Overseas for overseas sales). Similarly, Domtar Chemicals obtains its raw materials from its Tar and Chemical division, manufactures through Chemical Developments of Canada, and distributes its products, in part, through Canadian Overseas. Integration has many advantages for Domtar, not the least of which is the $30 million of internal sales it achieves annually.[16]

Holding companies are another mechanism by which concentration is increased and accelerated. Some of the main holdings operating in Canada are Argus Corporation, Power Corporation, and CPR-Cominco. Much publicized because of its extensive media interests,[17] Power Corporation is probably the most important Québec-based holding company. As is illustrated in chart 2, it controls a majority of the voting shares of six major corporations — Canada Steamship Lines, Campeau Corporation, Dominion Glass, Laurentide Financial Corporation, Imperial Life Assurance Company of Canada, and Investors Group. These subsidiary corporations, in turn, control other important subsidiaries of their own. Investors Group, for example, holds a voting interest of 50.01% in Great-West Life Assurance Company and a 24% interest in Montréal Trust.

CHART 2
ORGANIZATION OF POWER CORPORATION[a]

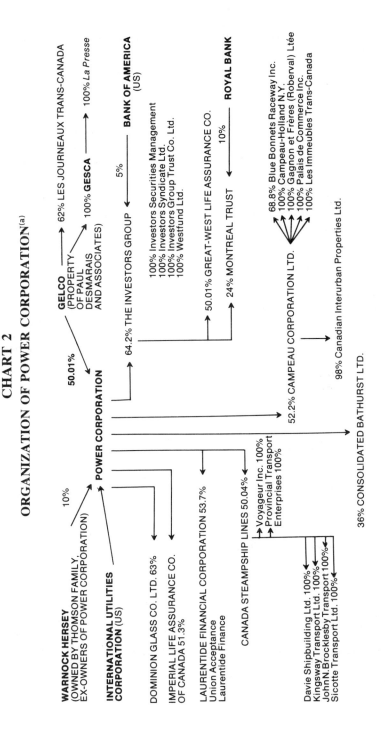

WARNOCK HERSEY 10%
(OWNED BY THOMSON FAMILY,
EX-OWNERS OF POWER CORPORATION)

INTERNATIONAL UTILITIES CORPORATION (US)

POWER CORPORATION

GELCO → 62% LES JOURNEAUX TRANS-CANADA
(PROPERTY OF PAUL DESMARAIS AND ASSOCIATES) 100% **GESCA** → 100% *La Presse*

50.01%

BANK OF AMERICA (US)

5%

64.2% THE INVESTORS GROUP

100% Investors Securities Management
100% Investors Syndicate Ltd.
100% Investors Group Trust Co. Ltd.
100% Westfund Ltd.

DOMINION GLASS CO. LTD. 63%

IMPERIAL LIFE ASSURANCE CO. OF CANADA 51.3%

50.01% GREAT-WEST LIFE ASSURANCE CO.

ROYAL BANK

24% MONTREAL TRUST 10%

LAURENTIDE FINANCIAL CORPORATION 53.7%
Union Acceptance
Laurentide Finance

52.2% CAMPEAU CORPORATION LTD.

68.8% Blue Bonnets Raceway Inc.
100% Campeau-Holland N.Y.
100% Gagnon et Frères (Roberval) Ltée
100% Palais de Commerce Inc.
100% Les Immeubles Trans-Canada

98% Canadian Interurban Properties Ltd.

CANADA STEAMSHIP LINES 50.04%

Voyageur Inc. 100%
Provincial Transport Enterprises 100%

Davie Shipbuilding Ltd. 100%
Kingsway Transport Ltd. 100%
John N. Brocklesby Transport 100%
Sicotte Transport Ltd. 100%

36% CONSOLIDATED BATHURST LTD.

(a) *McGill Daily*, 1 November 1971.

Finally, Power Corporation has important minority interests, for instance, 36% in Consolidated-Bathurst and 10.4% in Argus Corporation. In 1975, Power Corporation controlled about $5 billion worth of assets through an investment of some $350 million.[18] Although quite diversified, Power's main interests are in the financial sector, chiefly in insurance and investment companies.

Four of the companies mentioned above in the Power Corporation orbit appear in the list of the biggest 100 Québec-based corporations.[19] This underlines not only the financial power of a holding company but also the extent to which holding companies can increase the level of economic concentration by bringing together seemingly autonomous corporations or financial institutions.[20] The next chapter will show how the autonomy of the Power Corporation subsidiaries is decreased even further by a network of overlapping and interlocking directorships.

The economic advantages of a holding company are patently clear. In the first place, use of a holding company allows the creation of a managerial pool which, along with common technical services, is of assistance to the constituent companies. It can also create links between companies which are users of capital and those that are sources of capital. In the Power holding company, for example, Consolidated-Bathurst is a user of capital whereas financial institutions such as Investors Group are sources of capital. Finally, a holding company allows the constituent corporations to take full advantage of the possibilities of vertical integration. Consolidated-Bathurst, for example, not only owns logging companies but is provided with a market for its paper through Power's media interests. The daily newspaper *La Presse* alone consumes nearly 40,000 tons of paper annually.[21]

The precise influence of financial institutions on the industrial structure is an open question. Some have claimed that banks are the dominant economic institutions of capitalist economies. Others have maintained that the industrial sector can hold its own vis-à-vis the financial sector. The evidence gathered for this study is contradictory. However, financial institutions, particularly banks, play an important coordinating role in the economic structure, thereby enhancing the degree of concentration in the business system of power.

In the first place, financial institutions wield substantial economic power: They are one of the main sources of capital for industrial development. S. Menshikov estimated that between 30 and 40% of the financial needs of American corporations are met by financial institutions through the purchase of company stocks and bonds. He further estimated that about 75% of all bonds issued by private companies are held by financial institutions.[22] Potentially, this allows banks substantial power since it is up to them to determine which industrial sectors, investment projects, regions, or firms should be given priority. Indeed, according to Adolf Berle, "If 20% of the capital requirements [of a company] must be raised from the outside, then the outside certainly has a powerful voice in affairs."[23]

Banks also exercise power in that they are crucial sources of information for industry. They have an overall knowledge of economic conditions locally and internationally; they are in a position to give advice on the financial aspects of mergers, diversification, and how best to finance expansion. As Menshikov put it:

> Immeasurably more information about various industries, factories, regions and individuals is concentrated in banking institutions than in any industrial corporation. A banker is in a position to compare competing firms in one and the same sector which utilize his services and to suggest a *modus vivendi* to each one. [24]

Overall, then, banks have the effect of increasing the degree of economic concentration through their financial power and through the centralization of economic decision-making which is derived from their activities.

This hypothesis can be verified by examining the Canadian banking system, especially as it pertains to Québec. Peter Newman's analysis in *Maclean's Magazine* is particularly illuminating. He underlined not only the high level of concentration in the banking system, for instance, the Royal Bank of Canada, the Bank of Montréal, and the Canadian Imperial Bank of Commerce together control more than 70% of Canadian banking assets, but also the substantial economic power enjoyed by the 261 directors of the eight Canadian-owned banks:

> They control what is by quite a wide margin the largest pool of private investment capital in the country . . . Their board members hold among them some 3,152 corporate directorships, representing assets of about $581 billion . . . They put their mark not only on banking policies, but on just about every significant business decision in the country . . . [25]

One of the means by which banks exercise their coordinative function in regard to investment and information is through their boards of directors. Newman estimated that bank directors are "agents of the intelligence network which keeps any bank in competition" and that "each member of a bank board knows exactly what's happening in his own industry — who's on his way up, which companies are in trouble, what the prospects are for new banking business." [26]

A more detailed analysis of the composition of the boards of directors of banks indicates the existence of financial circuits surrounding banks. According to Newman, each bank has a special relationship with selected underwriters, law firms, auditing houses, and large insurance companies. Some 67 bank directors sit on the boards of the 17 largest Canadian insurance firms. In addition, banks have regular client corporations with which they develop very close ties. These ties are developed and maintained in part through common directors. The Bank of Montréal, for example, has 11 common directors with CPR, six with CIL, four with Bell Telephone, and three with Aluminum Company of Canada. In the financial sector, it is associated with Sun Life Assurance Company, the largest insurance company in Canada with six common directors, Standard Life with four common directors, and the Royal Trust with 14. [27] Similarly, the Royal Bank of Canada is closely linked to Imasco and to Power Corporation holdings, including Montréal Trust, Investors Group, and Imperial Life.

Board connections between banks and industry are significant in business terms. According to the source quoted by Newman, "About 30% of all authorized credit lines of $100,000 or more were to directors,

25

their firms or corporations of which they were officers or directors."[28] This was confirmed in the interviews. The main reason why senior industrial executives sit on bank boards is that it provides them with a source of credit and a source of information on business activity. Banks, on the other hand, invite on their boards representatives of the companies where they have investments or to which they would like to lend money. According to one of the vice-presidents of Imasco, the advantage of having Paul Paré, president of Imasco, on the board of the Royal Bank is: "When we ask for money, they give it to us." Another advantage is that Paré, or Imasco, gets "a hell of a lot of information on business, specifically on where to make investments or diversification moves . . . Paré can phone up McLaughlin [president of the Royal Bank], for example, and ask him if Grissol is a good buy.[29]. Our representation on the Royal Bank board helps us take advantage of investment opportunities quickly."[30]

The reverse relationship also holds true. Banking executives benefit from sitting on the boards of directors of companies because it permits them to keep a close watch on companies in which the bank has investments in capital stock or to which the bank has loaned money in the form of bonds. The chief executive officer of a major pulp and paper company stated: "Any banker is interested in doing business with a company on whose board he sits, and that is why he accepts the nomination." More specifically, he said: "Arnold Hart [chairman of the board of the Bank of Montreal, which is the company's senior banker] would probably resign from the board if our company stopped doing business with the Bank of Montreal."[31] From the point of view of the company, the reason for inviting a banker on its board is to get information on the investment community and access to the money market. A former executive of a major Québec company said that a banker on the board "adds respectability and helps the company's credit when it needs to borrow money."[32]

To conclude, as Newman said, it is difficult "to exaggerate the importance of bank boardrooms as concentrating forces of corporate power;"[33] and as Menshikov said, these boards have "increasingly turned into a meeting place for closely interconnected leaders of large banks and industrial complexes, into headquarters where the activities of the financial group as a whole and, more frequently, of a big part of it, are coordinated."[34]

Foreign ownership, although not directly related to the degree of economic concentration, has a significant impact on economic power and the business structure. First, the fact that many of the large corporations acting in Québec are themselves parts or subsidiaries of even larger, often multinational, interests, gives them additional financial power. Second, the firms that are foreign-owned enjoy an increased degree of decision-making autonomy. Thus, the report of the Task Force on the Structure of Canadian Industry claimed that when foreign ownership is embodied in firms which are large and have economic power and which are "no longer simply disciplined by the impersonal forces of the market," there is "a diminution of decision-making within the host country that would not result if the firms were small and fully subject to the discipline of the market."[35] This has political implica-

26

tions, according to the Task Force, because there is no natural coincidence between the interests of the host country and the large foreign-owned firms.

André Raynauld estimated that, in Québec, according to the value-added criterion, 41.8% of manufacturing in foreign owned, compared to 42.8% owned by English Canadians and 15.4% by French Canadians.[36] It has been alleged that Québec has developed mainly in accordance with the requirements of the United States economy, that is, the need for raw materials, and of the Ontario economy, that is, as a market for manufactured products, and that this has had a major impact on the structure of the Québec economy. Specifically, American and Anglo-Canadian control of the Québec economy has been blamed for this province's inadequate structure: the under-development of the manufacturing sector and the preponderance of light over heavy industry within the manufacturing sector. [37]

To return to the discussion of the autonomy and power of foreign-owned firms, many recent studies[38] have confirmed that subsidiaries are to some extent dependent on the head offices. The Task Force on the Structure of Canadian Industry argued: "In most cases the head office must be consulted on major policy changes, particularly on financing" and that the head office "exercises an overall coordination control."[39] Kari Levitt, in *Silent Surrender,* said that Canada is so dependent economically on the United States that it is impossible for provincial or federal governments to define or apply any long term policies. She also said that foreign companies are in a position to disregard the fiscal and monetary policies of the Canadian government.

Gilles Paquet's *The Multinational Firm and the Nation State* also emphasized the power and flexibility of multinational firms:

> A key characteristic of the multinational firm is its commercial flexibility . . .
> Once entered [a country], and confronted with an unfavourable economic or
> political environment, it can revise its initial plans, and, in extreme cases, shut
> down its operations.[40]

This flexibility can be particularly advantageous when dealing with labour problems: ". . . A multinational firm may have substantial bargaining power if it has the flexibility to switch production between affiliates in different countries and thus avert the impact of a strike in any one country.[41]

Finally, Christopher Tugendhat, in *The Multinationals,* made the point that the subsidiary's main reference point is the head office, not the local government:

> A characteristic feature of multinational companies is that their subsidiaries
> operate under the discipline and framework of a common global strategy, and
> common global control. The head office is their brain and nerve centre. It evolves
> the corporate strategy, decides where new market investment should be located,
> allocates export markets and research programmes to the various subsidiaries,
> and determines the prices that should be charged in inter-affiliate exchanges.
>
> The local subsidiary of a multinational naturally tries to meet the wishes of the
> government, and may be prepared to undertake a number of ventures of dubious
> commercial validity in an effort to secure its good will. But this does not alter
> the fact that it has an over-riding extra-territorial commitment to its parent company.[42]

The example of the Iron Ore Company reveals some of the characteristics of foreign ownership. As shown in chart 3, Iron Ore is owned jointly by three U.S. steel companies: National Steel (16.8%), Republic Steel (18%), and Bethlehem Steel (15.7%), which together control 50.5% of the company stock; and two mining companies: Hanna Mining of the U.S. (26%) and Hollinger Mines (11.6%).

The steel producers in the United States suffered a shortage of iron ore after World War II. Hanna Mining, the biggest iron ore producer, decided to associate itself with the Canadian-owned Hollinger Mines. Together the two companies created Labrador Mines and Exploration Company and began negotiations with the Québec government for exploration rights. At a cost of $100,000 a year, they obtained rights to 250 square miles of land in Québec. In 1954, three U.S. steel producers — National Steel, Republic Steel, and Bethlehem Steel — created Iron Ore, incorporated it in the U.S., and proceeded to sublet Labrador Mining and Exploration's exploration rights. [43]

These three companies, along with Hanna Mining, are the main customers of Iron Ore. In effect, they buy the iron from themselves and take a double profit. Hanna Mining, for example, not only gets dividends from Iron Ore, which account for one-third of Hanna's profits, but also sells the iron to the big steel producers which in turn sell it to car manufacturers or other users. Hanna benefits at this level, too. It has a 20% interest in National Steel and a 9% interest in Chrysler Corporation. [44] This is a good example of the benefits of vertical integration.

Not only has Iron Ore been developed in accordance with the interests of its foreign owners, but its benefits for Québec are open to question. In 1972, Eric Kierans, professor of economics at McGill University, asked for a full inquiry into the activities of Iron Ore in Québec. He claimed that Québec received only "a few salaries" from the company. It is estimated that Québec gets a maximum of $15 million a year from Iron Ore in royalties for the concessions and taxes. In return, the Québec government provides roads, bridges, ports, and other services. [45]. Kierans believed that there was no real advantage in having Iron Ore in Québec, especially since most of the transformation and manufacturing takes place in the U.S. [46].

Another relevant point is that Iron Ore was started with an initial investment of $250 million, half of which was paid for through a loan floated on the Québec bond market. [47] The value of the assets of Iron Ore are now estimated at some $1 billion.

In October 1972, a few months after Kierans's demand for an investigation, the Parti Québécois created a controversy in the press by publishing Iron Ore's 1971 financial statements. The statements showed that, in 1971, Iron Ore declared that only 1% of its total profits were in Québec, even though one-eighth of its mining activities were in the province. Indeed, since the mining operations are on both sides of the Québec-Labrador border, Iron Ore chose to declare most of its profits in Newfoundland where the tax rate is lower than in Québec. [48] It also declared most of its expenses in Québec in order to reduce its taxable income in the province.

CHART 3
THE OWNERSHIP STRUCTURE OF
IRON ORE COMPANY (1970)[a]

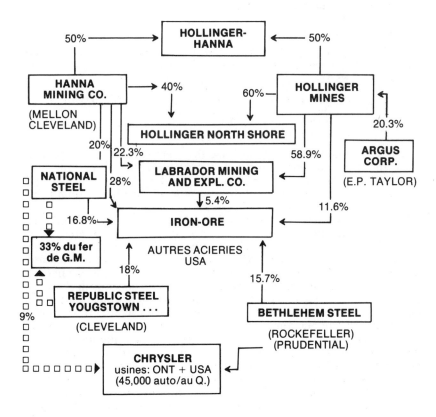

(a) Confederation of National Trade Unions, *Aide-mémoire au document "Ne Comptons que sur nos propres moyens"* (Montréal: Confederation of National Trade Unions, 1972), p. 36.

The Iron Ore case is a good example of the degree of autonomy and flexibility enjoyed by foreign-owned companies. Since most activities are not public knowledge, and since government control is minimal, nothing prevents subsidiaries from buying services, expertise, or legal services, for example, from the head office very expensively and selling its raw materials at a lower than market price to its parent company. Claude Ryan, publisher of *Le Devoir,* explained Iron Ore's position this way:

> "The company can fix special prices for its customer-shareholders and other prices for those who are not shareholders. It can decide to allocate more than 60% of its legal fees to American law firms, leaving only crumbs to Canadian and Québec firms. It can impute to services received from abroad a variable proportion of its planning, research, and consultation expenses. It can increase its capital — as in the case of Carol Lake — to the sole benefit of its American stockholders. All of this escapes the scrutiny and control of the real owners, the citizens of Québec."[49]

Some additional factors can increase the dominance of the large firms over the small or medium-sized corporations. As a prelude to a discussion of the political influence of the larger corporations, it is useful to examine the nature of these companies' economic dominance within the business system.

For many reasons, including the economies of scale, the high cost and economic advantages of modern machinery and equipment, diversification, advertising, distribution activities, research, and the financial security associated with size, there has been a trend towards larger production units. For many of the same reasons, it has become increasingly difficult for small companies to commence or survive.

The small companies tend to operate in a climate of fierce competition, usually in those economic sectors which are the least profitable.[50] The big companies, which are concentrated in the highly mechanized and more profitable industries,[51] have the advantage of having access to large amounts of capital. Another disadvantage suffered by many small companies is their dependence on big companies. In Québec, for example, Rémi Carrier Company makes seats for the Bombardier Skidoos. Companies like Rémi Carrier are in a position of continual jeopardy because nothing prevents the larger company from taking over that aspect of production which they have leased to a supplier. Small companies can also be eliminated through "price wars." For these and other reasons, it is not surprising that two-thirds of new companies set up in Québec go bankrupt within the first five years of their creation.[52]

As regards the establishment of new firms, the myth of going from "rags to riches" based on the initiative of free and bold individuals is dead. In the era of the Fords and the Carnegies, the myth could be kept alive in a certain way. In the present times, with a few exceptions, those who aspire to wealth must climb the steps of existing corporations or own substantial family capital at the start. The present system is closed and it would take more than brilliant graduates from business schools to start a steel mill. First there would be difficulties in obtaining the necessary capital. Few banks would be willing to encourage a competitor of Stelco, Algoma, Dofasco, or Sidbec. They would prefer to stimulate the growth of these larger corporations instead of helping rivals. Secondly, the new steel mill would face a supply problem. The best ore bodies being controlled by competitors, it would be difficult to obtain ore at a reasonable price. Finally, there would be a demand problem. There is no guarantee that the new firm would not be boycotted by the multi-nationals or the financial groups controlling the existing steel mills.

NOTES

(1) Miliband, p. 12.

(2) For discussions of economic concentration in the U.S., see Cohen and Mintz, Domhoff's *Who Rules America?*, Galbraith's *The New Industrial State*, and Baran and Sweezy. Miliband and Ernest Mandel, *Marxist Economic Theory* (London: Merlin Press, 1962), have some data for most advanced western countries.

(3) For details, see chapter 8 in Porter.

(4) See Gideon Rosenbluth, "The Relation Between Foreign Control and Concentration in Canadian Industry," *Canadian Journal of Economics*, vol. 3, February 1970, pp. 14-38, and Wallace Clement: *The Canadian Corporate Elite, McLelland and Stewart, 1975.*

(5) Parti Québecois, p. 28. According to Louis Reboud; "Les Petites et moyennes entreprises," *Relations*, no. 309, October 1966, pp. 268-270, only 3.5% of the total number of Québec companies hired 200 employees or more; moreover, these companies accounted for 60% of total industrial production.

(6) Interview with Québec business leader, May 1973.

(7) This information is derived from Parti Québécois. It is based on a list of the 62 largest companies operating in Québec, ranked on the basis of total number of employees.

(8) According to the Québec Bureau of Statistics, *Québec Cooperatives: Financial Statistics* (Québec City: Editeur Officiel du Québec, 1970), the cooperative sector has total assets of $4 billion — 95% of which are concentrated in the financial sector.

(9) *Financial Post,* "The Co-op That Turned Swinger," 4 March 1972.

(10) In the top 100 group, Northern electric is a wholly-owned subsidiary of Bell Telephone, and the Banque Provinciale is controlled by the Caisses Populaires Desjardins.

(11) Gilbert Athot, "Crise dans l'industrie des pâtes et papiers," *Le Soleil,* 29 May 1972.

(12) These are Consolidated Bathurst, Price Company, Domtar, Canadian International Paper, Anglo-Canadian Pulp and Paper, Québec North-Shore Paper, and E.B. Eddy Company.

(13) Philip Mathias, "Tighter Links May Alter World Paper Rivalry," *Financial Post,* 17 January 1970. Newspapers, and other large consumers of pulp and paper products, often buy substantial shares in pulp and paper companies. The *Chicago Tribune,* for example, wholly owns Québec North Shore Paper. The *New York Times* shares the ownership (49%) of Gaspesia Pulp and Paper with Price Company, and of Malbaie Paper (35%) with Donohue Brothers. These links facilitate agreements on the purchase price of pulp and paper and also allow the newspapers to recuperate a good portion of their own newsprint expenditures.

(14) When the ownership of stock is dispersed, control can often be exercised by a very small percentage of the total capital stock (5 to 10%). See Don Villarejo, "Stock Ownership and the Control of Corporations," *New University Thought*, vol. 2, Autumn 1961.

(15) The paper companies are also linked through their directors. For example, the Bank of Montreal board of directors has members from Consolidated-Bathurst, Domtar, and Price Company. The Toronto-Dominion Bank has directors from CIP and Consolidated-Bathurst.

(16) Information on Domtar comes from Sonja Sinclair, "Domtar: Case History of a Corporate Trend," *Canadian Business*, September 1964, and Confederation of National Trade Unions, *L'Avenir des travailleurs de la forêt et du papier* (Montreal: Confederation of National Trade Unions, 1972).

(17) For a list and evaluation of Power's media interests, see chapter 7.

(18) Data on Power Corporation holdings came from the 1971 annual report of the company. For a detailed history of Power Corporation, see Richard Brunelle and Pierre Papineau, "Le Gouvernement du capital," *Socialisme Québécois*, no. 23, 1972, pp. 111-125.

(19) These are Canada Steamship Lines, Dominion Glass, Consolidated-Bathurst, and Montréal Trust. Note that Investors Group has increased its interests in Montreal Trust from 24% to 47%. (Robert Pouliot, "Investors Group porte à 47 pourcent ses intérêts dans Montréal Trust," *La Presse*, 21 Septembre 1972.)

(20) Other important holding companies in Québec are CPR-Cominco and Imasco. CPR-Cominco has two crucial subsidiaries, Canadian Pacific Investments and Consolidated Mining and Smelting Company, and controls over $3 billion worth of assets. Imasco started off in the food and beverage sector, but has recently become much more diversified. Among other areas, it has expanded substantially in the sporting goods retailing sector.

(21) Confederation of National Trade Unions, p. 68.

(22) S. Menshikov, *Millionaires and Managers* (Moscow: Progress Publishers, 1969), p. 173.

(23) Adolf Berle, *Power Without Property: A New Development in American Political Economy* (New York: Harcourt, Brace and World, 1959), p. 41.

(24) Menshikov, p. 219. In Canada, according to Peter Newman, "The Bankers," *Maclean's Magazine*, March 1972, "All banks maintain experts in nearly every corporate lending category" (p. 77).

(25) Newman, p. 21. He also quoted R. G. D. Lafferty, a Montréal investment counsellor, as saying: "The banking system [in Canada] is a highly concentrated, monolithic structure with interlocking interests that employs restrictive practices to prevent new initiative and enterprise from challenging its dominant position" (p. 29).

(26) Ibid., p. 30.

(27) According to Newman, the Bank of Montreal has 53 board members who, among them, hold 455 corporate directorships, representing holdings of $124.9 billion. Some interesting hypotheses about the main financial networks operating in Québec are found in Louis Fournier, "Notre argent dans leurs banques," *Québec-Presse,* 27 January 1972.

(28) Newman, p. 30. The source quoted by Newman was the Royal Commission on Banking and Finance.

(29) Grissol was acquired by Imasco in 1972.

(30) Interview with Québec business leader, May 1973.

(31) Interview with Québec business leader, May 1973.

(32) Interview with Québec business leader, May 1973.

(33) Newman, p. 30.

(34) Menshikov, p. 221.

(35) Task Force on the Structure of Canadian Industry, *Foreign Ownership and the Structure of Canadian Industry* (Ottawa: Queen's Printer, 1968), p. 51.

(36) André Raynauld, *La Propriété des entreprises au Québec* (Montreal: Les Presses de l'Université de Montréal, 1974), p. 80. Chapter 3 will examine in detail the breakdown of these categories as well as the role differences between the English — and the French-Canadian elites.

(37) The Parti Québécois, for example, said: "La structure inadéquate de notre industrie découle avant tout de décisions d'investissements qui ont été prises par des non-québécois" (p. 39). By comparing the manufacturing sector of Québec with that of Ontario, the PQ said light industry is revealed as dominant in Québec, that it represents 45% of total manufacturing output compared to 28% for Ontario and that heavy industry is dominant in Ontario, representing 52% of total manufacturing output versus 31% for Québec.

(38) These include Kari Levitt, *Silent Surrender* (Toronto: MacMillan Company of Canada, 1970), Christopher Tugendhat, *The Multinationals* (New York: Random House, 1972), Gilles Paquet, ed., *The Multinational Firm and the Nation State* (Don Mills, Ontario: Collier-MacMillan, 1972), and Task Force on the Structure of Canadian Industry.

(39) Task Force on the Structure of Canadian Industry, p. 27.

(40) I. A. Litvak and C. J. Maule, "The Multinational Firm: Some Perspectives," in Paquet, p. 23.

(41) Ibid., p. 29.

(42) Ibid., pp. 95-96.

(43) In effect, the Hollinger group played the role of doorman for the U.S. steel interests.

(44) See chart 3. Information on Iron Ore is from "L'Iron Ore sait comment changer le fer en or," *Québec-Presse,* 20 August 1972.

(45) *Québec-Presse* estimated that 37% of the annual tonnage on the St. Lawrence Seaway is iron.

(46) Jacques Keable, "Kierans réclame une enquête sur l'Iron Ore", *Québec-Presse,* 6 August 1972. The only Québec user of Iron Ore's iron is the General Motors plant at Ste. Thérèse.

(47) Since Iron Ore is incorporated in the state of Delaware, it is under no obligation to file financial statements in Québec. Its assets, sales, and profits can only be estimated.

(48) Réal Bouvier, "Le PQ accuse l'Iron Ore de fraude fiscale," *La Presse,* 2 October 1972. Robert Pouliot, financial analyst at *La Presse,* agreed with the PQ analysis of Iron Ore's statements. He concluded that Iron Ore had reduced its income from its Québec operations in order to pay smaller taxes ("En réduisant ses revenus au Québec, l'Iron Ore a payé moins d'impôts," *La Presse,* 5 October 1972).

(49) Claude Ryan, "Les Révélations involontaires de l'Iron Ore," editorial, *Le Devoir,* 2 October 1972.

(50) For example, leather, food and beverages, printing, and clothing.

(51) For example, oil, steel, chemicals, transportation equipment, and pulp and paper.

(52) Information from Groupe de Recherche Économique, *Coopératives de production, usines populaires et pouvoir ouvrier* (Montréal: Éditions Québécoises, 1973). See pages 17-21 for a more detailed discussion.

CHAPTER 3

BUSINESS ELITES AND BUSINESS IDEOLOGY

THE MANAGERS of the institutions of business, that is, the business elite, further contribute to the operational unity of the business system of power, and they are also, by and large, ideologically homogeneous. I will argue here that industrial activity is not just concentrated but also controlled by a small number of individuals who are operationally united and ideologically homogeneous. Furthermore, I will show that there is no significant amount of pluralism within the business system of power.

Many studies dealing with business, while admitting the substantial economic power of business, have rejected the notion of corporate political power. According to Epstein, the crucial limitation upon corporate political power is "a degree of political pluralism within the corporate community that has prevented the emergence of a monolithic business political force." [1] Similarly, Richard Rose, in his analysis of England, claimed that "differences in values and goals" [2] of the corporate elite guarantees the existence of pluralism within the economic system.

To begin with, the business elite in Québec is small in size,[3] tightly knit, socially homogeneous, and largely self-perpetuating. This has already been demonstrated for Canada as a whole by Porter. His data showed that 907 Canadian individuals held 1,304 of the 1,913 directorships of the largest corporations, and further that 203 individuals held 45% of all the board seats in key companies. Porter went on to show that these individuals were socially homogeneous. He claimed that they were mainly university trained, with private school backgrounds, overwhelmingly Anglo-Saxon in composition, united in outlook, and self-perpetuating; he also demonstrated that they shared extensive contacts with one another.[4]

A doctoral thesis submitted to the department of management at Michigan State University by Laurent Bélanger largely confirmed the relevance of Porter's findings for Québec. With the help of 1,200 questionnaires, Bélanger found: "The largest part of the Québec economic elite originated from fathers who were already in business as large, medium and small owners, or as executives and foremen." [5] in addition to confirming the occupational continuity of businessmen. Bélanger's findings also indicated a degree of social homogeneity among the business elite. For example, 80% of the English and 68% of the French executives were found to be university trained.[6]

Overlapping directorships are one of the main mechanisms by which the business elite achieves operational cohesion. The case of Power Corporation is a good example. The ownership links between Power and its subsidiaries or dependent companies are strengthened by

the extensive overlapping among the boards of directors. In its subsid- ✓
iaries, six of the 16 directors of Power sit on the boards of both Campeau Corporation and Laurentide Financial Corporation; five Power
directors sit on the Dominion Glass and Investors Group boards; and
four directors sit on the Canada Steamship Lines board. In the companies in which Power holds important minority interests, seven directors
sit on the board of Consolidated-Bathurst and four are on the Montréal
Trust board. Paul Desmarais himself, chief executive of Power, is found
on the boards of most of the constituent companies of the holding,
including Canada Steamship, Consolidated-Bathurst, Dominion Glass,
Investors Group, Imperial Life Assurance, Laurentide Financial Corporation, and Montréal Trust. Desmarais is also a member of many boards
outside the Power Corporation "tree", including Churchill Falls Corporation, British Newfoundland Corporation (Brinco), Corporation des
Valeurs Trans-Canada, and Meagher's Distillery.[7]

The four senior executives of Power Corporation and the other
12 members of the board own, as a group, approximately 300,000 shares
of Power as well as substantial amounts of stock in its subsidiaries.
Further, Desmarais and Jean Parisien, chairman of the board and
president of Power Corporation respectively, and a few others own
Gelco, a private investment company which controls 50.1% of Power's
voting shares.[8]

The various elements of the leadership group in the large corporations, the owners, managers, and directors as well as the French and
English elements of the business elite, will now be examined. An
attempt will be made to determine whether these various elements can
be sources of conflict or disunity within the business elite.

The relationship between owners and managers will be analysed
first. For many years, a number of economists and other observers of
corporate behavior have argued that the control of large corporations
was rapidly passing from their owners to their managers, and that, in
fact, ownership and control had become separated. The adherents of the
"managerialist school"[9] went on to argue that this situation had
resulted in changes in business behavior and "was likely to have significant consequences for the criteria governing the use of business
power."[10].

The extent of the separation of ownership and control may have
been overestimated. It could be argued that, in many cases, the owners
have retained substantial power and influence.[11] However, there is no
doubt that the power of the managers has increased and that they
dominate the leadership of large corporations. In a detailed study of
business leadership in the U.S., Gordon concluded that the senior
executives play the key role:

> Of all the groups connected with the large corporation, the executive group
> far more than any other has come to perform the leadership function . . . Corporate
> executives as a group determine the volume and direction of investment in their
> firms; they set prices and formulate price policies; and, in general, they make the
> other important decisions which constitute the heart of what many economists
> call the entrepreneurial function — the function which we have called business
> leadership.[12]

A question which is much more important than the distribution of power between owners and managers is whether the separation of ownership and control is significant in terms of business unity and behavior. A detailed analysis makes it evident that there is no fundamental conflict between owners and managers. More important, and contrary to Berle's contention, there has been no significant change in the values or criteria underlying business behavior. The main motivation of the managers is the same as that of the owners: profit-making. As is shown later, an overwhelming majority of the Québec managers who answered the questionnaire felt that profits should be the principal objective of business activity.

There are many factors which ensure that the manager's motivation remains compatible with that of the owner-stockholder. One of these is that most managers themselves are holders of substantial stock in their company; and, as Epstein put it, "The substantial ownership interests that top executives usually have in their firms as a result of their managerial position will give them a general sense of identity with the shareholders." According to Gordon's data, the senior executives of large U.S. companies had average stock holdings of $298,700 according to the market value of stock.[13] This may not represent an important percentage of the total stock of the company, but it involves the possibility of substantial financial gains or losses.

The available evidence suggests that the pattern is similar in Québec. A bulletin published by the department of consumer and corporate affairs in Ottawa showed that the directors and managers of Canadian corporations often have important stock holdings in their companies. For example, in 1971 Taylor Kennedy, president of Canada Cement Lafarge, owned 5,868 common and 1,137 preferred shares in his company; Domtar executives T. N. Beaupré and H. R. Crabtree owned 9,007 and 19,000 shares respectively in their company; Louis Desmarais, president of Canada Steamship Lines, owned 19,900 shares in his company; and the two Molson brothers, Hartland and Thomas, owned $4 - $5 million in Molson Industries stock.[15]

The managerialist school has often reinforced its argument about the dominance of managers by claiming that "people's capitalism" or "economic democracy" has been achieved because of the decline of owner-families. The available evidence, however, does not suggest that stock ownership is diffuse. Moreover, shareholders have been largely impotent in the modern corporation. Adolf Berle admitted that the stockholder is so divorced from management that "he can hardly communicate with management even by megaphone."[16] Shareholders meetings were described by W. H. Ferry, a consultant to large U.S. corporations for 12 years, as "at best pathetic efforts by management to assure itself that it has obtained both participation and consent, at worst a deception aimed at maintaining for as long as possible the particular rule of a particular managerial hierarchy."[17]

Theoretically, it is the function of stockholders to choose management. In fact, however, "The selection procedure is largely ritualistic, since the incumbent management controls the proxy machinery, and the shareholders are largely impotent."[18] By and large, then, management is self-perpetuating and responsible only to itself. Since the business system of power is not democratic in any sense of the word, the conscience of managers becomes the only guarantee against "corporate irresponsibility."

It can now be asked if the board of directors can act as a check on management, and what is the likelihood that the interests of the directors could come into conflict with those of management.

First, the distinction between managers or senior executives and directors is largely artificial. The overwhelming majority of directors are themselves managers of the corporation itself or of another corporation. A study at the University of British Columbia showed that about 57% of company directors were senior executives; of the 1,408 directors surveyed, 269 were officers of the company, 424 were prominent businessmen, 284 owned or represented substantial stock, and 164 were prominent community figures. The rest were mainly lawyers, accountants, or consultants.[19] According to other research, company officers themselves were estimated to represent between 35% and 40% of board members.[20]

Second, the boards are only minimally involved in the day-to-day activities of the company, or, for that matter, in the formulation of corporate policy. Myles Mace, professor of business administration at the Harvard Business School, showed that the board's role is mainly advisory and that, most of the time, it is dominated by the company executives, particularly the president:

> In short, the generally accepted roles of boards — e.g. selecting top executives, determining policy, measuring results, and asking discerning questions — have taken on more and more the characteristics of a well-established myth . . . In the large widely held corporation, . . . the president determines in large part what the board of directors does or does not do.[21]

Gordon came to the same general conclusions:

> In practice, the careful scrutiny is frequently lacking; the necessary familiarity with the internal workings of the company is absent; and the board frequently voluntarily yields to the chief executive the authority it is supposed to have . . . The available evidence strongly suggest that ratification of management proposals by the board is a formality.[22]

Although the boards do not effectively play their generally accepted roles and although they only rarely challenge the power of management, they nonetheless perform an important coordinating role in the business system of power. The essential information about the financial markets, the conditions within the industry, and the general economic situation is usually found at the board level. It is also at the board level that some functional relationships crucial to the company are established. Thus, boards often include representatives of important suppliers, customers, creditors, or potential investors. One of the vice-presidents of Imasco, for example, claimed that Paré sat on the Canadian Pacific board of directors because Imasco was heavily involved in the transportation of finished products. Thus, Paré had a customer relationship within the CP board; his participation also allowed him to obtain the information necessary for his company. The executive of Imasco mentioned that some people were named to the board as representatives of regions, in order "to get information on the investment climate."[23]

In order to verify the general argument presented above concerning the unity of interests between managers and directors, the businessmen were asked in the questionnaire if "there are often serious differences of opinion between executive officers and the directors in a company?" Eighty-two per cent of the respondents, including 20 of the 22 directors, replied "no," and 17.2% replied "yes."[24] This suggests agreement between the two groups on most issues.

Another potentially divisive factor within the Québec business elite is its composition of French, English, and foreign (mainly American) elements. Raynauld, chairman of the Economic Council of Canada, estimated the distribution of control in Québec manufacturing as follows: French Canadian 15.4%, English Canadian 42.8%, and foreign 41.8%.[25] The possibility of conflicts between the three groups exists, especially considering that the French element, which represents 80% of the total Québec population, is underrepresented in the control of the Québec economy and considering the importance of foreign ownership.

As regards French relative to English participation in management, even the Montréal Chambre de Commerce complained about "the Anglophone domination of economic decision-making centres . . . which have the result of directly favoring investment in Anglophone areas as well as the development of companies and services owned by members of the same linguistic group [Anglophone]."[26] As noted earlier, in 1971 only 15% of head office employees earning more than $22,000 a year were of French mother tongue. In addition, the individuals of French mother tongue who reach the managerial level usually play secondary roles: "The role of the Francophone at the management level is generally limited to the interpretation and implementation, locally or regionally, of decisions relating to company guidelines — decisions in which he has not participated."[27]

These findings were corroborated by Raynauld's study for the Royal Commission on Bilingualism and Biculturalism. His analysis demonstrated that companies owned by French Canadians were not only underrepresented in the manufacturing sector, but also were concentrated in the traditional, low productivity, and labor-intensive sectors such as wood-cutting and leather manufacturing, where salaries and exports were found to be low.[28] For example, productivity in the firms owned by French Canadians was reported to be 14.8% lower than in those owned by English Canadians and 45.4% lower on the average than in the foreign-owned firms.[29]

Raynauld also found that French and English elements of the Québec business elite were, by and large, isolated and separated from each other.[39] His data came from an analysis of the boards of directors of Québec-based banks and companies. Raynauld discovered that the two "French banks," the Banque Provinciale du Canada and the Banque Canadienne Nationale, were linked to French-Canadian owned companies, including investment, trust, and insurance companies. Similarly, the boards of directors of French companies were almost entirely made up of French Canadians. Only three English-

Canadian members of Porter's corporate elite were represented on the boards of French-Canadian companies.[31] Raynauld concluded that French-Canadian businesses do not succeed or do not try to attract members of the English-Canadian elite to their boards.[32]

On the English side, the financial networks tended to be exclusively English; an English bank usually made loans to English companies and was usually associated with English trusts, insurance, and investment companies. At the board level, there was some French-Canadian representation: 36 French Canadians were directors of (Porter's) key Canadian companies. However, the evidence suggested that French-Canadian directors were accorded mainly public and political relations roles. Seventeen or 47% of the 36 French-Canadian directors were lawyers, and 15 or 42% were associated with a political party.[33] In Porter's overall picture of the Canadian corporate elite, only 18% were lawyers and 27% political "representatives." This led Raynauld to conclude:

> "The relative importance of lawyers and of the political factor in the French-Canadian group, within the English-Canadian group, leads us to believe that the French-Canadians who sit on the boards of large English companies act mainly as liaison officers between these companies on the one hand, and the government of Québec, the workers (through their unions), and the consumers, on the other hand."[34]

The above suggests that in many areas there are potential conflicts between French and English managers, chiefly in regard to the marginal role played by the French-Canadian elite. As will be seen below, however, there are no major ideological differences in either general policy or specific legislation between the English and French groups.

Regarding foreign control, the businessmen who received the questionnaire were asked if there were "significant differences of opinion between American directors and their Canadian colleagues?" Eighty-five point nine percent felt there were no such differences, and 14.1% thought there were. Considering the various policies which favour the development of the parent company at the expense of the subsidiary, this indicates a remarkable degree of agreement between the Canadian and American directors.

The study of the ideology of the Québec business elite has a dual relevance to this analysis: first, it permits one to determine whether, by and large, business is united ideologically and politically; second, it enables one to outline the main policy objectives of business and, more specifically, what business expects from government. This is useful background to the discussion of business influence on government policy in part II and to the determination of the responsiveness of government to the demands and expectations of business.

In an attempt to measure in a general way businessmen's perceptions of their own unity, the following question was put to them: "By and large, do you think there is agreement within the business community regarding the major social and political problems of the day?" Nearly 70% replied in the affirmative.[35] Since perceived group unity is usually low, this degree of agreement is significant.

Another question asked what businessmen considered should be "the most important objective of business." Seventy per cent answered "profitability," 20% chose "growth of the economy," and 5% opted for "social objectives.[36]

The interviews strengthened the conclusion that profit is the main motivation of business activity. The chairman of the board of an important trust company put it this way: "The businessman is not primarily interested in the general welfare. He does not want to abuse his work force, but his primary duty is to his shareholder.[37] The manager does not have much choice in the matter. Not only is it to his advantage to seek profit-maximization, as was argued earlier, but his performance is judged according to the profit yardstick. To quote Epstein: "Profits for the firm and stockholders stand as the primary criterion of the effectiveness with which he exercises his function.[38] The chairman of the board of a major Québec company spoke of profit as "the built-in mechanism by which the performance of business is tested."[39] The president of a business association claimed: "It would be difficult to evaluate management if businesses were administered on other criteria than profitability."[40]

The "external" or political goals of business are derived from the "internal" objective of business activity, that is, profits. Indeed, "business political activity is an integral part of profit-maximizing." In this context, the main political goal of business is "the creation of a political environment sympathetic to corporate goals and interests."[41] A related point is that business elites derive their power from the economic system. Any attempts to modify significantly the existing economic system of private ownership of the means of production would have a major impact on the distribution of wealth and power. Thus the maintenance of the present system is perhaps the crucial political objective of business. This was probably the essence of what V. O. Key had in mind when he spoke of the "network of common interests [which] pulls the business community together on major issues when its security is threatened."[42]

It is only in the context of the above discussion that the ideology of business towards the role of government can be properly understood. According to business leaders, the primary responsibility of government should be to create a favorable climate for business or, as the Canadian Manufacturers' Association put it, "a climate which generates confidence, encourages private saving, attracts external capital and provides adequate rewards for risk-taking."[43] Of course, it is "only if the climate for expansion is favourable" that the private sector is able to "achieve the required levels of investment in new plants and equipment which will reduce unemployment and provide new job opportunities for a rapidly growing labour force."[44]

Regarding the economic role of the government, the businessmen were asked what they thought "the main economic function of government" should be. As is shown in table 1, a large majority of businessmen (84.1%) answered it should be to "create the economic conditions for the growth of the private sector." Others (8.3%) chose "welfare and redistribution of income," while 0.7% preferred "protecting the environment and operating some public enterprises," and

5.5% chose the "other" category. The French respondents were
somewhat more oriented towards the social functions of government.
Their replies constituted a total of 19.6% for the first three options
(including 13.7% for "welfare and redistribution of income") compared to 5.3% for their English counterparts. The larger companies
also showed a more pronounced inclination towards "welfare and
redistribution of income" than the secondary companies by a margin of
10.3% to nil. Overall, however, there was substantial agreement in all
categories that the primary role of government in the economic field
was to act as a complement or adjunct to private enterprise.

That is not to say, however, that businessmen have maintained
their traditional nineteenth-century hostility towards the State; quite
the contrary, businessmen, especially the leaders of the large
corporations[45] have increasingly come to realize that an active state is
necessary not only for purposes of overall coordination of the economy
and planning but also for ensuring the survival of the economic system.
E. P. Taylor, for example, president of Argus Corporation, said in the
early nineteen-sixties:

> I think the time for longer-range planning or rationalization of our economic
> affairs is now upon us. Canadians have seen far too much in recent years of
> expedience and opportunism. The challenge, which all our leaders must accept, is
> that of economic statesmanship.[46]

Government planning, however, must have as its main objective
the improved efficiency of the private sector. As W. E. McLaughlin,
president of the Royal Bank of Canada, put it:

> The role of government [in cooperation with the Economic Council of Canada]
> should be to provide the environment within which private planning in a free
> market can be most effective.
>
> This end can be achieved if the Council takes as its main goal the most efficient
> allocation of the nation's resources of labour, capital, and enterprise and
> concentrates its efforts on the improvement of markets and the market mechanism
> through which the allocation is effected.[47]
>
> The general principle, or criterion, of indicative planning should be that, when
> policy alternatives exist, the choice should go to the one which involves the least
> (public or private) interference with the free competitive market.[48]

In light of the subordinated and generally complementary role
which business would like to see the government play, it is somewhat
surprising that 51.1% of businessmen thought government "should
take the iniative in making key economic choices for society; 32.4%
considered business itself should make the choices; and 16.5% thought
both government and business should be involved.[61] It is all the more
surprising in that, as will be shown later, the Québec government, for
one, does not have the means at its disposal to make the key economic
choices for society.

In the case of welfare and social policies, the heads of large
corporations in particular have moved away from laissez-faire. The
questionnaire demonstrated that 80.1% of businessmen thought government "should take the initiative in resolving social problems
compared to 5.7% for business and 14.2% for both government and
business. As expected, there was a significant difference in the

TABLE 1
DISTRIBUTION OF RESPONSES OF QUÉBEC BUSINESS LEADERS REGARDING MAIN ECONOMIC FUNCTION OF GOVERNMENT
(Question III C: "What should be the main economic function of government?")

	ALL RE-SPONDENTS	RESPONSES IN PERCENTAGES[a]				
		All Respondents	English Respondents	French Respondents	Respondents From Large Companies	Respondents From Secondary Companies
Welfare and Redistribution of Income	12	8.3	5.3	13.7	10.3	0
Protecting the Environment and Controlling Pollution	1	0.7	0	2.0	0	3.6
Developing and Operating Some Public Enterprises	2	1.4	0	3.9	0.9	3.6
Creating the Economic Conditions for the growth of the Private Sector	122	84.1	86.2	80.4	82.9	89.3
Other	8	5.5	8.5	0	5.3	3.6
No Answer	1	—	—	—	—	—
N	146[b]					

(a) The figures exclude the 0.7% of respondents who did not answer the question.
(b) N = 146 rather than 143 because some respondents gave multiple answers.

41

behaviour of the heads of large companies compared to those of the secondary corporations. The heads of the larger companies were more prone to accept "government interference" in social affairs than the less "liberal" leaders of the secondary companies. Thus, 84.2% of the large company executives opted for "government" compared to 63.0% of the secondary company executives; "business" was favored by 18.5% of secondary companies compared to 2.6% of large companies.

The interviews and several statements by senior executives confirmed that business is certainly not opposed to state intervention in the social arena.[49] This is true not only in general terms but also, as will be seen below, in the attitudes of business towards specific pieces of social legislation. There has been an increasing willingness on the part of business to admit that the free enterprise system left to itself is incapable of solving all problems. As a bank executive put it: "Control institutions are necessary because businessmen are often incapable of exercising sufficient self-control and of policing themselves adequately."[50]

Thus, by and large, business seeks to dispense with adversary relations with government. As Roy Bennett, president of Ford Motor Company of Canada, said:

> Business and government have a joint cause and a common ground for resolving the complex issues associated with Canadian economic growth . . .
> More direct, and better-coordinated methods for teamwork between the public and private sector are essential in view of new situations.[51]

Business has shown itself quite willing to accept government norms, taxation, and various other restrictions such as pollution control; as long as these are applied uniformly and equally to all businesses, they do not damage the relative competitive position of one company vis-à-vis another. Thus, business itself often desires government ground rules. An executive of Canadian Industries Ltd. put it this way: "The competitive system does not reward entrepreneurs for doing more than the minimum required by law. However, if government sets the ground rules for all competitors the system works satisfactorily."[52]

Similarly, C. Perreault, president of the Conseil du Patronat, said:

> Much as I dislike interference with my personal liberty as a businessman and much as I set relatively low values upon bureaucratic efficiency, I must reluctantly admit that certain functions can only be carried out by the State within our free enterprise system, paradoxical though this may seem. I fail to see, for instance, how a well-intentioned corporation can convince its shareholders to spend millions of dollars for environmental protection, and face a consequent increase in the cost of every unit of production sold, if this altruistic approach is not shared by its competitor. On the other hand, once appropriate regulations have been put into effect, Corporation A will have to internalize these costs and deal with the market imperative knowing that Corporation B is faced with generally similar restrictions. Thus I am led to conclude that some form of collaboration will produce better results . . .[53]

Finally, the chairman of the board of a major Québec firm said he did not oppose such measures as minimum wage laws, social legislation, and pollution control regulations as long as they were applied equally to every business, and since, in the end, the consumer had to pay for them anyway.[54]

For many of the same reasons that have led business to accept and even favour government intervention in certain areas, the corporate elite, particularly large corporation heads, have begun to emphasize in recent years the need for social responsibility in business. Two main reasons have encouraged this new insistence on social responsibility. First, business itself has recognized that social needs and the profit motive are frequently incompatible. Jean Brunelle, president of the Centre des Dirigeants d'Entreprise, said that many choices which are justified economically bring about nefarious social consequences.[55] Similarly, Pierre Shooner, president of the Montréal Chambre de Commerce, said the most crucial social needs will more and more be of the type that do not directly affect the individual consumer, and that an economy that limits itself to the classical competitive market would be less and less capable of responding to the real needs of the population.[56]

Second, the increase in economic concentration has made corporate power more visible and has made it obvious that corporations are responsible to no one but themselves. This has forced corporations to assure the public of the commonality of corporate and social interests:

> . . . The managerial search for the holy grail of social responsibility represents an explicit recognition by businessmen that the classic economic model is no longer in accord with the reality of an economy in which huge multinational corporations dominate their markets and exceed many governmental units in resources and social impact.[57]

In the end, the primary motivation for the emphasis on social responsibility is the survival of the economic system and the preservation of the autonomy of corporate decision-makers. Business realizes that the best way to avoid sharing its power and to avoid various governmental constraints is to take the initiative in assuring the people that business is responsive to social needs. The attitude of business towards social responsibility is thus essentially defensive, seeking to ensure that the changes which do take place are defined in business's own terms rather than imposed from outside.

Many public statements from senior businessmen confirmed this "strategy." J.K. Finlayson, deputy chairman and executive vice-president of the Royal Bank, gave an important speech on the "social responsibilities of international business" in May 1973. His message was clear:

> We are reaching the point where the social and political climate almost everywhere in the world will make it increasingly necessary [for corporations] to justify their existence on grounds other than purely economic success, as expressed in terms of profits to shareholders.[58]

> What I am saying, overall, is that without minimizing the importance of profit, businesses exist for other purposes as well, and those purposes must accord reasonably well with the expectations of the societies that support them.[59]

> . . . I do not consider that social responsibility should be assumed by corporations, sometimes at the expense of profits, for purely altruistic reasons. My point

is that if corporations are not seen to act, and do not in fact act, in a socially responsible manner, their long-term survival could be threatened. [60]

The above statements show that business has to accept some changes if it wants to survive and if the power structure is to remain intact. Brunelle thought business must accept the inevitability of social change and concentrate its efforts on making sure that business is not devaluated in social terms. [61] What is more, like Finlayson, he believed that if the behavior of business was not modified, the free enterprise system might well disappear. It was thus important to correct the "image of industry as an insensitive institution run by men more inspired by the profit motive than by concern for the general welfare" because "if this principle is not recognized by business, then revolutionary unionism or, ultimately, a political system controlled by an oligarchy will have to be accepted as valid." [62]

It is obvious from the statements of business that it is the outside threats of the labour unions, consumers, environmentalists, and others which are forcing it to revise its position. Perreault made it clear that the corporation cannot afford to ignore the open and systematic criticism to which business has been subjected by other social groups. [63] Brunelle, in an article entitled "Elements of a Strategy for Business," carried the point further:

> Criticism from within the population has now jelled into organized opposition threatening private enterprise on the political level as well as through direct action. If it remains idle, it will be compelled to agree to major changes and perhaps give up much of its freedom of action. [64]

> It must be recognized that the curiosity of Nader's raiders and of the public authorities is more than a transient phenomenon. If action is postponed too long, business might well find itself bound to a status that would be nothing less than a strait-jacket.

> If private enterprise does not avail itself of the means to operate in a suitable society, it will have no choice but to accept the society that will be imposed on it. [65]

In the case of social responsibility as well as in the case of intervention, the main preoccupation of business remains its freedom of action and its ability to earn profits. A.E. Levin, manager of public affairs for the Royal Bank of Canada, although arguing that "contemporary situations should be dealt with in a constructive manner before permanent organizations are formed to force corporations to do this," maintained nonetheless that business "should not take on activities which threaten or jeopardize its ability to earn a profit." [66] R. Ritchie, former senior vice-president of Imperial Oil and president of the Institute for Research on Public Policy, created by the federal government, argued that business could accept constraints such as air pollution controls because these "were entirely compatible with the market mechanism." What was important for Ritchie, then, was not to "let the market mechanism be interfered with in ways which undermine it to the point where we would wake up some years hence to find out that it no longer existed . . ." [67]

The above argument that "social responsibility" is the business response to public and governmental threats is strongly supported by the available literature on business leadership.[68] Epstein summarized it well.

Social responsibility . . . is based upon the desire of business managers to preserve their autonomy by demonstrating that corporations act in accordance with public expectations and interests and should not, therefore, be subjected to additional social controls . . .[69]

Now that business goals and ideology have been discussed in a general way, I will analyse some of the issues and policies which are specific to Québec businessmen. In order to get a better idea of what preoccupies Québec businessmen, and also in order to help choose relevant issue-areas for the analysis of business influence, businessmen were asked what they thought was "the most important problem facing business." As shown in table 2, a majority (56.9%) thought that economic policies were dominant — including 32.6% who selected "unemployment and inflation" and 24.3% who chose "weakness of Québec economic structure." [70] "Social unrest and labour problems" were considered most important by 29.8% of the respondents compared with 9.0% for the "language question" and 4.2% for "separatism." Although an "other" category was included, to make sure no important aspect had been left out, only 4% chose it, usually stating that the main problem faced by business was a combination of the options offered.

As revealed in table 2, 70% of the French respondents put more emphasis on the economic problems[71] and less on the social, labour, and "cultural" problems than their English counterparts. Secondary company executives were more concerned about social, labour, and language problems than the executives of the largest 100 companies. This fact was perhaps due to the greater strength and power of the larger corporations when faced with labour demands or language pressures.

The main objective of section IV in the questionnaire was to evaluate the degree of business satisfaction with specific governmental policies. A secondary objective was to measure the degree of homogeneity in business ideology.

In the economic field, business demonstrated support for the general economic policies of government (81.1%), for the delay of forest reform legislation (82.4%), for the nationalization of Hydro-Québec (72.3%), and for the recent economic initiatives of the Québec government (63.1%). In the social and labour area, business expressed satisfaction with Bill 19, which put an end to the common front strike in May 1972 (99.3%), with the Québec government's attitude during the FLQ crisis (98.6%), with unemployment insurance (93%), and with the Québec pension plan (97.1%). In the language and education area, businessmen approved the government's attitude regarding the language question (72.2%), Bill 63 (94.4%), and Bill 71 (54.7%).

Regarding party preferences, 87.2% of businessmen considered the Liberal Party was the "provincial party most favourable to business," compared with 6.7% for the Union Nationale, 6.0% for the Creditiste Party, and 0% for the Parti Québécois.[72] Businessmen were

45

TABLE 2
DISTRIBUTION OF RESPONSES OF QUÉBEC BUSINESS LEADERS REGARDING MOST IMPORTANT PROBLEM FACING BUSINESS IN QUÉBEC
(Question IIIA: "What is the most important problem facing business in Québec at present?")

	ALL RE-SPOND-ENTS	RESPONSES IN PERCENTAGES[a]				
		All Respondents	English Respondents	French Respondents	Respondents From Large Companies	Respondents From Secondary Companies
Social Unrest and Labour Problems	43	29.8	34.0	22.0	27.3	40.7
Language	13	9.0	11.7	4.0	6.8	18.5
Separatism	6	4.2	4.3	4.0	4.3	3.7
Unemployment and Inflation	47	32.6	28.7	40.0	35.9	18.5
Weakness of Québec Economic Structure	35	24.3	21.3	30.0	25.6	18.5
Other/No Answer	6	—	—	—	—	—
N	150[b]					

(a) The figures exclude the 4.0% of respondents who chose the "other" category or did not answer the question.
(b) N = 150 rather than 143 because some respondents gave multiple answers.

also strong partisans of Canadian unity; 99.3% of the respondents opposed separatism.[73]

A few other questions of a more hypothetical nature further confirmed the degree of business ideological unity. Thus, 98.6% of businessmen supported the elimination of strikes in public and essential services, 94.7% opposed any governmental attempts to fix prices to counteract monopoly power, and 95.6% opposed any governmental intervention regarding profits.

The only division of opinion concerned businessmen's attitudes towards cooperatives; 52.9% of businessmen thought that production cooperatives could be a threat to the smooth functioning of the economic system, while 47.1% disagreed. Also, only 27.3% expressed support for a government project to finance a pulp and paper cooperative in Cabano.

Overall, there was a substantial degree of homogeneity and agreement within the business elite in Québec. While there were a few differences between the English and French elements, and while executives of smaller companies tended to be more reticent towards government intervention in the social arena and more vulnerable towards labour problems, ideological unity was the dominant characteristic of business.

NOTES

(1) Epstein, p. 226.

(2) Richard Rose: *Politics in England*, Boston: Little, Brown and Co., 1964, p. 111.

(3) As Philip Resnick said: "The small size of elite groups facilitates communication between their members" ("The Dynamics of Power in Canada," *Our Generation*, June 1968, p. 137).

(4) According to Porter, 150 Montréal members of the Canadian "corporate elite" belong to the Mount-Royal Club and 146 to the St. James Club (p. 304).

(5) Laurent Bélanger, "Occupational Mobility of French and English-Canadian Business Leaders in the Province of Québec," (Ph. D. dissertation, Michigan State University, 1967), p. 152.

(6) Ibid., p. 154.

(7) Information is from the 1970-75 annual reports of Power Corporation and its subsidiaries. The other key men on the Power Corporation board — P. N. Thomson, W. I. M. Turner, Jean Parisien, and A. Deane Nesbitt — all have important directorships inside and outside the Power Corporation organization.

(8) Power Corporation of Canada, *1971 Annual Report* (Montréal, 1972), pp. 10-12.

(9) The best-known and first study of the managerialist school was that of Adolf Berle and Gardner Means entitled *The Modern Corporation and Private Property* (New York: MacMillan Company, 1933). The authors reported, among other findings, that salaried managers controlled 44% of the 200 largest non-financial corporations. Other managerialists include James Burnham, *The Managerial Revolution* (New York and London: Putnam Press, 1942) and Galbraith, *The New Industrial State*.

(10) John Child, *The Business Enterprise in Modern Industrial Society* (London: Collier-MacMillan, 1968), p. 34.

(11) According to Mills, the owner-manager dichotomy has been exaggerated: "The chief executives and the very rich are not two distinct and clearly segregated groups. They are both very much mixed up in the corporate world of property and privilege" (p. 119). Similarly, Menshikov claimed that the economy is controlled by "combinations of millionaires and managers" (P. 318). According to Ferdinand Lundberg, *The Rich and the Super-Rich* (New York: Bantam Books, 1969), managers are "a mere appendage to the leading tycoons" (p. 117).

(12) Gordon, pp. 114-115.

(13) Rogert Gordon: *Business Leadership in the Large Corporation:* University of California Press, 1966, pp. 302-303.

(14) Department of Consumer and Corporate Affairs, *Bulletin: Canada Corporations Act*, vol. 1, no. 1 (Ottawa: Queen's Printer, 1971).

(15) Management ownership of company stock is encouraged by the use of stock options, i.e., the sale of company stock to executives or sometimes employees at a less than market price.

(16) Adolf Berle, "Economic Power and the Free Society," in Hacker, p. 95.

(17) W. H. Perry, "Irresponsibilities in Metrocorporate America," in Hacker, p. 119. According to Epstein: "The general state of shareholder impotency is further compounded by the fact that at the end of 1966, institutions

(insurance and investment companies, banks, etc.) held more than $157 billion worth, or 33 per cent of the market value, of all stocks listed on the New York Stock Exchange" (p. 259).

The difficulty of mobilizing shareholders and the importance of institutional investors was made obvious in 1970 when some General Motors stockholders attempted to organize their fellow stockholders around social objectives — including black representation on GM's board. "Campaign GM," as it was called, only succeeded in obtaining 3% of the proxies. The main problem, apart from the large number of stockholders and the expense involved, was that half of the GM stock (about 233 million shares) was owned by funds, including the Chase Manhattan Bank, Rockefeller Foundation, and Morgan Guaranty Trust. These institutional buyers all refused responsibility for GM's policies. President Pusey of Harvard University, which owned 287,000 shares of GM, said the purpose of the investments was to make money and that Harvard could not be held responsible. See Alexander Ross, "Shareholder Power Takes on the System," *Financial Post,* 23 January 1971.

(18) Epstein, pp. 267-68.

(19) Eileen Goodman, "How Boards of Directors Keep Abreast of the Changing Times in Which They Must Operate," *Canadian Business,* September 1960, p. 85.

(20) Menshikov, in a study of the composition of the boards of the 110 largest industrial corporations in the U.S., found that 39% of directors were company officers in 1961 (p. 129). Some boards are made up entirely of company officers. Imasco and Steinberg's are two Québec examples of inside boards.

(21 Myles Mace, "The President and the Board of Directors," *Harvard Business Review* March - April 1972. Mace's data included interviews and participation on some boards.

(22) Gordon, p. 134.

(23) Interview, May 1973.

(24) Figures exclude 6.2% of respondents who did not answer the question.

(25) Raynauld, p. 80. The criterion used was value added.

(26) Chambre de Commerce du District de Montréal, p. 6.

(27) Ibid. p. 6

(28) André Raynauld, "La Propriété et la performance des entreprises au Québec," unpublished report prepared for the Royal Commission on Bilingualism and Biculturalism, May 1967, p. 110. The English-Canadian group was found dominant (i.e., ownership of 50% or more according to value-added criterion) in textiles, electrical appliances, clothing, pulp and paper, and food and beverages. The foreign group was concentrated in heavy industry — including oil, steel and iron, chemical products, transport equipment, metals, and machinery.

(29) Ibid., p. 137. Raynauld also reported that the foreign-owned concerns were on the average seven times larger than the French-Canadian firms (p. 120), and that foreign firms exported 60% of their production, compared to 48.6% for English-Canadian and 21.9% for French-Canadian concerns (p. 171).

(30) Ibid., p. 210.

(31) Porter's sample of key Canadian companies included 170 corporations, five banks, 10 insurance companies, and six trust companies.

(32) Raynauld, p. 206.

(33) Ibid., p. 206. One of the main reasons for the selection of French-Canadian lawyers on the boards of English companies is their knowledge of Québec legislation, in particular the Civil Code.

(34) Ibid., p. 207.

(35) 69.4% replied "yes" and 30.6% "no". These percentages exclude the 6.3% of the respondents who did not answer the question.

(36) In the answers to this question, there was a striking difference between the French and English respondents. 83.5% of English businessmen chose profitability compared to only 44.9% of French corporate leaders. Of the remaining French respondents, 12.2% opted for social objectives and 42.9% for growth of the economy. On the English side, the figures were 1.1% and 15.4% respectively. As far as can be determined, the discrepancy was not due to an error in translation. The most plausible explanation derives from the fact that one-sixth of the French sample was made up of executives working in cooperatives, including l'Assurance-Vie Desjardins, the Union Régionale des Caisses Populaires Desjardins, the Société Nationale de Fiducie, the Coopérative Fédérée du Québec, and the Coopérative Agricole de Granby. It was reasonable to expect that the executives of the cooperatives were less concerned with profit margins.

(37) Interview, May 1973.

(38) Epstein, p. 176.

(39) Interview, May 1973.

(40) Interview, May 1973.

(41) Gordon, p. 339.

(42) V. O. Key, *Politics, Parties and Pressure Groups* (New York: Thomas Y. Crowell Company, 1964), p. 72. Gabriel Kolko, *Wealth and Power in America: An Analysis of Social Class and Income Distribution* (New York: Praeger Books, 1962), described the political objectives of business in a similar way: "Political capitalism is the utilization of political outlets to attain conditions of stability, predictability and security" (p. 28).

(43) Canadian Manufacturers' Association, *An Industrial Policy for Québec* (brief submitted to Guy St. Pierre, minister of industry and commerce, 11 August 1972), p. 2.

(44) Ibid.

(45) Domhoff, in *The Higher Circles,* and Weinstein put substantial emphasis on the important role played by the leaders of the larger corporations and financial institutions. They maintained that these leaders were, on the whole, more "system conscious" (i.e., oriented toward the survival of the system) than the leaders of the smaller business units who tended to be more concerned with their own short-term interests. Thus, the leaders of the larger corporations were much more receptive towards "liberal values," i.e., the need for more labour and welfare legislation. Weinstein maintained, moreover, that few reforms brought in during the progressive era in American politics "were enacted without the tacit approval, if not the guidance, of the large corporate interests," and further that "the ideal of a liberal corporate social order was formulated and developed under the aegis and supervision of those who then, as now, enjoyed ideological and political hegemony in the United States: the more sophisticated leaders of America's largest corporations and financial institutions" (p. ix).

(46) E. P. Taylor, "A Canadian Industrialist's Four-Point Formula For Expansion," *Canadian Business,* November 1961, p. 27.

48

(47) W. E. McLaughlin, "Pitfalls of Economic Planning," *Canadian Business*, June 1965, p. 71.

(48) Ibid., p. 68. A recent advertisement by Gulf Oil Corporation in Newsweek, 25 June 1973, pp. 52-53, typifies the attitude of business towards the government. Gulf Oil first stated: "A strong private energy industry must be maintained." It then listed all the services that the government should provide for the oil industry. This included "increasing availability of public lands to energy industries," the "support of long-range research programs," the creation of "the economic environment needed to commercialize synthetic fuels," government encouragement to U.S. industry "to develop energy sources in foreign countries," and government encouragement of energy conservation.

(49) Business is often more than willing to give government the responsibility of dealing with social problems but not the means. To quote Arnold Hart, chairman of the board of the Bank of Montréal:
"There has been an ambivalence in the business attitude toward government on problems of welfare . . . On the one hand, we have tended to leave the welfare baby on the government doorstep and on the other have consistently inveighed against government spending, the stultifying effects of our welfare system and the disincentives to initiative and progress throughout the economy that are inherent in the approach.
". . . Some of us in the business community must revise our attitude towards government and be less reluctant to enter into partnership with the government to achieve our common goals" (quoted in Vithal Rajan, "The Challenge of Youth," *Canadian Business*, September 1969, p. 42).

(50) Interview, May 1973.

(51) Roy Bennett, "Government-Business Advisory Board Should be Established," *Financial Post*, 6 January 1973.

(52) CIL executive quoted in Vithal Rajan, "The Challenge of Youth."

(53) C. Perrault, "The Business-Bureaucracy Interface," speech to the 17th annual business conference at the University of Western Ontario, London, 1 June 1973, pp. 4-5.

(54) Interview, May 1973.

(55) Centre des Dirigeants d'Entreprise, *Fonction de l'entreprise et regroupement des cadres* (Montréal: Centre des Dirigeants d'entreprise, 1970), p. 5.

(56) Pierre Shooner quoted in Michel Roesler, "L'Homme d'affaires efficace est un homme de gauche," *La Presse*, 29 February 1972.

(57) Epstein, p. 149.

(58) J. K. Finlayson, "Social Responsibilities of International Business," speech given at a luncheon of the Canada/United Kingdom Chamber of Commerce in London, England, 2 May 1973, p. 2.

(59) Ibid., p. 4.

(60) Ibid., p. 6. In "The Fourth Circle," *Canadian Banker*, July 1972, H. C. Byleveld, director of corporate development for the Banque Provinciale du Canada, said: "Accepting social change as a steady procession of manageable problems is preferable to rigidly resisting it as long as possible. Inflexibility may ultimately sow the seeds of some future crisis and of ill-considered, excessive government intervention" (p. 17).

(61) Centre des Dirigeants d'Entreprise, p. 4.

(62) Jean Brunelle, "Business in Québec: Bystander or Partner in Development," speech given at the annual meeting of the Centre des Dirigeants d'Entreprise, 7 December 1972, p. 6.

(63) Conseil du Patronat du Québec, *Rapport Annuel: 1971-1972* (Montréal: Conseil du Patronat du Québec, 1972), p. 2.

(64) Centre des Dirigeants d'Entreprise, "Elements of a Strategy for Business," *Industrial Relations*, vol. 26, December 1971, p. 993.

(65) Ibid., p. 1001.

(66) A. E. Levin, "Social Responsibility is Everybody's Business," *Canadian Banker*, July 1972, p. 15.

(67) Ronald Ritchie, "Analysing Competitive Enterprise," *Canadian Business*, November 1972, p. 28.

(68) See Berle, Gordon, and Child.

(69) Epstein, p. 150.

(70) This is not to say that "unemployment and inflation" do not have an important social dimension.

(71) The 70% figure was arrived at by adding the 40% of French respondents who opted for "unemployment and inflation" to the 30% who chose "weakness of the Québec economic structure."

(72) The PQ obtained 23.8% of the vote in the Québec provincial election of April 1970 and 30.1% of the vote in the election of October 1973.

(73) Only one respondent favoured separatism, but there is strong reason to believe this was a mistake. The same respondent expressed support for the Liberal Party and was in general agreement with governmental policy. The Figure of 99.3% should therefore be 100%.

CHAPTER 4

BUSINESS ASSOCIATIONS

BUSINESS ASSOCIATIONS are a component of business power in three important ways: they provide formal channels of access to governmental decision-making structures; they constitute a significant pool of business resources and a visible tool of business public relations and other propaganda activities; they are vehicles for business unity because they present a common business point of view to government or to other social groups. Since the main focus is big business, emphasis is placed on the links between large corporations and business associations. However, before analysing each Québec business association separately in terms of the three elements outlined above, a few general points must be made.

In the first place, a number of recent studies suggest that the public relations function of business associations is on the upswing. In Germany, according to Gerard Braunthal, the Federation of German Industry has become "increasingly active in its public relations campaign."[1] The Federation, along with the German Employer's Association, has also put more stress on defending the economic system and in 1951 founded the Institute of Research and Public Relations to "help lay the foundations of the entrepreneurial conception of economic and social policy and to make it part of public consciousness."[2] Similarly, in Italy, the main business association, Confindustria, publishes a regular newsletter, designed for distribution to workers, "which stresses the important role of private enterprise and the necessity of maintaining harmony betwen labour and management."[3]

Opinions differ on the degree of homogeneity and unity within business associations. Some observers claim that opposing points of view and goals within the membership make it very difficult for associations to reach a consensus;[4] others state qualifications. According to Braunthal, for example:

> Although their [business associations affiliated to the Federation of German Industry] internal cohesion is less than the leadership would desire, neither does it amount to a state of anarchy . . . It is perfectly true that on some measures the leadership cannot achieve a compromise among competing industries; but on broad issues of policy it can usually obtain a degree of accord — either because all industries would benefit or because of a common ideology.[5]

In Québec, 97.1% of the questionnaire respondents thought "business associations reflect the views of the business community".[6] This indicates a high level of ideological cohesion within big business[7] and confirms the hypothesis that the various statements and public representations of business associations are a reflection of the feelings of the larger corporations.

The question of the associations' access to governmental decision-makers is complex. As will be seen below, they have easy access to top governmental decision-makers, but the senior executives use the associations infrequently to present their views. Thus, despite the large degree of functional success enjoyed by the associations, businessmen still prefer to deal directly with government.

This view is supported by a large body of literature. Joseph La Palombara, in his analysis of Confindustria, concludes:

> There is a tendency on the part of industrial giants like Fiat and Montecatini to have one foot inside and one foot outside the Confederation [of Italian Industry] . . The industrial giants are often strong enough to effect in their own way interaction with political parties, other interest groups, and the branches of government . . .[8]

Or, as Jean Meynaud says: "Siemens, Montecatini, Courtaulds, GM need no intermediaries to deal with the authorities.[9] Epstein, too, speaks of the "tendency for [U.S.] corporations to 'go it alone' in their political involvement rather than rely predominantly on trade and business associations."[10]

The interviews confirmed the fact that large companies often bypass business associations in their attempts to influence government. One senior executive said that when an issue was significant, his company presented its own briefs and made its own representations.[11] One of the vice-presidents of a bank said that although business associations were sometimes useful as pressure groups, "We prefer to organize ourselves."[12] The vice-president of a holding in the food and beverage sector claimed that informal contacts with government were more productive than working through business associations.[13] Others said the groups were "not particularly useful" or "a lot of wasted time."[14]

In addition, the smaller companies are the main beneficiaries of the services provided by business associations. According to Paul Diment, who analysed trade associations for *Canadian Business:* "It seems probable that the smaller businesses within any given industry benefit more from their associations than do the larger firms."[15] This is confirmed by an executive of the Canadian Manufacturers' Association: "Quand il y a des problèmes d'interprétation du Code du Travail, ce ne sont pas Dupont et les grosses compagnies qui nous appellent, mais les petits employeurs, surtout des petites entreprises francophones."[16]

If large corporations do not use the associations' services, and if, in addition, they use them only marginally for access to decision-makers, one might ask why big businesses are the main supporters of associations in terms of financial and personnel resources.[17] First, the associations play an important public relations role: They engage in the more overt forms of political activity which, by and large, the large corporations shy away from. Second, large corporations participate actively in the business associations to keep them to some extent under control and to make sure that the public positions taken by the associations represent the interests of big business. The bigger corporations, being the main sources of expertise, resources, personnel, and research reports, can, of course, "present their point of view much more effectively than the smaller ones."[18] Executives of smaller companies, on the other hand, "do not have enough time and have too many functions to be able to study legislation and express an opinion."[19]

A bank executive acknowledged the essentially defensive stance adopted by big businesses within associations:

> "The large companies belong to associations for defensive purposes, by tradition, in order to obtain information concerning their industry and to control other companies a little. They do not want to be disturbed by the associations. When they have a problem, they decide what to do outside the associations."[20]

Chart 4 gives a bird's eye view of the operation of the main business associations in Québec. As is readily seen, there are three associations which group firms or corporations and two which group business leaders or individuals. The Conseil du Patronat regroups most of the associations themselves. The General Council of Industry (GCI), which will be discussed at length in the next chapter, also appears on the chart even though it is not properly speaking a business association. Suffice it to say for the time being that formally the CGI is an advisory board composed of important business leaders who make periodic recommendations to the minister of industry and commerce.

The questionnaire data indicated a high degree of participation among Québec businesses and businessmen in the various business associations. Businessmen were asked to which associations their company belonged; on the average, slightly more than three associations were listed per respondent.[21] Table 3 makes it clear that the French element favored the predominantly French associations, namely, the Chambre de Commerce and the Centre des Dirigeants d'Entreprise, whereas the English respondents leaned more towards the predominantly English associations, such as the Board of Trade, CMA, and trade associations.

Corporate leaders were also asked what they thought was the "most effective business association in dealing with the Québec government." Table 4 shows that the Conseil du Patronat, founded in 1969, has acquired a dominant position in the minds of businessmen. Almost 40% of business executives thought it was the most effective organization. As expected, French respondents considered their own associations had more influence, while the English respondents opted for the Board of Trade and the CMA.

There is also a significant difference between the responses of the major and secondary companies. The executives of the smaller companies favoured the Chambre de Commerce and the CMA while the larger company executives chose the Conseil du Patronat. This is perhaps due to the fact that the Conseil du Patronat deals with the larger issues of business concern and is more clearly dominated by the heads of the large corporations. On the other hand, the other associations, including the CMA and the Chambre de Commerce, deal with many of the basic problems of smaller businesses and tend to give the smaller businessmen greater participation in decision-making. There is also the fact that, as will be shown later, big businessmen are much more aware and conscious of what individuals wield influence at the governmental level.

CHART 4
BUSINESS ASSOCIATIONS IN QUÉBEC: FORMAL ACCESS STRUCTURES

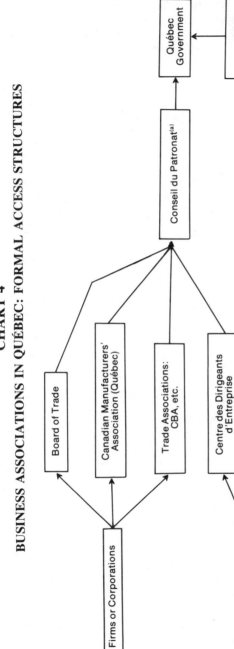

(a) The Conseil du Patronat is a member of several Québec government advisory boards, the most important of which is the Advisory Council on Labour and Manpower.

TABLE 3

PERCENTAGE DISTRIBUTION OF RESPONSES OF QUÉBEC BUSINESSMEN REGARDING MEMBERSHIP IN BUSINESS ASSOCIATIONS
(Question II C: "Which business association(s) does your company belong to?")

	All Respondents	French Respondents	English Respondents
Board of Trade	79.7	63.8	86.9
Chambre de Commerce	86.3	90.1	83.7
Canadian Manufacturers' Association	51.8	36.0	59.7
Trade Associations	61.8	38.3	73.9
Centre des Dirigeants d'Entreprise	23.7	42.5	14.1

N = 425[a]

(a) N = 425 because businessmen and corporations usually belong to several associations.

The Canadian Manufacturers' Association (Québec)

Across Canada, in 1972, the CMA had about 8,300 member firms, representing approximately 75% of total manufacturing output. It had more than 100 full-time employees.[22] Although its head office is in Toronto, the CMA maintains an active Québec division centered in Montréal but including eight regional branches. According to a CMA executive, there are 1,800 member firms in Québec, of which 80% employ less than 100 workers, and the CMA permanent staff numbers 12.[23]

The CMA is probably the most homogeneous management association because it speaks only for manufacturers. But even if its main focus is the "problems specific to manufacturers," it deals also with the more general problems facing the business community.[24]

Like most business organizations, it claims to be non-political:

> The CMA does not adopt political positions . . . makes no political statements . . .
>
> Yet it does express its views on matters of local, provincial or federal concern insofar as they affect the manufacturing industry. It has recently submitted its views on such matters as competition policy, foreign ownership policy, amendments to the Unemployment Act and the Canada Labour Code. [25]

It is evident from the above that only the most narrow definition of politics, i.e., as competition between political parties, allows the CMA to describe its activities as non-political. In keeping with contemporary business ideology, the association tends to identify its interests and policies with the public's: "We believe that in the overwhelming majority of cases the interests of the nation as a whole are similar and in most cases identical with the interests of the manufacturing industry . . ." [26]

The functions of the CMA include information services to members, public relations, and government representation. Regarding information and advice functions, the Québec CMA "maintains a full-time staff of experts which make available, at no charge, specialized services covering all manner of management problems and queries affecting a company's provincial operations." [27] These include labour relations, wage rates and working conditions, pollution legislation, provincial income, and investment incentives. The Québec division also publishes its own news bulletin which features digests of legislative enactments, details of new provincial regulations, or orders in council of import to Québec industry. [28]

Altough the CMA is less active on the provincial front than the Chambre de Commerce or the Conseil du Patronat, it has nonetheless submitted a good number of briefs on most aspects of Québec governmental policy, including language, labour relations, economic development, education, and social problems. Most of the dealings with government, however, are secret and not put in the form of briefs. As D. H. Fréchette, CMA executive vice-president, said:

> . . . The overwhelming bulk of CMA input is, and will continue to be, in the form of unpublicized informal discussions — the constant interchange of visits between government officials and the CMA staff and committee personnel.
>
> In its relations with a number of Ottawa departments, this process of consultation has virtually eliminated the need for formal submissions, except for those cases in which it is appropriate to provide rather full documentation in support of a particular policy proposal. [29]

The same applies to the Québec level. A CMA executive working in Québec declared that he was satisfied with his access to government. He claimed the CMA's day-to-day relations were with the deputy minister and his assistants, though there were frequent dealings with ministers and the premier:

> When we have a problem, we usually go see the relevant minister and explain the situation to him. He then chooses a civil servant who will be responsible for solving the problem. This allows us to follow up on the problem and to always know who is responsible for its solution. [30]

Concerning the degree of business consensus within the CMA, one company executive said: "There are occasional disagreements, but they are rarely insurmountable." [31] A CMA executive remarked: "There are no difficulties in obtaining a consensus." [32]

The CMA is active in the public relations field. It noted with satisfaction that "general items quoting the CMA have appeared an average of 3,830 times each year in newspapers and periodicals," and that "editorials from *Industry* [CMA publication] have been reproduced an

TABLE 4

PERCENTAGE DISTRIBUTION OF RESPONSES OF QUÉBEC BUSINESSMEN REGARDING BUSINESS ASSOCIATIONS JUDGED MOST EFFECTIVE IN DEALING WITH QUÉBEC GOVERNMENT[a]

(Question II B: "In your opinion, which business association has been most effective in dealing with the Québec government?")

	All Respondents	English Respondents	French Respondents	Respondents From Large Companies	Respondents From Secondary Companies
Board of Trade	9.5	14.3	1.9	9.8	8.0
Chambre de Commerce	27.0	23.8	32.1	25.3	36.0
Conseil du Patronat	39.4	35.7	45.1	42.9	24.0
Canadian Manufacturers' Association	13 1	15.5	9.4	11.0	24.0
Trade Associations	9.5	9.5	9.4	8.8	8.0
Centre des Dirigeants d'Entreprise	1.5	1.2	1.9	2.2	0

N = 125

(a) The figures exclude the 12.6% of the respondents who did not answer the question.

average of 578 times a year."[33] The aims of the CMA public relations efforts are to "explain to the people of Canada the achievements, rights and responsibilities of business" and "to tell the truth about business to a public that was plainly out of touch with the economic facts of life."[34] The main tool for achieving this is an "economics education programme." In a brief to Guy St. Pierre, Québec minister of industry and commerce, the CMA asked for "an immediate start in imparting to high school students a minimum but basic understanding of the economic realities of the society in which we live," including, for example, "how commercial banks function, an understanding of saving, investing, government and taxation, the function of money."[35]

A CMA executive working in Québec was blunt about the program's aims: "The guys who get out of high school must know that profit is not the fruit of the exploitation of workers. Potential revolutionaries must be stopped."[36] He claimed the CMA held at least one yearly meeting at each regional level for CMA business representatives, students, and professors. It also cooperated with Québec junior colleges in establishing courses. Finally, he said, the CMA maintained a committee on the business climate whose function was "to counteract and respond to the accusations made against business."[37]

The Chambre de Commerce

The Chamber of Commerce has three levels: Canadian, provincial, and local. The position of the Québec Chambre de Commerce is unique in that it is autonomous from the Canadian Chamber and has no official links with the Canadian organization. The separation came after World War II when the Canadian Chamber offered to finance all provincial chambers on the condition they agreed to forego their direct contributions from companies. All provincial chambers accepted the proposal except that in Québec. Though the Canadian Chamber's offer would have provided at the time about three to four times more money than the Québec Chambre's budget, the Québec group wanted to keep its right to solicit its own contributions. The decision was apparently costly at first, but now, with a budget of more than half a million dollars annually, the Québec Chambre has the largest income of any provincial chamber in Canada.

The Québec Chambre is a federation of 235 local chambers and boards of trade. The local chambers are affiliated separately to the Canadian and Québec chambers. However, almost all are affiliated to the Québec Chambre while only half are connected to the Canadian group. Some of the local chambers are in fact important in their own right. In 1971, the Chambre de Commerce du District de Montréal, for example, had 4,000 members, assets of $719,395, and revenues of $219,087.[39] It is active in the public relations field and publishes a monthly magazine, *La Revue Commerce,* which has more than 60,000 subscribers. The Montréal Chambre is affiliated to both the Canadian and Québec chambers.

The affiliates of the Québec Chambre have a total of 30,000 individual members and 2,000 corporate members. Ninety per cent of the membership is made up of businessmen and professionals.[40] However, they all claim officially to be "community organizations," and it is for this reason that the Québec Chambre did not join the Conseil du Patronat. All the evidence indicates, however, that the chambers are business associations. An executive of the Québec Chambre admitted that the chambers were trying to camouflage the fact that they were indeed business spokesmen.[41] Other business association executives supported this statement. A senior executive of the Board of Trade argued that both the Québec and Canadian chambers of commerce were financed mainly by the corporate community and were "corporate organizations whether they recognized it or not."[42] A spokesman for the Conseil du Patronat, commenting upon the last-minute decision by the Québec Chambre not to become a member of the Conseil, rejected the Chambre's contention that it was not a business association.[43]

Though without formal links with the Conseil, the Chambre maintains many informal ties. An executive of the Québec Chambre said there were monthly meetings at the executive level among business associations to coordinate action. These meetings include discussions of government legislation and suggestions of how to avoid overlapping among the various groups. In most cases, the associations agree on a division of labour; when the issue is considered crucial, however, they all get involved in the pressure activity. The same executive claimed there is an "agreement on the basics" with the Conseil du Patronat and other business associations.[44]

The decision-making process within the Québec Chambre is another indication of business dominance. According to an executive of the Chambre, business not only provides most of the funds, but also controls the board organizations, particularly in urban areas. He added that, though the local chambers were theoretically supposed to make all the main decisions, in practice it was the experts of the Québec Chambre who made the choices. Given the complexity of the problems involved, the regional groups have neither the time nor the competence to fully understand and evaluate the various proposals made, he maintained.[45] The executive and board of directors of the Québec Chambre are made up mostly of middle-level businessmen. The board of governors, however, is dominated by senior businessmen — including Desmarais, L. Beaudoin, president of Bombardier, L.G. Rolland, president of Rolland Paper, R.C. Scrivener, president of Bell Telephone, and S. Steinberg, president of Steinberg's.[46]

Even though the Chambre de Commerce is probably the most heterogeneous of the business associations, the evidence indicates that the degree of consensus within it is considerable. An executive of the Chambre claimed that "compromise is not too difficult," and the main source of friction was between the small and large companies. This problem is often accentuated, he said, because small companies are usually local and French, whereas the large ones tend to be multinational and English.[47] This does not prevent the Québec Chambre from succeeding at its annual convention in adopting long lists of specific resolutions dealing with a wide range of issues. In 1971, for example, it published a 100-page brochure containing proposals on most spheres of governmental activity, including such areas as communication, public works, industry and commerce, and education.[48]

The Québec Chambre de Commerce and its regional branches are mainly oriented towards the interests of French business leaders. To quote the Montréal Chambre:

> It is the French fact that represents the exclusive justification for the existence of the Chambre de Commerce du District de Montréal . . . For your Chambre, the goal is not only bilingualism! Its goal, its role, is the economic and social advancement of a nation, the French-Canadian nation[49] (p. 4).

Further, according to the Montréal Chambre, the French fact is the only raison d'être for its existence alongside the Montréal Board of Trade:

> The French fact is so closely identified with your Chambre that to ignore it would be the equivalent of provoking its disappearance or its integration within the Board of Trade, with which it would then overlap completely. If it is easy to imagine a bilingual Board of Trade, it is certainly not easy to imagine a Board of Trade advocating the increase of French-Canadian influence in all areas, and more particularly in the leadership positions of the large corporations and the state[50].

Like the CMA, the chambers are active in the public relations field and put substantial emphasis on economic education. The Canadian Chamber published pamphlets explaining the benefits of profits and the free enterprise system.[51] John Ellis, president of the Canadian Chamber in 1972, said the teaching of economics in schools was the only way to silence critics of the free enterprise system.[52] Similarly, the Québec Chambre stated that the deficiencies of economic education were one of the main reasons for current social problems.[53]

Regarding access to government, an executive of the Québec Chambre said that his association has almost daily contacts with ministers, deputy ministers, and divisional heads; also, the Chambre has four direct telephone lines to Québec City, and an executive goes there almost every week. Most of the pressure activity is at the ministerial level, although civil servants are useful sources of information for the preparation of briefs, for knowledge on what is behind a piece of legislation, and for preparation of discussions with ministers. The executive of the Québec Chambre usually meet ministers and deputy ministers one at a time at least once a year. Furthermore, the executive has a meeting with the entire Québec cabinet every year. The meetings usually lasted from four to five hours. The Chambre is the only association which has this kind of formal relationship with the Québec government, excluding, of course, the various advisory boards.[54]

The Montreal Board of Trade

The Montreal Board of Trade is the English counterpart of the Chambre de Commerce du District de Montréal. Unlike the Chambre, though, the Board of Trade has only corporate members. The Board represents about 3,000 business establishments in the Montreal area, 2,200 of which have fewer than 100 employees. It controls assets worth approximately $2 million and has a yearly revenue of $250,000. The Board of Trade is a member of both the Canadian and Québec chambers of commerce. [55]

As will be described in part II, the Board is active in many debates over policy at the Québec governmental level, including consumer protection, economic development, language, and education. It provided many of the same services which are available from other business associations, such as business training courses, personnel management workshops, an employee relations section, and transportation clinics. The Board also publishes semi-monthly circulars which are distributed to all members and which include advice on any new legislation or regulations at the local, provincial, or federal levels which affect business. [56]

Regarding the participation of big businesses in the Board, an executive of the Board of Trade gave three reasons why the companies having more than 100 employees are dominant. First, small companies have relatively little time to devote to Board activities; second, many of the experts used by the Board are employed by the large corporations, and they are responsible for most of the briefs submitted to government and the research reports; third, the large companies provide considerably more than 50% of the Board's expenses. [57]

Such businesses are well-represented in the upper echelons of the Board. In 1972-73, the 21-member council-elect included K.A. White, president of the Royal Trust, as president, and representatives from the Bank of Montreal, Aluminum Company of Canada, Canadian International Paper, Dominion Glass, Imperial Tobacco, Zeller's, Toronto-Dominion Bank, Robert Morse Corporation, T. Eaton Company, and Air Canada. [58]

An executive of the Board of Trade said that member companies of the Board have no difficulty reaching a consensus on most matters, including regional development, taxation, language, and labour legislation. "We reach a common point of view very easily on most things within the Board of Trade and within the Québec Chambre de Commerce," he said. [59]

The Board is also satisfied with its access to government and most of the time makes its representations directly to the government rather than going through the Québec Chambre de Commerce. A spokesman for the Board claims to deal directly and regularly with ministers and deputy ministers and thinks the minister and officials of the department of industry and commerce are particularly helpful because they "understand the business mentality." [60] He adds that ministers often came to business for advice and that several of them spend three to five days in Montréal when the National Assembly is not in session. [61]

The Centre des Dirigeants d'Entreprise

The Centre des Dirigeants d'Entreprise comprises about 1,000 businessmen representing approximately 400 companies. According to an executive of the CDE, its membership is dominated by small and medium-sized companies and is estimated to be 90% Francophone. Attempts to recruit members of English mother tongue have met with little success. Unlike the Québec Chambre, the CDE is not a federation; its eight regional offices are under the direction of the Montréal office.[62]

Although the CDE operates nine committees, including labour relations, regional development, and language, and provides various services to its members, such as advice on mergers, its primary function is social and ideological. To quote an executive of the CDE:

> The CDE does not first and foremost provide concrete services or act as a pressure group. Its action seeks to promote the integration of business to the socio-economic milieu in Québec. We are working on a long-term action plan to change business from within and also to change business's image in the eyes of the government and public opinion.[63]

The CDE is unquestionably the most progressive business association in Québec. It focusses almost exclusively on the social and human aspects of business, including such internal questions as the frustration of middle-managers. It is also the only association not located in the financial heart of Montréal; it has modest headquarters in a predominantly lower middle-class residential neighborhood in the northeast end of Montréal. Overall, its position in the business world is paradoxical. Though its membership is composed of predominantly small and conservative businessmen, its policies are more liberal than those of any other business association. A 1971 policy statement said the CDE's main objective was "the integration of man into business," "the adaption of business to the economic and social needs of the environment in which it operates," and the "broadening of businessmen's outlook."[64]

The CDE is credited with being the driving force behind the regrouping of business associations under the umbrella organization of the Conseil du Patronat[65], as well as the creation of the Québec Planning and Development Council in 1970[66], and the renewal of the Consultative Council on Labour and Manpower. Further, the CDE has put substantial emphasis on the creation of "concertation" mechanisms among labour, business, and government. Its main goal in this respect is to avoid labour and social crises by meeting problems head-on in advance:

> By pressuring governments to create really functional consultation (cooperation) mechanisms, the CDE seeks to dampen the more virulent aspects of social protest and to propagate a more ordered view of common problems.[67]

Inevitably, the creation of the Conseil du Patronat in 1969 led to questions about the role and even raison d'être for the continued existence of the CDE. An executive of the CDE considered that, even though the Conseil du Patronat had taken over the representative functions with governments and the "concertation" functions with unions, the CDE still has an important role to play as the "social conscience" of business and as a committee for the elaboration of long-term survival and defense strategy for business.[68] This role is described by C. Dessureault, the CDE president in 1973 and a CIL executive:

> The CDE, despite the Conseil du Patronat and the Montréal and Québec chambers of commerce, still believes it is a useful element for the world of business and that it can offer something different: the acceleration of the evolution of business towards the realization of its social and community, thus economic, role.
>
> The CDE has a more advanced philosophy than the Chambre de Commerce, aims less at the defense of the private enterprise system as such, wants to concentrate on long term research within the business community, preoccupies itself, in fact, with the evolution of business in the world of tomorrow.[69]

According to a CDE executive, the financial difficulties which plagued the CDE since 1971 were due mainly to the fact that "long-term preoccupations were not profitable on St. James Street [the locale of finance in Montréal].[70] In 1972, it launched a fund raising campaign to erase its $70,000 deficit. Some larger companies, including the Bank of Montreal and the Royal Bank of Canada, joined at the end of 1972.[71] This was not enough, however, and in April 1972 the Québec government announced its decision to grant $25,000 to the CDE to help cover its deficit.[72] In 1975, the Department of Industry and Commerce granted an additional $49,000 to the CDE and $60,000 to the Québec Chamber. Considering that business itself, despite its substantial resources, did not consider the survival of these associations essential to its aims,[73] one can wonder why the Québec government decided to finance them. The most plausible hypothesis is that the government was trying to encourage the development of more progressive views within the corporate elite on the presumption the improvement would result in greater social harmony.

Finally, regarding access to decision-makers, the CDE, like other business groups, is in a good position. An executive of the CDE claimed most of his contacts were with deputy ministers and ministers. He dealt mainly with St. Pierre.[74]

Trade Associations: The case of the Canadian Bankers' Association

Almost every industry, including pulp and paper, insurance, mining, and retailing, has an active and well-organized trade association. In dealing with the government, most of these associations focus mainly on the problems of the specific industry they represent, rather than on the more general problems faced by business as a whole. Since it is of little value to examine all these associations, concentration is placed on the Canadian Bankers' Association because it is probably the most powerful of the trade associations.

The CBA had a total staff of 100, of whom 60 are in the Toronto head office and 40 in Montréal. Its executive council is comprised of senior executives of the major Canadian banks, and it deals mainly with the federal government since little provincial legislation affects banking. The CBA nonetheless has a Québec section which, according to a CBA executive, "does not play a crucial role because the head offices of five major banks are located in Montréal and because the executives of these banks are very close to Québec and its issues and get together regularly with government officials."[75]

The CBA maintains a committee in Québec City, made up of senior bank executives in the area and a few local lawyers. Its primary function is dealing with minor problems and keeping the CBA informed on provincial legislation; as much as possible, the committee attempts to obtain copies of bills before they became public. Most of the secondary problems are dealt with by Renaud St. Laurent, the son of former Canadian Prime Minister Louis St. Laurent, who practises law in Québec City and who is also a member of several boards of directors. As the CBA's legal counsel in Québec City, his job is to try to solve problems at the deputy ministerial level. If new legislation is involved or if the problem is important, it is referred to the CBA's Montréal office.[76]

Like other business associations, the CBA has an active public relations department. Along with the CMA and the Chambre de Commerce, it is involved in a project to stimulate the study of economics. According to an executive of the CBA, "The CBA is under pressure from its membership to beat the drum for private enterprise."[77] By and large, the public relations activities are aimed at improving the "corporate image." To that end, "The CBA has produced a good number of radio spots which are currently [1973] being used by 40 to 50 radio stations" and has published a few pamphlets, including a book on "money management" which has sold over a quarter of a million copies, primarily in schools.[78]

The evidence indicates that banks are satisfied with the CBA, and the association has no problems reaching a consensus among its members. A CBA executive said: "There is no problem finding common views on issues. We get active support from all banks. Ranks close pretty quickly despite the fact that our membership includes three of the 15 biggest banks in the world."[79] This view is confirmed by two senior banking executives. Said one: "Consensus is almost automatic within the CBA."[80] Said the other: "The CBA is listened to by government" and plays an important role in "getting together with government officials to draft regulations."[81]

The Conseil du Patronat du Québec

The Conseil du Patronat is an employers' federation regrouping the horizontal business associations,[82] except the Chambre de Commerce, and most of the trade associations. The Conseil has some 130 member associations representing the employers of more than 80% of Québec's manpower. Founded January 20, 1969, it has rapidly become the most effective spokesman for management vis-à-vis the Québec government and Québec society as a whole.[83]

One might ask why business in Québec felt it needed a common voice when in most of the Canadian provinces and in the U.S., no such structure exists. The main reason, according to the president of a business association, is "the need for a common business point of view in face of a more militant labour movement and the various common fronts."[84] Another business association spokesman said there was "a feeling among certain associations and businessmen that the existence of one voice would be more efficient and would facilitate communication with the state."[85]

The Conseil is the first business association in Québec to have French-Canadian leadership, though it has largely English-Canadian financial backing.[86] According to a senior executive of a major Québec company, who is also a member of the Conseil's board of governors, "The French-Canadian leadership is good because it allows more effective communications with government and a more effective public relations job for business."[87] Here again, the public relations function of French-Canadian business leaders comes to light.

An executive of the Conseil estimates that at least 90% of the Conseil's activities are at the Québec provincial level. It represents the business viewpoint on many governmental advisory boards, such as the Québec Planning and Development Council on which it has three representatives, the Consumer Protection Council on which it has five representatives, and the Advisory Committee on Labour and Manpower on which it has five representatives. It also submits briefs on such subjects as taxation, sectorial bargaining, labour legislation, and language and makes representations to committees of the National Assembly. There is, also, an annual meeting between the Conseil's executives and Québec's premier and finance minister concerning the budget.[88]

During its first three years of existence, the Conseil concentrated its efforts on labour legislation, but, according to one of its executives, "This was due to circumstances — like an active labour period and a heavy legislative output by the government in the labour field. After 1972, the Conseil spent at least as much time on economic matters.[89]

In regard to public relations, the Conseil devotes considerable energy to the defense of federalism and the free enterprise system. In 1972, for example, it published a brochure entitled *Détruire le système actuel? C'est à y penser*[90] which gave a detailed outline of the benefits of the free enterprise system and also spelled out a series of long-term objectives for business.

The interviews confirm that the Conseil du Patronat and its president, C. Perrault, are rated very highly by top Québec businessmen who think both have been helpful in "opening up new links with government,"[91] "particularly effective in dealing with labour-management relations,"[92] and "excellent as the voice of business in Québec."[93] The chairman of the board of a major company said: "Nothing is done in Québec that the Conseil du Patronat does not have something to say about."[94] An executive of the Conseil du Patronat concurred that the Conseil has excellent contacts at all levels of government in Québec City.[95]

The Conseil du Patronat has also been successful in presenting a unified business viewpoint on nearly all important social, economic, and political questions. According to an executive of the Conseil,

"During the last four and a half years, the Conseil has been successful in reaching a consensus on all critical questions,"[96] even though, he continued, cultural issues, particularly language, were difficult to deal with. Two senior executives supported his claim regarding unity within the Conseil.[97]

A final point of interest is the relationship between the Conseil du Patronat and large corporations. For the same reasons cited in the instances of the other associations, the larger companies have the upper hand in the Conseil. This is not surprising in that the majority of funds are provided by a relatively small number of large corporations. In 1971, the Conseil spent $168,477, but only $10,000 of that was contributed by member associations. The rest was provided by about 100 big corporations.[98] In 1974, the Conseil du Patronat published a list of the 117 corporations which made financial contributions to its operations. The list was made up mainly of the largest Québec companies. Surprisingly, the list included two companies owned by the Québec government — Hydro-Québec and Sidbec. CIL, Royal Bank of Canada, and Canada Cement Lafarge were among those companies which were involved in the formative stages of the Conseil du Patronat, and they continued to make regular contributions.[99] The Conseil did try to finance itself through it's member business associations, but its attempts were unsuccessful.

The Conseil du Patronat has modified its structure to allow for corporate membership. The companies which finance it are now allowed to become members and to elect their own delegates to the board of governors. This has, in effect, created a parallel structure to the board of directors which is made up mainly of business association representatives. The relationship between these structures is not clear, but, according to an executive of a business association, the reorganization has allowed the large corporations who foot the bill to exercise control within the Conseil at the expense of the federated members. He said he thought the large companies had fought to dominate the Conseil because they realized how successful it had become.[100] He further claimed that the smaller companies within the Conseil had been opposed to the larger companies' efforts to obtain special status through corporate membership.

An executive of the Conseil du Patronat maintained that corporate members were essential to the survival of the Conseil and were justified by the principle "no taxation without representation." He maintained, however, that the new structural arrangements "will not give that much to the companies."[101] If this is so, one can wonder why some companies pushed so hard to obtain the changes. A senior executive of a large corporation claimed the changes were made to "placate some companies."[102] The vice-president of an insurance company argued that making the big companies full participating members of the Conseil was advantageous for financial reasons and also "because the big companies were the source of most of the expertise and manpower for the committees, reports, etc."

In an open letter to *La Presse* on January 28, 1976, J. Arthur Bédard, former president of the CDE, complained bitterly that the CPQ did not adequately represent Québec employers as a whole but rather only the largest and mainly foreign corporations. He claimed that the CPQ reflected the interests of the firms which financed it and this explained the Conseil's position against the Tetley and Descoteaux reports, which recommended stiffer requirements for foreign investments.

When asked about the influence of the large companies within the Conseil, a Conseil executive replied their pressures were discreet and that only two or three companies had withdrawn their contributions because they were not satisfied. The fact remains, however, that the Conseil was dependent on corporate contributions. That only two or three companies were sufficiently dissatisfied with the Conseil to withdraw their contributions was proof of the substantial degree of consensus within the organization.

NOTES

(1) Gerard Braunthal, *The Federation of German Industry in Politics* (Ithica: Cornell University Press, 1965), p. 345.

(2) U. W. Kitzinger, *German Electoral Politics* (Oxford: Clarendon Press, 1960), p. 245.

(3) Joseph La Palombara, *Interest Groups in Italian Politics* (Princeton: Princeton University Press, 1964), p. 414.

(4) See Lewis Edinger, *Politics in Germany* (Boston: Little, Brown and Company, 1968), p. 177, and R. A. Rose.

(5) Braunthal, p. 345.

(6) The question was not answered by 4.2% of the respondents.

(7) This evidence contradicts other findings. Epstein, for example, claimed there was a "feeling on the part of some officials of large companies that business organizations do not adequately represent the political interests of large corporate constituents" (p. 52).

(8) La Palombara, p. 416.

(9) Jean Meynaud quoted in Miliband, p. 163.

(10) Epstein, p. 50.

(11) Interview, May 1973.

(12) Interview, May 1973.

(13) Interview, May 1973.

(14) Interview, May 1973.

(15) Paul Diment, "How Your Trade Associations Help You," *Canadian Business*, May 1969, p. 63.

(16) Interview, May 1973. "When there are problems of interpretation with the Labour Code, it is not Du Pont or the other large companies that call us, but rather the small employers, especially the small Francophone firms."

(17) Several executives from business associations have admitted that business association funds come from a handful of large corporations (from interviews, May 1973).

(18) Interview, May 1973.

(19) Interview, May 1973.

(20) Interview, May 1973.

(21) If one included the Conseil du Patronat, to which all companies belong through their associations, the figure would be four per respondent. It should also be noted that French executives seemed to participate somewhat less in the business associations than the English executives; they were members, on the average, of 2.7 associations compared with 3.2 for the English executives.

(22) For more details on the activities of the CMA, see D.H. Frechette, "The CMA — Spokesman for Industry," Paul Fox, ed., *Politics: Canada*, 3rd ed. (Toronto: McGraw-Hill of Canada, 1970), pp. 172-175.

(23) Interview, May 1973.

(24) Interview, May 1973.

(25) Letter to the author from K. W. Counsell, manager of the CMA's public relations department, 14 April 1972, p. 2.

(26) Ibid., p. 3.

(27) Canadian Manufacturers' Association, CMA in Québec (Montréal: Canadian Manufacturers' Association, 1972), p. 4.

(28) Ibid.

(29) D. H. Fréchette, quoted in *Financial Post*, "Improve Business-Government Ties," 7 October 1972.

(30) Interview, May 1973.

(31) Interview, May 1973.

(32) Interview, May 1973.

(33) Canadian Manufacturers' Association, *What It Is and What It Does* (Montréal: Canadian Manufacturers' Association, 1972), p. 2.

(34) Canadian Manufacturers' Association, *The First Hundred Years* (Montréal: Canadian Manufacturers' Association, 1971), p. 17.

(35) Idem, *An Industrial Policy for Quebec* (Québec City: Canadian Manufacturers' Association, 1972), app. M, pp. 1-2.

(36) Interview, May 1973.

(37) Interview, May 1973.

(38) Information from an interview with an executive of the Québec Chambre, May 1973.

(39) Chambre de Commerce du District de Montréal, *Rapport de son 84ᵉ exercise annuel 1970-1971* (Montréal: Chambre de Commerce du District de Montréal, 1971), pp. 12-13.

(40) La Chambre de Commerce de la Province de Québec, *Mémoire annuel* (Montréal: La Chambre de Commerce de la Province de Québec, 1972), p. 1.

(41) Interview, May 1973.

(42) Interview, May 1973.

(43) Interview, May 1973.

(44) Interview, May 1973.

(45) Interview, May 1973.

(46) Chambre de Commerce de la Province de Québec, *Faits et tendances*, vol. 25, no. 4, March 1973, p. 2.

(47) Interview, May 1973.

(48) Chambre de Commerce de la Province de Québec, *Déclaration de principes* (Montréal: Chambre de Commerce de la Province de Québec, 1971). Similarly, at its 1973 convention, the Chambre adopted detailed recommendations which it published in *Politiques d'action 1973* (Montréal: Chambre de Commerce de la Province de Québec, 1973).

(49) Chambre de Commerce du district de Montréal, *Rapport de son 84ᵉ exercise annuel 1970-1971*.

(50. Ibid.

(51) These include *L'Economie et vous* (Montréal: Canadian Chamber of Commerce, 1969) and *Le Profit: c'est quoi?* (Montréal: Canadian Chamber of Commerce, 1972).

(52) John Ellis quoted in La Presse canadienne, "Etablir une communication suivie entre gouvernants-hommes d'affaires-syndicats," *Le Devoir*, 20 September 1972.

(53) Chambre de Commerce de la Province de Québec, *Mémoire Annuel*, p. 9.

(54) Information is from an interview with an executive of the Québec Chambre, May 1973.

(55) Montreal Board of Trade, *Annual Report 1970-1971* (Montréal: Board of Trade, 1971), pp. 14-15.

(56) Ibid., p. 17.

(57) Interview, May 1973.

(58) *Montreal Gazette*, "Supplement on the Board of Trade," 4 May 1972.

(59) Interview, May 1973.

(60) Interview, May 1973.

(61) Interview, May 1973.

(62) Interview, May 1973.

(63) Interview, May 1973.

(64) Centre des Dirigeants d'Entreprise, "Elements of a Strategy for Business," *Industrial Relations*, vol. 26, December 1971, pp. 999-1,000.

(65) This is the opinion of a CDE executive as well as that of Laurent Bélanger in *Evolution du patronat et ses répercussions sur les attitudes et pratiques patronales dans la province de Québec*, Study no. 14, Privy Council Office (Ottawa: Queen's Printer, 1970), p. 107.

(66) See chapter 5 for details on the Québec Planning and Development Council.

(67) Centre des Dirigeants d'Entreprise, *Structures et fonctionnement* (Montréal: Centre des Dirigeants d'Entreprise, 1972), p. 3.

(68) Interview, May 1973.

(69) Pierre Vennat, "Claude Dessureault à la barre d'une CDE qui cherche une vigeur nouvelle," *La Presse*, 27 November 1973.

(70) Interview, May 1973.

(71) Rhéal Bercier, "Le CDE pourra éffacer son déficit," *La Presse*, 10 October 1972.

(72) Idem, "Le Gouvernement du Québec finance un organisme patronal," *La Presse*, 27 April 1973.

(73) Only 1.5% of questionnaire respondents chose the CDE as "the most effective business association in dealing with the Québec government."
A very different conclusion was reached by Bélanger who claimed the CDE was considered the most important business association at the Québec level (p. 105). Even though Bélanger's analysis covered the period before the creation of the Conseil du Patronat, the discrepancy is substantial.

(74) Interview, May 1973.

(75) Interview, May 1973.

(76) Interview, May 1973.

(77) Interview, May 1973.

(78) Interview, May 1973.

(79) Interview, May 1973.

(80) Interview, May 1973.

(81) Interview, May 1973. He also said the CBA assists government because "we have a lot of experience, and government officials do not know what we need and what will work."

(82) Horizontal business associations are open to all corporations or firms, whereas vertical associations regroup only those firms in a specific industrial sector.

(83) According to the CDE, "Elements of a Strategy for Business:" "After two and a half years of existence, the Conseil du Patronat is remarkably successful. It is recognized as a spokesman for management by both government and the trade unions" (p. 998).

(84) Interview, May 1973.

(85) Interview, May 1973.

(86) Interview, May 1973.

(87) Interview, May 1973.

(88) Conseil du Patronat, *Rapport Annuel: 1971-1972* (Montréal: Conseil du Patronat, 1972,). pp. 2-3.

(89) Interview, May 1973.

(90) Conseil du Patronat, *Détruire le système actuel? C'est à y penser* (Montréal: Publications les Affaires, 1972).

(91) Interview, May 1973. An executive of a business association thought that Perrault was on very friendly terms with Robert Bourassa, Québec premier, because they had worked together on the Bélanger Commission, which dealt with Québec's tax system.

(92) Interview, May 1973.

(93) Interview, May 1973.

(94) Interview, May 1973.

(95) Interview, May 1973.

(96) Interview, May 1973.

(97) Interview, May 1973.

(98) Interview, May 1973.

(99) Information from interviews, May 1973.

(100) Interview, May 1973.

(101) Interview, May 1973.

(102) Interview, May 1973.

CHAPTER 5

BUSINESS ACCESS TO GOVERNMENT

ACCESS TO DECISION-MAKERS is absolutely essential in attempts to wield influence. Without access, it is difficult if not impossible for a political actor to convey his views and to exert pressure. I will analyse here both the informal and formal aspects of business access to the Québec government. First, I will try to determine the extent and the quality of the contacts which are established between business and government. Special attention will be paid to the specific mechanisms of access, e.g., the individual in the company who deals with the government and the method. In the process, the chapter will also assess the position and the weight of business within the overall governmental decision-making environment. Second, some potential sources of governmental dependence on business will be examined, i.e., electoral finance and the need for government to borrow on the money market. These factors are closely related to access because they may lead directly or indirectly to greater receptivity on the part of government to the demands of business.

In addition to the formal and informal mechanisms of access, I will deal with the mutual institutional penetration which links business and government, i.e., the interchange and overlap of personnel between the two systems of power. As could be expected, very little data is available on the matters treated here, and reliance had to be placed almost exclusively on the questionnaire and interviews. In fact, a substantial portion of the research effort had to be focused in this area.

At the outset, it should be remembered that wealth and economic power are closely linked to access. This is true in a general way in that government recognizes its dependence on business in the performance of key economic functions. As Epstein said:

> Business leaders have considerable influence as a consequence of their capacity as the managers of the most important economic enterprises in the country, whose cooperation and assistance is critical to the national interest.[1]

> The concentration of substantial wealth in the hands of a relatively small number of firms provides these companies with the potential (even if unexercised) for behavior of political significance, which governmental decision-makers must take into account in formulating policy.[2]

But wealth also has some more specific advantages. To quote Epstein again:

> Wealth also enables business firms to fund the numerous governmental and electoral activities that are essential to promoting company political interests. It is expensive to finance such ventures as maintaining employees who concentrate full time on political matters; contributing to political parties and candidates; engaging in administrative, legislative and executive lobbying; conducting litigation; and purchasing media time and space. [3]

Informal Access

Many observers have argued that business, especially big business, has privileged access to the upper echelons of government, including cabinet ministers and senior bureaucrats.[4] The questionnaire and interview data unequivocally validate this hypothesis in the case of Québec where businessmen not only enjoy substantial access to cabinet ministers and senior civil servants, but also usually succeed in dealing with whom ever they chose in the government. The evidence also points to a high degree of satisfaction among the businessmen regarding the perceived effectiveness of their contacts with government.

Québec businessmen were first asked if they had "reasonably quick access" to senior civil servants and cabinet ministers. In the case of civil servants, 94.1% of the executives of the 100 major companies answered "yes," and 85.1% claimed access to cabinet ministers. While there were no major differences in the degree of access between French and English, the data showed that the access enjoyed by the executives of the secondary companies was substantially less than that of major companies. Thus 65.2% of the secondary company executives maintained they had quick access to civil servants and 57.1% of them reached cabinet ministers. The particularly privileged position of the major company executives will be made more obvious as this chapter progresses. At this point, however, it is clear that the government itself realizes the particular importance of these businessmen.

Two other questions sought to compare the usual methods of approach to the government with what the businessmen thought was the most effective method of influencing the Québec government. The purpose was to determine if businessmen succeeded in dealing with the government in the way they judged most effective. The corporate leaders were first asked how they usually approached the government. The choices given were "personal contact," "public opinion campaigns," "acting through business associations," and "other." As is shown in table 5, 76.7% of the senior executives of the large companies approached the government through personal contacts, whereas 20.7% opted for business associations. The secondary company executives were somewhat more likely to deal with the government through associations (27.6%) and somewhat less likely to use personal contacts (69.0%). As will be shown below, the quality of the personal contacts of the secondary company executives tended to be inferior; they dealt less with senior people than did the major company executives.

The businessmen were then asked what they thought was "the most effective method of influencing the government." The options given were the same as for the preceding question. Table 6 shows that 65.8% of major company executives chose "personal contacts," 2.6% public opinion campaigns, and 30.7% acting through business associations.[5]

Thus the perceived effectiveness of business associations was far less than personal contacts. Here again, there were significant behavioral differences between the executives of major and secondary companies. While 50% of secondary executives thought personal contacts were more effective, a substantial 42.9% favoured business associations. This was probably due in large part to the fact that secondary company executives had less access to senior government officials, as shown below. This would explain why secondary companies not only tended to rely more on business associations but thought they were more effective.

If a correlation is drawn between the two questions, the extent to which the individual businessman dealt with the government in the way he perceived most conducive to influence can be determined. Thus, if the answers to the two questions are identical, it can safely be assumed that the businessman was dealing with government in the way he thought was most effective. In the case of the major companies, 87.2% approached the government in a manner estimated most conducive to influence. In the case of secondary companies, the relationship was 75.0%.

Two other questions sought to determine the individuals or groups in the government with whom business executives dealt, and which individuals or groups were considered most crucial in the decision-making process. Table 7 shows that 81.8% of major company leaders dealt at the upper echelons of government, including 46.2% with cabinet ministers or the premier and 35.6% with deputy ministers. Other civil servants accounted for 11.4% of the major companies' governmental contacts.

TABLE 5

PERCENTAGE DISTRIBUTION OF RESPONSES OF QUÉBEC BUSINESSMEN REGARDING USUAL METHOD OF APPROACH TO THE QUÉBEC GOVERNMENT[a]
(Question II H: "How do you usually approach the government?")

	All Respondents	English Respondents	French Respondents	Respondents From Large Companies	Respondents From Secondary Companies
Personal Contact	75.2	75.3	76.5	76.7	69.0
Public Opinion Campaign	0	0	0	0	0
Acting Through Business Associations	22.0	22.6	21.6	20.7	27.6
Other	2.8	3.2	2.0	2.6	3.4

N = 138

(a) The figures exclude the 3.5% of respondents who did not answer the question.

TABLE 6
PERCENTAGE DISTRIBUTION OF RESPONSES OF QUÉBEC BUSINESSMEN REGARDING MOST EFFECTIVE METHOD OF INFLUENCING QUÉBEC GOVERNMENT[a]
(Question II G: "In most cases, what do you find is the most effective method of influencing the government?")

	All Respondents	English Respondents	French Respondents	Respondents From Large Companies	Respondents From Secondary Companies
Personal Contact	62.7	65.9	56.9	65.8	50.0
Public Opinion Campaign	2.8	0	7.8	2.6	3.6
Acting Through Business Associations	33.1	31.9	35.3	30.7	42.9
Other	1.4	2.2	0	0.8	3.6

N.B. = 135

(a) The figures exclude the 5.6% of respondents who did not answer the question.

73

TABLE 7

PERCENTAGE DISTRIBUTION OF RESPONSES OF QUÉBEC BUSINESSMEN REGARDING INDIVIDUALS OR GROUPS IN THE QUÉBEC GOVERNMENT WITH WHOM THEY USUALLY DEAL[a]

(Question II D: "When you deal with the Québec government, with whom do you usually deal?")

	All Respondents	English Respondents	French Respondents	Respondents From Large Companies	Respondents From Secondary Companies
Individual MNAs	4.0	5.2	1.7	3.8	6.2
Deputy Ministers	32.8	31.9	34.4	35.6	31.3
Party Officials	0.6	0	1.7	0.7	0
Cabinet Minister or Premier	40.2	39.6	41.4	46.2	28.1
Legislative Committees	1.1	1.7	0	1.5	0
Other Civil Servants	20.7	20.7	20.7	11.4	34.4
Other	0.6	0.9	0	0.7	0

N = 133

(a) The figures exclude the 7.0% of respondents who did not answer the question.

The quality of the personal contacts enjoyed by senior executives seemed to leave little doubt that business considered the civil service, particularly senior officials, to be an important cog in the decision-making machinery. The businessmen interviewed confirmed that the role of the civil service in decision-making and in business-government relations had increased. The president of a chemical company maintained: "The need for contact below the ministerial level has increased substantially in recent years, due mainly to the expanded role of government."[6] The vice-president of a holding in the food and beverage sector claimed: "In early days, the Québec civil servants were incompetent, and the company dealt directly with the political people. But now the civil service has become more competent and influential."[7] Several executives mentioned "stability" as one of the main advantages in dealing at the deputy-ministerial level.

The answers to the next question showed that business bypassed almost entirely political parties, National Assembly members, and committees of the National Assembly, even though they can be considered in many ways the "normal channels" of access to government. Many groups in Québec society had no choice but to seek to influence government through these channels.[8] In general the businessmen interviewed had low opinions of MNAs and the committees. The chairman of the board of a pulp and paper company thought that committees had the advantage of "permitting the opposition to get at least some insight in the government-industry dialogue."[9] An executive of a business association said he felt sorry for MNAs because "they do not know what is going on and cannot keep up with legislation."[10]

The behavior of the executives of secondary companies highlighted some significant differences. First, 34.4% of them dealt with "other civil servants," which was three times more than for the executives of the major companies. The access of the executives of secondary companies to cabinet ministers (28.1%) was substantially lower to that enjoyed by the large companies (46.2%). Considering the inferior quality of the personal contacts of the secondary company executives, it was not surprising, as argued earlier, that they found personal contacts somewhat less effective in influencing government.

The business leaders were then asked who they felt usually played the most important role in molding a government decision. Table 8 shows that 63.3% of all the respondents thought that cabinet ministers or the premier played the most important role, followed by deputy ministers with 30.6% and other civil servants with 4.8%. As was the case previously, MNAs (0.7%), legislative committees (0%), and party officials (0.7%) were deemed to be insignificant. Considering the very low perceived effectiveness of these three latter categories, it was not surprising that, as shown in the previous question, businessmen chose to ignore them almost totally as a means of access to government. Thus, businessmen avoided parliamentarians and party officials not because they did not have access to them, but because they did not consider them useful or influential. Here again, the attitudes of the secondary company respondents were somewhat different from those of the major companies. Indeed, executives of secondary companies give somewhat more weight to deputy ministers in the decision-making process — that is, 38.5% as opposed to 28.9% for the major company executives — and somewhat less weight to cabinet ministers — 57.7% as opposed to 64.5%. This was either because their access to cabinet ministers was more limited or because they were less likely to be listened to by cabinet ministers than were the larger companies' executives.

A correlation was set up between the last two questions to determine if businessmen dealt with the individuals or groups in government which they thought played the most important role in molding a decision. Of major company executives 65.7% gave identical answers for both questions, indicating that two out of three senior executives dealt directly with the individual or group who they considered was most influential in the decision-making process. In the case of secondary company executives, the relationship was 56.5%, some 10% lower than for their major company counterparts.

The quality and extent of business access to government having been determined, some attention must be paid to the specific mechanisms of business-government relations. First, various studies and the interview data made clear that business, particularly its senior executives, had become increasingly involved in relations with government.

A study of senior Canadian executives by a Chicago-based consultant firm in 1973 concluded that heads of large corporations, which were defined as corporations having annual sales of $100 million or more, spent on the average 11% of their time on "relations with government bodies." [11] This study stated further that one of the greatest challenges that a Canadian president will have to face in the future will be that of being a "mediator between government and the private business sector, adept at influencing legislation." [12] A *Financial Post* survey of Canadian businessmen in 1971 found that many firms were spending $250,000 to $500,000 a year on governmental contacts and that senior executives were spending as much as 25% of their time dealing with Ottawa. [13] The study also revealed that many Canadian companies, including CIL, had either set up a "special department of governmental affairs headed by an executive level official" or had "delegated top-management personnel to deal with governmental affairs on a full-time basis." [14]

The results of another question showed that only 27.7% of major companies "maintain a section or department (public relations, government relations, etc.) whose function it is to deal with government." The corresponding figure for secondary companies was 14.8%. The interview data also indicated that very few companies had offices in Québec City. Apparently, most of the contacts were by telephone, and executives were sent to Québec City only if the problems were serious or complex.

According to the businessmen interviewed, contacts with government were maintained at all levels of the company. In fact, there was a corresponding hierarchy between business and government. The senior executives usually dealt with the cabinet ministers or premier, the middle executives conferred with deputy ministers or their

TABLE 8

PERCENTAGE DISTRIBUTION OF RESPONSES OF QUÉBEC BUSINESSMEN REGARDING INDIVIDUALS OR GROUPS PLAYING MOST IMPORTANT ROLE IN MOLDING GOVERNMENTAL DECISIONS[a]

(Question II E: "Who do you feel usually plays the most important role in molding a government decision?")

	All Respondents	English Respondents	French Respondents	Respondents From Large Companies	Respondents From Secondary Companies
Individual MNAs	0.7	1.0	0	0.8	0
Deputy Ministers	30.6	28.1	35.3	28.9	38.5
Party Officials	0.7	1.0	0	0.8	0
Cabinet Minister or Premier	63.3	62.5	64.7	64.5	57.7
Legislative Committees	0	0	0	0	0
Other Civil Servants	4.8	7.3	0	5.0	3.8
Other	0	0	0	0	0

N = 136

(a) The figures exclude the 4.9% of respondents who did not answer the question.

assistants, while lower level executives or managers dealt with lower echelon civil servants. This was the pattern at Aluminum Company of Canada and Domtar, among others. Even in the companies which had government relations departments, such as CIL and Northern Electric, "Government relations were everybody's business," and the vice-president who headed government relations played mainly a "coordinative role," that is, "he opened doors and told people who to see."[15]

When a particular problem needed to be solved, the pattern was usually to "start at the bottom and keep going up the line," said the vice-president of a pulp and paper company. "If we are getting nowhere with the section heads or other civil servants, we go one step higher to the deputy minister. If we are still dissatisfied and the matter is serious enough or involves millions of dollars, the president of the company goes directly to Bourassa."[16] Similarly, one of the vice-presidents of an insurance company said: "We start with the superintendent of insurance and work up if we are not getting anywhere. If the problems involve major impingements of our business activity, the president deals with the minister."[17] Two other senior executives confirmed that was the usual pattern. "There is no confrontation at the high levels [cabinet ministers] unless we failed lower down; it is only if there is an obstruction or misunderstanding of a persistent nature that we go to the ministers," said the chairman of the board of an important trust company.[18]

The interviews made it clear that the senior executives had the primary responsibility for government relations, that these relations usually took place at the ministerial level,[19] and that business associations played a marginal role in the process. Senior officers, often the president or chairman of the board, usually handled government relations at Montreal Trust, Royal Trust, Consolidated-Bathurst, Domtar, CIL, Imasco, Northern Electric, Canada Cement Lafarge, Bank of Montreal, Royal Bank of Canada, among others.[20] These contacts were usually at the ministerial level. Some senior executives, including the president of a bank and the president of a large pulp and paper company, dealt almost exclusively with Premier Bourassa himself. Business associations and public relations departments played a secondary role because "direct links at the senior level are more effective."[21]

There was general satisfaction among senior executives concerning the accessibility of cabinet ministers. The chairman of the board of a large corporation claimed he knew a lot of cabinet ministers and had "no trouble getting appointments with Bourassa [Labour Minister Jean] Cournoyer, and St. Pierre."[22] His vice-presidents also had good contacts; the vice-president for labour relations, for example, had close ties with Cournoyer. He said relations with the Union Nationale government (1966-70) and other preceding governments were just as satisfactory and effective as those with the Bourassa government.[23] In the 1970-74 period, Bourassa, Finance Minister Raymond Garneau, and St. Pierre were considered particularly accessible and receptive to the business point of view.[24]

Relations with government were not only based on an ad hoc problem solving basis. Business attempted to cultivate its access to government on a permanent long-term basis. According to one executive, "Government relations are nurtured through a lot of our people getting to know people they should know in government. This allows us to find a solution quickly if and when a problem comes up."[25] Similarly, a bank president said: "Contacts with government are constant and mainly informal. We get to know the ministers and premiers on a first name basis, so that if a problem comes up, we can contact them rapidly and easily."[26]

But it was not just business that sought contacts with government. The evidence indicated that the initiative for contacts often came from the ministers themselves and that government courted business perhaps more than business courted government. According to the director of a trust company, "Cabinet ministers often come to see us to ask how things are going and to discuss the effects of laws and regulations. We discuss such things as the investment climate and consumerism."[27] This was confirmed by an executive of a bank: "A lot of cabinet ministers come to Montréal and have a quiet dinner with us." The purpose was usually to "chew the fat and get to know each other better. Ministers like contacts with us; they get pretty isolated. There is a lot going on that no one knows anything about," he concluded.[28] The president of a cement company was more blunt: "Ministers often seek our advice. They want to know what they should do."[29]

The interview data also revealed that most of the meetings between businessmen and government officials were kept secret because the government preferred confidentiality. Said one bank president: "Ministers prefer not to have it known they are meeting with executives of our bank."[30] Similarly, the chairman of the board of a pulp and paper company stated that the government told the pulp and paper executives "not to broadcast the fact that they were having meetings [with cabinet ministers] because there could be criticism they were getting preferential treatment."[31]

Secrecy, of course, has serious implications for the policy-making process in general and underlines the significance of non-decisons. The vice-president of a major corporation made the point clearly: "On many issues, compromise is reached well in advance of any public debate. The public has a lot of difficulty in understanding what is going on. We work directly and secretly with government, and we manage to avoid government regulations as a result." He concluded: "The government is not brave enough to take a shot at the business community."[32]

During the interviews, several examples of recent meetings between senior executives and high government officials were related. At Aluminum Company of Canada, it was learned that a meeting had been held a few months earlier in Vermont between several senior executives, including M. Leman, president of Aluminum Company of Canada, and Bourassa.[33] At the Royal Bank, "a long private chat" over policy matters between the president of the bank and Bourassa was mentioned as having taken place a week previous to the interview.[34] At a pulp and paper company, it was learned that regular meetings, about once a month, had been held for the past five or six years between senior pulp and paper executives and key ministers, including Bourassa occasionally. At the time of the interview, there had been no meetings in the past four months because the pulp and paper executives had succeeded in "obtaining what we wanted."[35] A somewhat broader point was made by another senior executive who said: "Ministers are easy to meet" in part because of the numerous informal ties between businessmen and ministers "on the golf course, for example."[36]

Another question attempted to measure the perceived effectiveness or satisfaction of business with respect to government relations. It asked: "By and large, do you feel that business (and its associations) is effective in its attempts to influence government policy?" A high affirmative answer was not expected since studies have shown that an individual's or group's perceived effectiveness is usually low.[37] Nonetheless, 42.9% of senior businessmen answered "yes." Here again, secondary executives seemed to be in a less favourable position since only 30.8% answered in the affirmative.

I then sought to assess perceived effectiveness in a specific, and perhaps more significant, way. Businessmen were asked if "over the last two years your company has made oral or written representations to the Québec government concerning legislative issues." Sixty-seven per cent of senior company executives and 44.4% of secondary company executives answered in the affirmative.

A supplementary question, asked if the businessmen had been "satisfied with the reaction of government." Of The 62.7% who made representations to the Québec government, 72.3% expressed satisfaction with the government's response.

Finally, in an attempt to determine if the government frequently took the initiative in establishing contacts with companies, corporate leaders were asked if in the last two years, their opinion had been solicited by a government official concerning policy questions. Of the heads of large companies, 51.4% answered that their views had indeed been sought, compared with 25.9% of the secondary company leaders. This seemed to add to the evidence, which was already strong in the analysis of access differentials, that the government recognized the crucial importance of the major companies and accorded them preferential treatment. Thus, secondary companies seemed to enjoy less access to government, qualitatively and quantitatively, and to be less effective in influencing decisions.[38]

The interviews with the senior excutives revealed a more substantial degree of satisfaction vis-à-vis the government than did the questionnaire. Executives of Northern Electric, CIL, Aluminum Company of Canada, Royal Trust, Montreal Trust, and the Bank of Montreal, among others, were particularly pleased with the effectiveness of their contacts with the government of Premier Bourassa. The president of a chemical firm put it this way: "Our relations with the present [Bourassa Liberal] government are working well. People of our own kind are much more numerous in government, and this makes it easier to deal with the government."[39] One of the senior executives of a trust company claimed: "The Quebec government sees our point most of the time" and that "our relations with them are not tinctured with nationalism or bilingualism."[40]

Even though it was quite obvious that senior executives were the main business participants in governmental relations, the interviews sought to determine if the board of directors, or some of its members, played a supportive role. The evidence was inconclusive. Some companies, including Aluminum Company of Canada, Domtar, and Consolidated-Bathurst, did not use their boards at all in dealing with the government. Others used specific board members to improve their access, as a source of information on governmental activities, and, once in a while, to apply pressure. A senior executive of a trust company claimed that an influential board member occasionnally met or arranged a meeting with a minister. Several years ago, he said, his company had used a couple of its influential directors to apply pressure when the company was in the process of obtaining a public charter and wanted to retain some of the features in its former charter.[41] Similarly, another executive of a trust company claimed: "There is the odd instance when a board member is a personal friend of a cabinet minister or official and is useful." He mentioned one occasion when a board member, who had a personal contact in the government, was used to pressure the government into introducing its new trust act more rapidly.[42] According to the president of a chemical firm, the chairman of the board of the company was "very active in organizing 'entrées' for us and in making representations to government."[43] The same company also had Senator Hartland Molson on its board. "If it was necessary," said the chemical company president, "he could put us into contact with the right people in government."[44]

Board members who were practising lawyers or former politicans seemed to offer particular advantages for government relations. Regarding former politicians, a retired senior executive said: "They are aware of the social environment, know their way around, and are sometimes useful in getting an introduction to see important people, particularly if they had a cabinet post."[45] The president of a cement company claimed that many individuals on his company's board, including a senator and a former cabinet minister, were well connected politically and that their functions were "to tell us what is going on in Québec City, give us advice, and open doors to help us see the right people."[46]

Regarding lawyers, the case of Antoine Geoffrion was revealing. According to Kendal Windeyer of the *Montreal Gazette,* Geoffrion, who held a number of directorships in important companies, had, thanks to his "friendship with some of the most powerful politicians in the country," earned himself "the reputation in the business community of being one of the most effective lobbyists in the country." [47] Geoffrion himself claimed that the problem was in "getting to the right person who can make a decision," and "If you can get the door open and get your foot in, you can successfully plead almost any legitimate request." [48]

Finally, I tried to determine if the nature and extent of access had changed significantly during the past couple of decades. Specifically, one wondered if access was much different during the Duplessis government years (1939 to 1960) than it had been since then. According to the businessmen interviewed, there was some nostalgia for the pre-1960 days, but, overall, the pattern of business-government relations had remained the same.

The Duplessis years were marked by close and personal ties between senior executives and Premier Maurice Duplessis. It seemed that all contacts of significance were exclusively at the top level. The two former senior executives who were interviewed, for example, always dealt directly with Duplessis. One claimed to have had a close friendship with Duplessis whom he described as "very cooperative" and "helpful to business."[49] The other thought Duplessis was "a good businessman who knew how to encourage industry."[50] Similarly, according to an executive of the company, R. E. Powell, former president of Aluminum Company of Canada, was on very close terms with Duplessis: "Powell would send cigars to Duplessis and they would go fishing together."[51] The comments of the Aluminum Company of Canada executive on the Duplessis years brought out an interesting facet of the former premier's relations with business. Apparently, Duplessis made a habit of "blasting the aluminum companies or other companies one day and calling up the president the next morning to tell him not to worry about it, that he had only sought to pacify a faction — explaining that the needs of the situation required him to criticize or threaten business but that he would never follow up on it." As will be seen when the budgetary process is discussed, [52] Bourassa seemed to have inherited from Duplessis this particular approach to public relations.

Some of the present day executives who were also active during the Duplessis years confirmed the pattern of interaction described above. According to the vice-president of a pulp and paper firm, "The company always dealt directly with Duplessis — for anything at all. It was not worth bothering with the ministers. In the past 10 years or so, there had been a gradual change in the pattern."[53] A senior executive of a trust company put it this way: "During the Duplessis era, if you knew the rules there were no problems. Dealings were usually handled directly by powerful men over the telephone."[54]

It seems that the relations between senior executives and Bourassa were somewhat de-personalized in comparison with the Duplessis years. With the increase in the scale of governmental activity, the premier was no longer capable of handling all relations with senior executives. Other ministers and senior civil servants had to play a more important role. Overall, however, no fundamental changes in business-government relations had taken place since 1960.

Business-Government Personnel Links

The personnel links between business and political elites are a means by which indirect business access to government is provided and also contribute to breaking down the autonomy between the two systems of power. An exhaustive analysis of personnel interchanges between business and government in Québec will not be attempted.

Instead, the thesis will outline a few examples in an attempt to verify Miliband's hypothesis that "the world of administration [political] and the world of large scale enterprise are now increasingly linked in terms of almost interchanging personnel."[55]

First, there is the case, mentioned above, of politicians who, upon leaving parliament or their cabinet posts, become involved in business positions, often as members of boards of directors.[56] The example of Jean Lesage, Québec premier between 1960 and 1966, is one of the better-known cases. After retiring from politics, Lesage acquired eight company directorships, including those in the Montreal Trust, Reynolds Aluminum, and Campbell Chibougameau Mines. Lesage, however, continued to occupy important "public functions."[57] Indeed, he was the government representative in the lengthy and controversial negotiations with International Telephone and Telegraph-Rayonnier. The ITT representative, Marcel Piché, who was Lesage's "opponent" in the negotiations, sat with the former premier on the Reynolds Aluminum board of directors.

Lesage was also legislative counsel to the government:;he read all legislation before it was submitted to the National Assembly. Although his integrity was not questioned, a conflict of interest clearly existed. It is questionable for an individual to be allowed to read and evaluate a secret piece of proposed legislation on mining, for example, while sitting on the board of Campbell Chibougameau Mines at the same time.[58] The mining company could easily benefit from this advance knowledge of legislation; among other things, it could exert pressure on the government before this proposed legislation became public. When questioned about the problem, Bourassa said simply that Lesage was a "very responsible man;"[59] he did not attempt to deny that the problem was genuine. One can wonder, of course, if the presumption of integrity was a sufficient safeguard.

Another example was George Marler, who was transport minister in the federal Liberal government from 1954 to 1957 and minister without portfolio in Québec between 1960 and 1965. When he was a Québec cabinet minister, he was considered "the government's link with the financial community of St. James Street."[60] After resigning his provincial cabinet post, Marler was named chairman of the board of Canada Cement Lafarge and director of Royal Trust, Imperial Bank of Commerce, and other companies. According to an executive of Canada Cement Lafarge, the company derived some specific advantages from having Marler on its board of directors. Government being one of the principal cement buyers, Marler was given the task of keeping up good relations with the department of roads.[61] A more recent example, finally, was that of Claude Castonguay, who was health and welfare minister in the Québec Liberal government until October 29, 1973. A few months later, he had acquired several directorships, including one in Imasco.

The flow also goes the other way. Many executives are loaned by their companies to government or are brought in by government to fill important posts. Shortly after he was elected in 1970, Bourassa announced his intention of recruiting senior businessmen on a temporary basis for high-level civil service posts. The executives brought in by Bourassa included Pierre Côté, president of Laiterie Laval, who was appointed to head the Québec Development and Planning Council; Gérard Plourde, chairman of UAP, Inc., who was appointed to the part-time office of president of Québec's Industrial Development Agency; Pierre Shooner, a former director of the Montreal Chamber of Commerce who was named associate deputy minister of Industry and Commerce; and Pierre Delagrave, vice-president of Domtar, who was recruited as a special adviser to the department of industry and commerce.[62] According to one of Delagrave's colleagues at Domtar, Delagrave was loaned for a three-year period; the company, however, continued to pay part of his salary. Delagrave's main function was to act as a liaison between government and some specific industrial sectors, including pulp and paper and textiles. Delagrave, according to the executive of Domtar, had not only "made government more aware of the problems of industry"[63] but had also been involved in specific problem areas such as pollution control and forest reform legislation. Here again, it certainly could not be assumed that the interests of Domtar and the pulp and paper industry in general would in every case be compatible with the interests of the government or citizens of Québec. Apparently, Delagrave was also involved in defending Domtar's position on the language problem vis-à-vis the Québec government.[64]

Epstein, in his analysis of business-government links in the U.S., drew out some of the implications of senior business officials being recruited to government posts:

> Men who come from private corporations and intend to return to them have tended to follow ingrained response patterns when confronted with issues for which "public interest" is not abundantly clear. Bias, not corruption, is the real problem . . .[65]
> The fact that many of these officials [recruited from business] are still actively engaged in corporate activities or intend to return to business firms after their tour of government service reinforces their pro-business propensities . . .[66]
>
> . . . Here, too, the accessibility of former business associates is enhanced by the prior associations. This is not the result of malfeasance or corruption but rather a consequence of the natural inclination to be available to one's friends.[67]

Another aspect of the business-government personnel links question is the politically partisan involvement of senior businessmen. A glance at the executives and board members of Power Corporation, for example, showed clear ties between the Liberal Party and the holding. Claude Frenette, vice-president of Power, was former president of the Québec federal Liberals; P. N. Thomson was ex-treasurer of the provincial Liberals; and Paul Martin, Jr., also a Power vice-president, was a son of the federal Liberal senator.

Formal Access to Government

The General Council of Industry

Advisory boards are another means of access to the government although their importance in policy formation is not always clear.

The Conseil du Patronat, for example, is represented on the Conseil Consultatif du Travail et de la Main d'Oeuvre and the Conseil Consultatif des Accidents de Travail. Perhaps the most interesting and unquestionably the most powerful advisory board is the General Council of Industry of Québec.

Created on February 26, 1969, the GCI was made up of about 60 senior-level businessmen.[68] Among the powerful executives were G. A. Hart, chairman of the board and president of the Bank of Montreal; McLaughlin; Scrivener; N. R. Crump, chairman of the board of Canadian Pacific; and Desmarais. All the main holdings (CPR-Cominco, Argus, and Power) and financial institutions (Royal Trust, Bank of Montreal, Royal Bank of Canada, etc.) were represented. The GCI also represented various national industrial interests, such as the main Americain companies (Iron Ore, Texaco, Alcan, Chemcell, among others), English-Canadian companies (Dominion Textiles, Domtar, Price Brothers, Steinberg's, etc.), and French-Canadian corporations (Bombardier, Rolland Paper, Dupuis Frères, etc.).[69]

The GCI was set up by the Québec government in an official advisory role. According to the statute establishing it, tne GCI's functions were to advise the minister of industry and commerce on the evolution of the business community opinion regarding Québec, to suggest ways and means to orient or modify this opinion, to make concrete proposals about government economic policy, to serve as a source of information for the department of industry and commerce and the government, and to help the Québec government in its industrial promotion outside the province. In its information brochure, the GCI felt the need to make clear it was "apolitical" and that "its members are chosen without regard to political sympathies . . ."[70]

The initiative for the creation of the GCI came from within business. Paul Ouimet, legal counsel to the Iron Ore Company of Canada and president of the GCI, claimed that it was he who suggested setting up the GCI in conversations with Daniel Johnson, Union Nationale premier, and J. P. Beaudry, UN industry and commerce minister: "Je leur ai fait observer que le Québec avait besoin d'un groupe important d'hommes d'affaires pour assister le gouvernement dans l'établissement d'un meilleur climat au Québec."[71]

According to Richard Brunelle and Pierre Papineau, the creation of the GCI was part of a series of measures to re-establish business confidence in Québec.[72] More specifically, they claimed that in the 1967-68 period the business community launched a campaign to show that investment was declining in Québec and that capital would leave the province unless the government stabilized conditions. By an extensive analysis of the press, Brunelle and Papineau showed how the media, especially the *Montreal Gazette* and the *Montreal Star,* had created a climate of panic which was unsupported by any concrete evidence. They argued further that the Québec government finally gave in to the pressures and made the following concessions to business: the nomination of Marcel Faribault, director of about 15 companies including Dosco, IBM, and Bell Telephone, as special adviser to the cabinet on economic and constitutional matters;[73] the creation of an Office du Crédit Industriel guaranteeing loans to business (Bill 70); the appointment of Charles Neapole, former executive of the Royal Bank, to the board of directors of the Québec Deposit and Investment Fund;[74] and, finally, the creation of the GCI. [75]

Between its creation in February 1969 and the election of a Liberal government in April 1970, the GCI was the subject of unfavourable rumors and much public criticism concerning its alleged influence on government. Claude Beauchamp of *La Presse* called the GCI "the tribunal of business" and claimed that barely two weeks after its creation the GCI had "invited" four UN cabinet ministers — Marcel Masse, Jean-Guy Cardinal, Mario Beaulieu, and Jean-Noël Tremblay — to a closed-door session to answer questions concerning their ideas on unilingualism and the constitution.[76] The arrogance of some GCI members was an additional source of embarrassment for the government. For example, one GCI member was quoted as saying: "When we submit recommendations to the government, we intend that they be applied. We now have the tool that we need with this council to force the government to act."[77] As can be seen from the above quotation, the GCI certainly had high expectations in its ability to influence government.

After the election of the Liberal government in April 1970, the GCI's only public activities have involved representing Québec business abroad. Thus, in March 1971, a large GCI delegation went to New York to reassure investors about the climate of investment in Québec. [78] Also, in November 1972, another delegation led by the GCI attended the European Institutional Investor's Conference in London. Overall, however, newspapers and other media have carried no news on GCI activities since 1971, and many observers were left with the impression that the Council was quietly defused by the Bourassa government.

In fact, it was almost impossible to get any significant information concerning the Council's activities from the GCI itself. In a 20-minute conversation with a GCI consultant, it was impossible to find out, for instance, what the topics of the GCI meetings were, how many meetings were held, or how effective the GCI activities were.[79] The only thing the consultant said was that the meetings dealt with "hot issues." He also mentioned that the GCI research staff was working on two long-term projects: an inventory of managerial talent in Québec and an analysis of the Québec economy in order to determine which industrial sectors offered the most potential for Québec's economic development.[80]

In the interviews held with the four GCI members, it became obvious that the above activities were quite secondary and a very small part of the Council's overall concerns. The interviews made it clear that the GCI was not only active, but effective and influential. The main thrust of GCI activities involved five or six annual meetings which were held between the members and Québec cabinet ministers — usually including Bourassa, St. Pierre, Cournoyer, Gérard D. Levesque, and a few top civil servants. The topics discussed embraced the whole field of Québec politics: economic development, education, language, labour problems, foreign investment, etc. Even though economic problems were the priority, "anything can be put on the agenda by a GCI member."[81] This was a far cry from the purely advisory role which the council was supposed to play.

More important, however, was the fact that GCI members were informed of and in a position to influence governmental policies and legislation before they were made public. This was the crux of the privileged position and the power of the General Council of Industry.[82] At the beginning of April 1973, for example, there was an important meeting concerning the Gendron Report, dealing with language in Québec, and the forthcoming governmental legislation on language. As will be shown later, the language legislation only became public in May 1974, or more than a year later. It will also be seen that senior businessmen, including the GCI members, were not only informed of the contents of the legislation well ahead of the public but succeeded in influencing the legislation in a way that suited their interests. Similarly, in May 1973, a meeting was held on the Québec government's energy policy, particularly oil. Subsequent discussions of Soquip, the Québec government's oil exploration company, and the government's overall energy policy will make it clear that many of the issues involved were of interest to other groups than business. At the time of writing, the government's policy had not been made public. Some of the GCI's meetings, finally, involved an overall review by its members of the activities of a specific government department. The minister was present to answer questions on general policy and on details.[83]

The GCI was also active between meetings. In fact, much of its activity focused on small informal meetings between senior executives and cabinet ministers. According to an executive of a trust company: "The GCI sponsors many informal meetings; smaller groups which are interested in specific problems or legislation will meet directly with a minister."[84] He also claimed that he received frequent telephone calls from Ouimet informing him that "the government is worrying about this and that" and asking him if he had "any idea of what should be done."[85] Finally, according to the vice-president of a holding in the food and beverage sector, "Ouimet can get any minister to meet any group of businessmen who have something on their minds."[86]

Interviews with GCI members and other executives who were aware of its activities revealed unanimous satisfaction with the effectiveness of the General Council of Industry. According to a senior executive and member of the GCI, the Council "plays a key role. I go out of my way to attend meetings. Ministers are prepared to listen; we feel our presence is effective."[87] A bank president said: "The GCI has done extremely good work and is most useful."[88] He maintained that "the government has been quite receptive" and that "Bourassa picked up enthusiastically on the GCI after his election in 1970."[89] Another executive said the Council "has helped improve business contacts with government."[90] Finally, an executive of a business association expressed satisfaction with the important impact on government policy of the GCI document on economic development.[91] Another indicator of business satisfaction was the great degree of participation in GCI activities, including the high rate of attendance at meetings.

The interviews showed that it was at the government's initiative that absolute secrecy had been imposed on GCI proceedings. Thus, no formal agendas were distributed and no minutes were taken during the meetings; members got an abbreviated list of topics to be discussed a few days before meetings.[92] According to two members of the GCI, the government insisted on the meetings being kept secret. Another executive claimed: "Secrecy is maintained because cabinet ministers could not say what they think otherwise. The press is so goddamn irresponsible."[93] Perhaps the best evidence of the degree of secrecy which surrounded the Council's activities was that business association heads and the various executives who were not part of the GCI seemed to have very little knowledge of what the GCI was doing.[94] The only information that could be obtained about the GCI's activities came from its members.

According to the chairman of the board of a trust company, the Council, as opposed to business associations, was "distinctly top level."[95] In fact, there was some indication that business associations and the smaller businesses were "jealous" of the access and power enjoyed by GCI members. An executive of a business association even suggested to the department of industry and commerce that the GCI should be abolished because it was "not representative enough of the business milieu."[96]

The evidence presented above indicated clearly that the GCI was in a particularly privileged position vis-à-vis the Québec government. It was not only made up of the senior executives of the most crucial financial and industrial concerns in Québec, but it also enjoyed unlimited access to cabinet ministers and was even allowed to discuss and attempt to influence governmental policy and legislation before they were submitted to the National Assembly or the public.

The Québec Planning and Development Council

Like the General Council of Industry, the Québec Planning and Development Council was an advisory board to the government. However, unlike the GCI, its membership was not made up exclusively of businessmen. It was one of a handful of advisory boards created after 1969 to try to "work out a consensus" between the various social groups, including business and labour. Other such boards were the Advisory Council on Labour and Manpower, the Advisory Council of Social Affairs, and the Superior Council of Education. It is noteworthy that the Development Council was set up as a result of business initiative.[97] Indeed, business seemed to be particularly favourable to the creation of boards or commissions which brought together the various sectors of society.

The Québec Planning and Development Council had 35 members, all named by the government. Among the ex-officio members were 11 representatives of the Regional Development Council, the mayors of Montréal and Québec City, the president of the GCI, three representatives of the Conseil du Patronat, and three union representatives. The Development Council had the right to retain expert advice and to request research reports. Formally, the Development Council was under the umbrella of the Québec Planning and Development Bureau. Its functions were defined very broadly by the Québec National Assembly: "to advise the Bureau on any matter which the Bureau submits to it respecting the development of Québec and the plans, programs and projects for economic, social and territorial development prepared by the Bureau."[98]

Even though the Development Council was created officially on July 5, 1968, it was not before 1971 that its executives were named. On February 26, 1971, Côté was named chairman, and on June 3, 1971, C. Harrington was sworn in as vice-chairman; both were members of the GCI. It was also in 1971 that a special order in council attempted to define some of the topics that could be dealt with by the Development Council. Although the Development Council kept the right to meet when it wanted, at least once every two months, and to discuss the topics it so desired, the government recommended several areas of interest, including governmental wage policies, governmental policies to stimulate industrial activity, the participation of state institutions in economic development, e.g. the General Investment Corporation and the Québec Deposit and Investment Fund, governmental policies dealing with regional inequalities, environmental planning and social policies.[99]

It was difficult to properly evaluate the effectiveness and activities of the Development Council because it had been in operation for only a few years and also because all of its members were sworn to secrecy. According to an executive of a trust company, the Development Council dealt mainly with specific issues, such as the James Bay project, the food industry, the projected deep-water port at Gros-Cacouna, and the problems of the agricultural sector. His overall evaluation of the Development Council's impact was one of satisfaction: "After three years of hard work," he said, "we find the whole thing very encouraging. We are more and more finding things we suggested beginning to pop up in the budget, in legislation, and in various projects."[100]

This seemed to contrast with the overall opposition and disillusionment of Québec labour unions towards the "mixed" advisory boards. The Québec Federation of Labour, for one, had complained about the "co-optation" which resulted from participation in consultative mechanisms. They also claimed that their participation on advisory boards did not signify an increase in the power of unions and workers:

> "It is clear that for governments which are tied to financial interests, the consultation which they have with workers does not represent a transfer of power. For them the purpose is simply to install antennas within key societal groups.[101]

Sources of Government Dependence on Business

Electoral Finance

The need for political parties to obtain funds to contest elections and to maintain their organizations between elections, as well as the need for most governments to borrow on the financial markets to finance their long-term and short-term activities, create additional potential dependency links between business and government.

There can be little doubt that money is a crucial resource for any party which seeks a degree of success in its electoral activities. K. Z. Paltiel, in his study of Canadian party finance, described the advantage of money:

> Election campaigns cannot be fought or won without the expenditure of large amounts of money . . . The winners in Canadian election do tend to spend more money than their rivals at the party and constituency level; and winning candidates of a particular party tend to spend more than their losing colleagues. . . In 1965 overall party spending per seat was more than $60,000 and in 1968 these combined costs rose to over $90,000 . . . Money can be exchanged and used to purchase resources such as manpower and command over the communications media.[102]

H. G. Thorburn supported Paltiel's conclusion. He claimed that "the new type of campaign [media, public relations, advertising] is extremely expensive" and that "the party with the largest purse has the best hope of victory, other things being equal." He said this results in increasing "the dependence of the parties on their financial angels, and, in turn, enhances the influence of the big contributors over the parties."[103]

The next question involves the political consequences of party financing. According to Paltiel again:

> . . . Overdependence of parties on any single source or socio-economic group inevitably narrows the freedom of action of political decision-makers. Such parties tend to become the spokesmen of narrow social interests losing the aggregative function attributed to parties in liberal-democratic thought. An examination of policy outputs in relation to the fund raising structures of the dominant parties casts light on the nature of the polity and its principal beneficiaries.[104]

It is well known that business is the main source of party finances in Canada, at both the federal and provincial levels. At the federal level, the Committee on Election Expenses estimated that the two major parties, the Liberals and the Progressive Conservatives, obtained some 90% of their campaign funds from business, of which 50% came from corporations and 40% from businessmen. It also found that the national Liberal office itself was financed by the regular annual contributions of 30 to 50 corporations.[105] Imperial Oil for example, according to its president M. Armstrong, contributed an average of $234,000 a year to the Liberal, Progressive Conservative, and Social Credit parties between 1970 and 1975. He stated that the objective of these contributions was to support the "democratic process." He also said that Imperial Oil would not support financially a party advocating the nationalization of oil companies.

90

There is much speculation as to the rationale for business financing of political parties. Porter thought: "Businessmen are interested in a party's ability to stabilize the field for corporate activity;[106] he added that, by supporting parties favourable to corporate interests, business achieved the indirect result of keeping "socializing" parties, for example, the New Democratic Party, down.[107] Paltiel claimed: "Contributions have assured access to the decision-making authorities in party and government."[108] And as Epstein argued: "While contributions by no means guarantee favourable results, they do assure corporations of a forum in which to present their case."[109] Finally, some corporate donations are related to specific acts of patronage and other favours, such as the defense of corporate interests in specific policies or legislation.

To come back to the Québec situation, there have been specific allegations with respect to patronage. A front page story in the *Montreal Gazette* in 1973 reported: "A carefully guarded policy of political favouritism in awarding government contracts has been flourishing in Québec ever since Premier Bourassa's Liberal party was swept to power nearly three years ago," and that "lucrative contracts with a cumulative value running into the millions of dollars have been used to reward friends of the party who have assisted in campaign work and contributed generously to the Liberal party election fund."[110] Going back in time, Jerôme Proulx, ex-member of the National Assembly for the Union Nationale, claimed to have been under heavy pressure from his party between 1966 and 1970 to accord specific favours to companies and individuals who were known to have supported the party.[111] Similarly, René Lévesque, head of the opposition Parti Québécois, stated that when he was minister of natural resources in the Liberal government between 1960 and 1966, he had been under pressure to give in to large corporations which had been generous to the Liberal Party.[112]

It is unlikely, despite the above examples, that patronage plays an important part in justifying business contributions to political parties. The most probable reason for business financing the Liberal Party in Québec is that the party is the most favourable to business objectives. The interviews also suggested, although businessmen tended to be discreet on the subject of party financing, that contributions to the Liberal Party helped improve business access to governmental decision-makers. According to the president of a cement company, "We get access to top men by financing them."[113] Another senior executive claimed that a provincial fund collector "promised special favours and access to cabinet ministers and civil servants in return for a contribution."[114] These statements would seem to cast some doubt on Bourassa's contention that the Liberal Party was in no way bound by electoral contributions from business.[115]

After the October 1973 provincial election in Québec, it seemed that only one political party, the Liberals, was financially secure. The large and regular contributions from business had allowed the Liberals to by-pass fund-raising activities and demands for contributions from their members. They had also allowed the party to out-do opposition parties at election time with regards to organization and especially media publicity.[116] The Union Nationale Party, which was virtually eliminated from the Québec political scene on October 29, 1973, fell into disfavour with the business community because of its nationalist leanings after 1969. It had, however, succeeded in keeping itself afloat by selling its assets, including a newspaper which it had acquired during better days.[117]

The Parti Québécois and the Créditiste Party have had to rely on fund-raising campaigns among their supporters to be able to contest elections. The PQ managed to collect $800,000 from its members and sympathizers in a two-month campaign at the beginning of 1973; it received 31,086 donations worth an average of $23.78 each.[118] Although the party waged a strong campaign at the organizational level in October 1973, similar to that of the NPD in Canada, it did not succeed in competing with the Liberals in the media, particularly television advertising. The Créditistes, whose supporters come from less favoured socio-economic groups, were even more hampered by their lack of funds.

An interesting case study in the political importance of financial contributions was the Liberal Party leadership convention in the fall of 1969.[119] Although opinion polls showed Claude Wagner to be the clear favourite of the Québec population, it was Robert Bourassa who, thanks to an extensive business-backed publicity campaign, was carried to victory. Pierre Laporte, former Liberal cabinet minister and also a contender in the leadership race, accused Bourassa of spending $1 million in an effort to convince 1,636 delegates to vote for him. Laporte was angry to the point that he promised Liberal delegates he would take the party out of the hands of St. James Street and give it back to its members. He added:

> Mr. Robert Bourassa should avoid giving Mr. René Lévesque and his friends proof for their argument that the Liberal Party, like the Union Nationale, is dominated by St. James Street and high finance. The kind of remote-controlled campaign we are witnessing shows clearly that powerful private interests are giving their full support to one of the candidate, [i.e., "all weapons of war"][120]

Further, Claude Wagner accused the Bourassa organization of paying for the transportation and accommodation costs of all those wishing to participate in the convention.

According to Gilles Racine, Bourassa's funds allowed him to do the following: rent 60 large bill boards along all major access routes to Québec City where the convention was taking place; rent television time on Channel 4, Québec City's private French television network, for the evening preceding the vote; rent 1,000 hotel rooms for his organization, and delegates, according to Wagner; mail out 70,000 cards to Liberal militants expressing interest in the way they viewed the problems of the day; nominate 28 regional and 108 constituency representatives; sponsor 110 pro-Bourassa hostesses on the convention floor, including beauticians and hairdressers; and hold a $25,000 party for his supporters at the Queen Elizabeth Hotel in Montréal.[121] Thus, in the space of a few weeks, Bourassa succeeded in eclipsing his two better-known rivals.

Québec government officials have been promising for a long time to reform party financing. Premier Jean-Jacques Bertrand of the

Union Nationale promised the National Assembly in 1969 that he would substantially amend the laws regarding party financing. This was not done however.[122] Bourassa, in a 1970 campaign speech at Rouyn, promised that "campaign chests" would be eliminated once and for all if he were elected. He even accused the UN of having wasted millions of dollars because of the patronage which resulted from that party's financing.[123] Despite criticism and specific accusations of patronage, as noted above, the Bourassa government, at the time of writing, had not yet dealt with the problems of electoral finance.

The Financial Market

Several observers have noted that business, and in particular the heads of the largest financial institutions, has been capable of wielding substantial political power because of the dependence of governments on access to the financial markets. Miliband and Meynaud, among others, explained how many reform-minded European governments have been held in check by the threats of the financial oligarchy that if they lost confidence in them, they would cut their sources of credit.[124] Although overt blackmail is rare, a government that needs capital or investments is always in a precarious position if it provokes the displeasure of the financial community.

Jacques Parizeau, former chief economic adviser to the Québec government, was the only source of public information on the "financial cartel" in Québec.[125] Since the nineteen thirties, a financial group headed by the Bank of Montreal and the Toronto-based brokerage house A. E. Ames had the exclusive responsibility for distributing Québec government bond issues on the Canadian market.Each broker had to agree in writing at the beginning of each year that he would go through the "syndicate" or cartel exclusively to distribute new bond issues.

As a result of the cartel's attempts to block the nationalization of electricity,[126] and as a result of various other pressures from the cartel, Eric Kierans, then minister of revenue in the Québec government, decided to break the cartel in two. Thus, in 1963 Kierans created another group centered around the Royal Bank of Canada. However, the two managing groups, each made up of four institutions, decided to "take turns in managing Québec issues"[127] rather than compete with each other. They formed a steering committee with another six institutions; and each of the 14 institutions was given one vote on decisions affecting an underwriting.

In addition to the episode of the nationalization of electricity, and the various warnings of the cartel with regards to the threat of separatism or various other "nationalist" issues, the financial syndicate was also alleged to have intervened in 1966 to "pressure the Québec government to be more generous in its grants to McGill University."[128] Finally, according to Parizeau, the syndicate enjoyed substantial political power: "The syndicate is . . . a political lobby of first importance, a means to pressure the Québec government to orient some of its policies . . ."[129]

The discussion on the access of business to government presented above demonstrates beyond reasonable doubt that Québec businessmen enjoyed substantial formal and informal access to decision-making structures. [130] The quality and quantity of this access are vital political assets in attempts to exercise influence and also contribute to shaping the decision-making environment within which government operates.

NOTES

(1) Epstein, p. 199.

(2) Epstein, p. 196.

(3) Ibid.

(4) Among others, Braunthal, Ehrmann, Domhoff, and Mills. Mills argued: "As the corporate world has become more intricately involved in the political order, the corporate executives have become intimately associated with the politicians, and especially with the key politicians who form the political directorate of the United States government" (p. 167).

(5) The perceptions of major company executives are supported by Meynaud's argument that it is usually at the level of direct contacts that the most effective pressure can be exerted (Jean Meynaud, "Groupes de pression et politique gouvernementale," Réflexions sur la polituque au Québec, no ed., (Montréal: Editions du Sainte-Marie, 1968), p. 80.

(6) Interview, May 1973.

(7) Interview, May 1973.

(8) According to Miliband, "It is now only the weakest groups which seek to wield influence primarily through legislatures, precisely because they have little or no hold over the executive. The major 'interests' use both means, with the greater emphasis on the government and the administration" (p. 161).

(9) Interview, May 1973.

(10) Interview, May 1973.

(11) Heindrick and Struggles, Inc., Profile of a Canadian President (Chicago: Heindrick and Struggles, Inc., 1973), p. 5.

(12) Ibid.

(13) W. L. Dack, "Running to Ottawa — Big New Business Cost," Financial Post, 8 December 1971.

(14) Ibid.

(15) Interview, May 1973.

(16) Interview, May 1973.

(17) Interview, May 1973.

(18) Interview, May 1073.

(19) An executive of an important aluminum producer, on the other hand, claimed his company dealt mainly at the deputy ministerial level because "they can usually make the point for us at the ministerial level" (interview, May 1972).

(20) This was confirmed by inrerviews with the executives of these companies.

(21) Interview, May 1973.

(22) Interview, May 1973.

(23) Interview, May 1973. The same executive maintained further: "Even if the Parti Québécois came to power, our contacts would be maintained. They would have to face the same economic facts of life as other governments and could not change the environment very much."

(24) Confirmed by interviews with representatives of Imasco, Canada Cement Lafarge, and Bank of Montreal.

(25) Interview, May 1973.

(26) Interview, May 1973. The pattern is the same at the federal level. The same bank president said: "I have gone through seven ministers of finance. I make a point of getting to know them on a first name basis shortly after their appointments. I saw [finance minister in Liberal cabinet John] Turner almost immediately."

(27) Interview, May 1973.

(28) Interview, May 1973. He added that many of the quiet dinners with ministers took place around elction time "because they [the ministers] want to get on the right side of us."

(29) Interview, May 1973.

(30) Interview, May 1973. In Ottawa, the Royal Bank has a special suite adjoining the cafereria in the Royal Bank building where executives can lunch with politicians and cabinet ministers without it being known. The bank also has a private dining room on the 41st floor of Place Ville-Marie in Montréal.

(31) Interview, May 1973.

(32) Interview, May 1973.

(33) Interview, May 1973.
(34) Interview, May 1973.
(35) Interview, May 1973.
(36) Interview, May 1973.
(37) See, for example, Angus Campbell, Gerald Gurin, and Warren Miller, *The Voter Decides* (Evanston: Row, Peterson and Company, 1954).
(38) A senior executive from a small bank stated unequivocally that smaller companies like his own were much less likely to be listened to by government. The government, on the other hand, was almost forced to listen to the big companies. "If Claude Primeau of the Banque Provinciale calls up St. Pierre to complain about a piece of legislation, he will be listened to," he said (interview, May 1973).
As regards Questions II J, L, and N, it should be noted that the rate of response was high for both the major and secondary company executives.
(39) Interview, May 1973.
(40) Interview, May 1973.
(41) Interview, May 1973.
(42) Interview, May 1973.
(43) Interview, May 1973.
(44) Interview, May 1973. A bank executive said that in 1971 the banks launched a concerted offensive against federal Labour Minister Bryce Mackasey's white paper on the new labour code. The banks decided to urge all their Canadian directors to attempt to influence those ministers with whom they were familiar. The directors were successful in obtaining important modifications in the white paper and also some changes in the legislation. Although the final version of the bill was not exactly what the banks wanted, they had by and large obtained satisfaction on the crucial points (interview, May 1973).
(45) Interview, May 1973.
(46) Interview, May 1973. A bank executive said: "We try to put people on our boards who have good access to government" and that it is "helpful to have a couple of lawyers and a senator on our board" (interview, May 1973).
(47) Kendal Windeyer, "Geoffrion: Opening the Right Doors," *Montreal Gazette,* 8 August 1972.
(48) Geoffrion quoted in Windeyer.
(49) Interview, May 1973.
(50) Interview, May 1973.
(51) Interview, May 1973.
(52) Interview, May 1973.
(53) Interview, May 1973.
(54) Interview, May 1973.
(55) Miliband, p. 125.
(56) Porter noted that successful ex-politicians were often called upon to sit on the boards of directors of companies which wanted to improve their links with the government. According to Meynaud in *Technocracy* (New York: Free Press, 1969), corporations also attempted to recruit top level bureaucrats "who, thanks to their personal links with former colleagues, can iron out difficulties" (p. 173).
(57) Information from Maurice Giroux, "Que fait Jean Lesage? Il pantoufle!" *La Presse,* 15 April 1971. Giroux stated that Lesage "occupe maintenant des fonctions importantes dans des grandes entreprises, tout en continuant de conseiller à l'occasion le gouvernement de M. Bourassa." Giroux also showed how, at the federal level, Robert Winters, Maurice Sauvé, Louis St. Laurent, Lionel Chevrier — all former Liberal cabinet ministers — inherited multiple functions and directorships with large corporations when they left active political life.
(58) See Jacques Keable, "Lesage, chef non élu, divise le parti libéral et domine Bourassa," *Québec-Presse,* 18 April 1971.
(59) Robert Bourassa interviewed by Jacques Keable, "Notre marge de manoeuvre est très mince," *Québec-Presse,* 23 January 1972.
(60) L. Chisholm, "Just What is Mr. Lesage Doing in Québec," *Financial Post,* 23 September 1961.
(61) Interview, May 1973.
(62) Amy Booth, "Businessmen Recruited to Spur Quebec Growth," *Financial Post,* 15 May 1971.
(63) Interview, May 1973.
(64) Interview, May 1973. Michel de Grandpré, assistant vice-president of Power Corporation, was another example of an executive loaned by business to the department of industry and commerce.
(65) Epstein, P. 35.
(66) Ibid., P. 201.
(67) Ibid.
(68) Information on the GCI was obtained mainly through interviews with four senior executives who were members of the GCI.
(69) General Council of Industry, *The General Council of Industry* (Montréal: General Council of Industry, 1971), p. 1.
(70) Ibid. The ideology of the GCI, which followed the same lines as that of big business as analysed in chapter 3, was revealed in a report entitled *Towards Economic Objectives and a Development Strategy For Québec* (Montréal: General Council of Industry, 1970), written by Louis Riopel and N. Takacsy of the CPR's research department. The report made the following recommendations: The government's main function should be to maintain a favorable investment climate and to encourage "a generally positive attitude towards work, competition and risk-taking" (p. 60); nationalizations or expansion of the public sector would be futile and self-defeating (p. 62); the government should play a service role vis-à-vis business, including providing fiscal incentives, encouragement of corporate mergers, and technical assistance for firms (p. 55).
(71) Paul Ouimet, "Le Climat d'investissements au Québec s'est amélioré," *La Presse,* 15 August 1969. "I made them understand that Québec needed an important group of businessmen to help the government establish a better investment climate in Québec."

(72) Brunelle and Papineau, pp. 84-90.

(73) Faribault's nomination came on October 31, 1967. As special adviser, he was called on to attend a large number of cabinet meetings. It should be noted that Faribault had access to the main "secrets" of Québec's economic policies, but nevertheless maintained all his directorships in the private sector.

(74) Neapole was named on July 21, 1967.

(75) According to Brunelle and Papineau, it was not just the possible loss of investments which forced the government to back down. It was also due to the fact that the financial cartel (explained later) had put the squeeze on the Québec bond market. Only after the government had made important concessions to business was it in a position to successfully launch a bond issue (November 2, 1967).

(76) Beauchamp, "Le Tribunal du monde."

(77) GCI member quoted ibid.

(78) Michel Lefevre, "Une Présence québécoise à New York," Le Devoir, 2 March 1971.

(79) Interview, May 1973.

(80) According to an executive of Aluminum Company of Canada, his company lent its vice-president of chemical sales, Donald Evans, to the GCI on a full-time basis for a year (interview, May 1973).

(81) Interview, May 1973.

(82) A senior executive and member of the GCI stated: "We are informed of proposed new policies and get a chance to discuss them with ministers" (interview, May 1973).

Another GCI member was more blunt: "The government comes and tells its story. We tell them what should be done" (interview, May 1973).

Finally, a spokesman for a business association argued that the GCL's main function was "to help the government evaluate the repercussions of its actions at the level of high finance" (interview, May 1973).

(83) To quote a senior executive: "We usually meet with one minister at a time and go through the activities of his department in detail" (interview, May 1973).

(84) Interview, May 1973.

(85) Interview, May 1973. Paré claimed to get "two phone calls a week from Ouimet" (interview with Paul Paré by Paul Tétrault, MA student in political science at McGill University, May 1970).

(86) Interview, May 1973.

(87) Interview, May 1973.

(88) Interview, May 1973.

(89) Interview, May 1973.

(90) Interview, May 1973.

(91) Interview, May 1973.

(92) Interview, May 1973.

(93) Interview, May 1973. The vice-president of a bank thought the meetings were secret "to avoid misquoting by journalists" (interview, May 1973).

(94) Confirmed in interviews, May 1973.

(95) Interview, May 1973.

(96) Interview, May 1973.

(97) The Centre des Dirigeants d'Entreprise stated: "Management has called for and obtained the setting up of the Québec Planning and Development Council" ("Elements of a Strategy for Business," p. 993).

(98) Québec National Assembly, National Assembly Debates, Chapter 14 (Québec City: Editeur Officel du Québec, 1968), p. 125.

(99) Executive Council of Québec, Order in Council No. 609 (Québec City: Editeur Officiel du Québec, 1971), p. 5.

Apparently, the Development Council was not satisfied with the original functions which were granted it by the 1968 legislation, i.e., the council did not simply want to give advice on matters submitted to it by the Bureau. It was then that Arthur Tremblay, president of the Québec Planning and Development Bureau, decided to get around the legal restrictions ("nonobstant la rigidité actuelle des textes législatifs") and to arrange a formula by which it was left up to the presidents of the Bureau and the Council to decide jointly on the topics to be referred to the Council. In fact, the Bureau was prepared to seek the advice of the Council on any question which the Council saw fit to advise it on. This arrangement, according to Tremblay, would enlarge the mandate of the Council in practice without having to obtain legislative approval and without provoking a debate in the National Assembly. See Arthur Tremblay, "Arrangements administratifs relatifs aux objets et modalités de communication entre l'office de planification et de développement du Québec et le conseil de la planification et du développement du Québec," letter to Pierre Côté, president of the Council, Québec City, 14 May 1971.

(100) Interview, May 1973.

(101) Québec Federation of Labour, Un Seul Front (Montréal: Québec Federation of Labour, 1971), p. 61.

(102) K.Z. Paltiel, Political Party Financing in Canada (Toronto: McGraw-Hill of Canada, 1970), pp. 159-60.

(103) H. G. Thorburn, "Politics and Business in Canada," in H. G. Thorburn, ed., Party politics in Canada (Toronto: Prentice-Hall, 1963), p. 153.

(104) Paltiel, p. 161.

(105) Committee on Election Expenses, Studies in Canadian Party Finance (Ottawa: Queen's Printer, 1966), p. 172.

R. G. Rankin, chairman of the Liberal Party's Red Carnation Fund, told a fund-raising gathering before the 1972 federal elections: "The Liberal party has operated for many years on the support of 95 major Canadian corporations" (Canadian Press, "Liberal Spills Secret," Montreal Gazette, 14 February 1972).

(106) Porter, p. 296.

(107) Ibid. See also pp. 373-79.

John Bird of the Financial Post, after an analysis of NPD successes in by-elections as opposed to general elections, concluded "The New Democrats are not as well heeled as the Liberals and PC's and their handicap in the big general elections is more a matter of money than organization" (NPD Handicap is Shortage of Money, Not Organization," Financial Post, 27 November 1971).

(108) Paltiel, p. 161.

(109) Epstein, p. 158. Epstein quoted John L. McLellan, Senator of Arkansas, to support his case: " 'I don't think anybody that gave me a contribution ever felt he was buying my vote or anything like that, but he certainly felt he had an entrée to me to discuss things with me and I was under obligation at least to give him an audience when he desired it to hear his views". (. 198).

(110) Derek Hill, "Québec Liberals Favoring Friends," *Montreal Gazette*, 21 February 1973. Hill went on to explain that no public tenders were called for the contracts in question, and the contracts were for the most part "awarded to companies or individuals selected from a confidential list compiled by party authorities shortly after the 1970 elction victory." The list apparently was a catalogued index of "company names suggested by individual Liberal members of the National Assembly and top party advisers working close to Premier Bourassa." Finally, Hill enumerated several specific cases where party subscribers had been awarded contracts and also where contractors had been replaced after the Liberal victory.

Gérald Godin estimated that in the year 1971-72, according to the public accounts of the province of Québec, 4,000 contracts valued at some $75 million were awarded by the Bourassa government without public tenders ("Le Gouvernement a dépensé plus de $75 millions sans soumission," *Québec-Presse*, 6 April 1973.

Hill's story was in part confirmed on March 15, 1973, when Robert Burns, house leader of the Parti Québécois, published a copy of a letter from Maurice Rioux, president of the Rimouski Liberal riding association, which asked for subscriptions to a Liberal fund-raising dinner. The letter asked for contributions to be remitted to Rioux's office so as to "permit me to furnish a list of subscribers to the party to our deputy minister" (Canadian Press, "Contracts To Be Prize For Grit Support," *Montreal Gazette*, 15 March 1973).

(111) Jérôme Proulx, *Le Panier de crabes* (Montréal: Parti Pris, 1971).

(112) Lévesque also complained about the "marée quotidienne de recommandations dont on nous inondait en faveur des grosses firmes que nous avions baptisés les 'ministérielles,' i.e. celles qui donnent aux deux caisses et partant sont toujours au pouvoir..." He said that in 1960 he was told to keep Perini enterprises on a public contract because they had been generous to the Liberal Party although, according to Lévesque, it was not in the public interest ("Les Caisses électorales, ça ne presse jamais," *Le Devoir*, 2 December 1971).

(113) Interview, May 1973.

(114) Interview, May 1973. The same executive added that he refused the offer. He considered his access to governmental decision-makers was adequate to begin with.

(115) Gérald Leblanc, "Bourassa se tient loin de la caisse," *Le Devoir*, 27 September 1973.

(116) One of the companies which contributed regularly to the Liberal Party was Northern Electric. This company donated about $100,000 annually to federal and provincial parties in Canada (interview, May 1973).

Richard Lafferty, president of Lafferty, Harwood and Company, a Montréal-based investment firm, complained in a speech to the North American Society for Corporate Planning of the "collusion entre les milieux politiques, judiciaires et financiers." He went on to say that banks controlled political parties because they were the most important contributors to election funds. Quoted by Laurier Cloutier. "Les Banques contrôlent les partis politiques," *La Presse*, 15 December 1972.

(117) See Don MacPherson, "UN Hopes Cash Key to Revival," *Montreal Star*, 19 May 1973.

(118) For information on PQ finances, see Parti Québécois, *Qui finance le Parti Québécois?* (Montréal: Les Editions du Parti Québécois, 1972).

(119) See Gilles Racine, "Les Etapes indédites de l'ascension de Robert Bourassa," *La Presse*, 14-17 Septembre 1970.

(120) Ibid.

(121) Ibid.

(122) See Proulx, p. 24. See also Gilles Lesage, "La Loi sera amendée avant les prochaines élections," *La Presse*, 16 October 1969.

(123) Bourassa quoted in *Le Nouvelliste*, 18 March 1970.

(124) See Meynaud, especially pp. 85-90, and Miliband.

(125) Jacques Parizeau, "De Certaines manoeuvres d'un syndicat financier en vue de conserver son empire au Québec," *Le Devoir*, 2 February 1970.

(126) According to Parizeau, ibid., the cartel opposed nationalization and had particular sympathies for Shawinigan Water and Power Company, the largest electric company, and its principal shareholder, Power Corporation. It thus refused to lend the $500 million or so that was needed to buy up the private power companies. Québec, however, began negotiations with Halsey Stewart of New York, from which it got a credit opening of $350 million. When it became obvious that Halsey Stewart was more than willing, the First Boston Bank, which is part of the Bank of Montreal-A. E. Ames group, took over as intermediary for the loan.

(127) See Ian Rodger, "Politics or Finance First in Bond Sales?" *Financial Post*, 16 October 1971.

(128) Rodger, "Politics or Finance." The grants to McGill University were increased shortly after the controversy broke out.

(129) Jacques Parizeau, "Le Syndicat financier," *Québec-Presse*, 16 September 1971.

(130) Birnbaum argued: "The intricate network which unites the property managers to the political managers is all the more effective for being informal; not a conspiracy, not even a club, but simply a happy coincidence — a set of common perspectives shared by men well aware of their responsibilites" (p. 14).

CHAPTER 6

INSTITUTIONAL PENETRATION: THE CASE OF MEDIA

THE ABILITY OF BUSINESS to penetrate, influence, or dominate other institutions constitutes another component of its power. This is particularly true of social systems which have a direct bearing or impact on the ideology and general political attitudes within a society. According to Miliband, the church, the media, and the educational system all play a role in "legitimating" the power structure within advanced capitalist societies.[1]

I will concentrate here on the relations between business and media in Québec, and particularly on the pattern of ownership of media, the degree of dependence of media on business, and some of the political consequences of the links between media and business. Media are emphasized because, as many political scientists and others have argued, they play a crucial role in shaping political attitudes and public opinion.

The pattern of ownership suggests the greatest source of dependence of media on business. First, the media have become, by and large, an industry dominated by big businessmen,[2] and this has meant media have been operating with the same fundamental objective as other businesses — that is, profitability. There is, however, no guarantee that profitability will in every case be compatible with high quality and stimulating information, or any other objective which is deemed desirable. Second, it should be underlined that many of the businessmen involved with media have extensive outside economic interests; and this connection constitutes a potential threat to the autonomy of the media vis-à-vis other industries.

In Québec, as in the rest of Canada,[3] media were not only owned and controlled by big business but they were also highly concentrated. According to the *Report on Mass Media,* better known as the "Davey Report," 49 of the 72 media units in Québec were group-owned, including nine of 14 newspapers, 29 of 41 radio stations,[4] and 11 of 17 television stations.[7]

In regard to radio and television, nine groups or individuals controlled all private French-language AM stations in Montréal, Québec City, and Trois-Rivières, as well as 11 out of 14 private television stations. One of the key groups in radio and television was the Pratte, Baribeau, and Lepage companies. Chart 5 outlines the organizational structure of this group. The Davey Report described the group as consisting of an "interlocking assortment of media interests of four groups which are involved in 12 broadcasting outlets in the province of Québec." As for the press, two groups — Power Corporation and Québecor — were associated with eight of the 11 French-language dailies as well as 80% of the weeklies.[7]

CHART 5

ORGANIZATION OF THE PRATTE, BARIBEAU, AND LEPAGE COMPANIES(a)

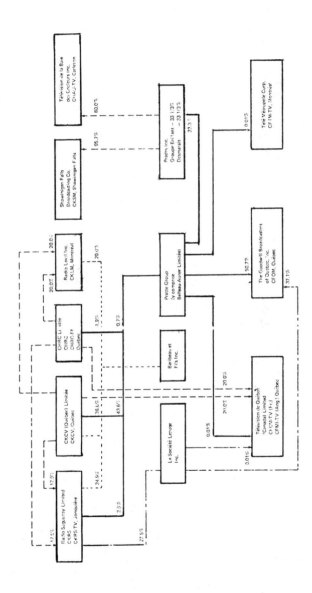

(a) Senate Committee on Mass Media. *Report on Mass Media*, vol 2. p. 98.

In 1972, Québecor, of which 75% was owned by Pierre Péladeau, was made up of two dailies, the Journal de Montréal and the Journal de Québec; seven weeklies with a total circulation of 434,083; five printing plants; a distribution agency, Messageries Dynamiques, which handled the company's own publications as well as approximately 100 non-affiliated publications; and a graphic ink company, Les Encres du Québec, which supplied some 50% of the internal ink requirements. The yearly sales of the Péladeau group amounted to $23 millions.[8]

In a strict sense, Power Corporation no longer owned any radio and television stations or newspapers. Through indirect means, however, it controlled vast media interests. As was seen earlier in chart 2, the two senior executives of Power, Desmarais and Parisien, together controlled Gelco, a private holding company, owning 75% and 25% of the stock respectively. Gelco owned 50.01% of the stock of Power Corporation as well as 100% of the stock of Journaux Trans-Canada and Gesca. La Presse in turn was a wholly-owned subsidiary of Gesca.[9] Finally, on August 10, 1973, La Presse acquired the rival Montréal-Matin from the Union Nationale, thereby controlling two-thirds of the circulation among French-language dailies.

Table 9 shows the media holdings of Power's two senior executives as well as the holdings of Francoeur and Télémédia, which, as will be shown below, were closely linked to Desmarais and Parisien and Power Corporation. Les Journaux Trans-Canada was controlled by Desmarais, Parisien, and Francoeur, who owned 46.6%, 15.56%, and 33.7% of the stock respectively.[10] The holdings of this company included three dailies — La Voix de l'Est in Granby, La Tribune in Sherbrooke, and Le Nouvelliste in Trois-Rivières — 11 weeklies, five weekend newspapers — Dernière-Heure, La Patrie, Dimanche-Matin, Le Petit Journal, and Photo-Journal — and one radio station — CHEF-AM in Granby.[11]

In addition to being president and holding a one-third interest in Les Journaux Trans-Canada, Francoeur owned 100% of a weekly, Le Guide du Nord, and had acquired the Québec City daily Le Soleil in 1974. The latter transaction aroused considerable controversy and at the time of writing its implications were still not entirely clear. In August 1973, Desmarais announced his intention to buy Le Soleil from the Gilbert brothers. Journalists, through the Fédération Profession-nelle des Journalistes du Québec, the Conseil de Presse, several editorialists, including Claude Ryan of Le Devoir, and other groups, including the three major unions, strongly opposed the sale on the grounds it would threaten freedom of the press. Bourassa, who was preparing for a provincial election in October, managed to convince Desmarais and the Gilbert brothers that no sale should be effected during a three-month waiting period. Then, on January 11, 1974, it was announced that Francoeur has just bought Le Soleil for $8.2 million.[12] It was learned that Francoeur had invested only $200,000 in the purchase and that the remainder had been covered by a $5 million loan from the Banque Canadienne Nationale and by a $3 million loan from the Gilbert family.

The evidence was overwhelming that Francoeur could not have bought Le Soleil without the help of Desmarais. An analysis by Claude

TABLE 9

MEDIA INTERESTS OF DESMARAIS, PARISIEN, FRANCOEUR, AND TELEMEDIA[a]

Newspapers	Circulation

Dailies

La Presse (Montréal)	222,184
La Tribune (Sherbrooke)	38,885
Le Nouvelliste (Trois-Rivières)	46,926
La Voix de l'Est (Granby)	11,775
Montréal-Matin (Montréal)[b]	100,000
Le Soleil (Québec City)[b]	225,000

Weeklies

Le Journal de Rosemont (Montréal)	16,000
Le Flambeau de l'Est (Montréal)	21,500
L'Est Central (Montréal)	20,000
Les Nouvelles de l'Est (Montréal)	21,000
Le Progrès de Rosemont (Montréal)	16,000
Le Saint Michel (Montréal)	19,000
Le Courrier de Laval (Laval)	40,000
Métro Sud (Longueuil)	29,035
Roxboro Reporter (Pierrefonds)	16,000
L'Écho du Bas St. Laurent (Rimouski)	5,668
Écho Expansion (St. Lambert)	24,000
Le Guide du Nord (Montréal)	16,500

Weekend

Dernière Heure	59,541
Dimanche-Matin	287,745
La Patrie	130,874
Le Petit Journal	208,348
Photo-Journal	131,273

Radio Stations		Audience
CHLN-AM	(Trois-Rivières)	59,000
CHLT-AM	(Sherbrooke)	34,900
CHLT-FM	(Sherbrooke)	10,000
CJBR-AM	(Rimouski)	
CJBR-FM	(Rimouski)	96,100
CJBR-AM	(rebroadcast Causapscal)	
CKAC-AM	(Montréal)	264,900
CKCH-AM	(Hull)	33,400

(a) Senate Committee on Mass Media, *Report on Mass Media*, vol. 2, table 19 on page 83 and table 32 on page 109. Circulation figures are for 1969.
(b) *Montréal-Matin* and *Le Soleil* were acquired after the *Report on Mass Media* was published.

CKCH-FM	(Hull)	
CKTS-AM	(Sherbrooke)	18,600
CHEF-AM	(Granby)	9,400
CKSM-AM	(Shawinigan)	16,300

Télévision Stations		Audience
CHLT-TV	(Sherbrooke)	411,200
CJBR-TV	(Rimouski)	128,400
CJBR-TV	(rebroadcast Edmundston)	
CHAU-TV	(Carleton, P.Q.)	122,500

Ryan showed how Francoeur was financially dependent on Desmarais and suggested that Francoeur had acted as a "front" for Desmarais.[13] Further evidence was added when it was learned that the Gilbert brothers had committed themselves in writing to sell the daily to Desmarais and that the two parties had decided to annul this commitment only a few hours before the purchase by Francoeur.[14] This confirmed, in effect, that Desmarais had approved the sale. It also meant that Desmarais and Power Corporation controlled over 70% of the French-language daily newspaper circulation in Québec.

Until July, 1970, Power Corporation also had substantial direct interests in radio and television through its subsidiary Québec Télémédia. These included 10 radio stations and three television stations. As a result of pressure from the Canadian Radio and Television Commission, Power Corporation decided to sell its broadcast holding company to Philippe de Gaspé Beaubien. Beaubien formed a new company, Télémédia (Québec). The transaction was reported to have totalled $7.5 million. Beaubien himself contributed $100,000; the rest was provided for by a $7.3 million loan from Power and a $100,000 loan from the Royal Bank, the president of which is McLaughlin, one of the directors of Power.[15]

This raises the question of what advantages, if any, business derives from media ownership or from its ability to influence media. A number of observers have argued that the most important long-term effect of the media has been to maintain a public opinion favourable to business and the economic system. Speaking of corporate expenditures, Key said: "The great political triumph of large-scale enterprise has been the manufacture of a public opinion favourably disposed toward, or at least tolerant of, gigantic corporations."[16] Similarly, Epstein stated:

> If nothing else, the mass media have historically been the primary agents for disseminating the fundamental tenet of American business ideology — that a capitalist economic order is the necessary precondition of a democratic political system. By their continuous stress upon the equation capitalism = democracy the media have placed those groups that propose change in the American economic order in an unfavorable light, since any deviation from a traditional free enterprise system is, by definition, considered to be antidemocratic . . .[17]

A study by Martin Goldfarb consultants for the Senate Committee on Mass Media showed that a large element of the Canadian population felt that media coverage was discriminatory against labour.

According to the survey, 61% of the Anglophone and 50% of the Francophone population in Québec thought that newspapers had a direct influence in creating a "poor image for labour."[18] This survey also revealed that "nearly 70% [of the Canadian population] believe that news in the press is subject to some form of exterior control" and that "nearly two-thirds of Canadians suspect big business and over half suspect the federal government of biasing the media."[19] Finally, 80% of Canadians were shown to be opposed to any one company being allowed to own most newspapers in one area.[20]

In the last decade or so, Québec journalists and other groups, including the unions[21] and citizens' committees,[22] have become increasingly critical of media coverage and of the various direct and indirect forms of censorship imposed by media owners.[23] The major newspapers, television, and radio stations, as well as governmental institutions such as the Canadian Broadcasting Corporation and the National Film Board, have all been the subject of protests and controversy. At the CBC, reporter Robert Mackay was fired for writing a column on international affairs in the separatist monthly *Point de Mire*.[24] At the NFB, at least two films have been blocked by Chief Commissioner Sidney Newman: "Vingt-quatre heures et plus," by Gilles Groulx, and "On est au coton." The latter film was highly critical of the textile industry in Québec, and Newman admitted that executives of Dominion Textiles put pressure on him.[25] He claimed that such films are undesirable because it is not the NFB's role to put into question the existing economic system, capitalism.[26]

To get a clearer idea of the political effects of media ownership, the example of the Montréal daily *La Presse* was used. The first element of control stemmed from the fact that board chairman Desmarais and his directors had the exclusive responsibility of naming the editors, and in the hiring, firing, promoting, and transferring of staff. Ryan emphasized very deliberately, when he testified as an expert witness in the trial of K. C. Irving enterprises for monopoly in Moncton, that the owner of a newspaper wields substantial control over the editor which he names:

> The main [person] responsible for each newspaper in the Irving group remains an employee of the owner, and it is inconceivable that he would be hired and kept employed if he did not share the options and fundamental opinions of the owner as regards the functioning and future of our socio-economic regime. We cannot expect the editor of a newspaper belonging to the Irving group to act, in the exercise of his functions, in a manner that could be considered detrimental to the interests of the owner. The problem is all the more complex and serious in the case of the Irving newspapers because the ownership group is a powerful conglomerate whose ramifications plunge into many spheres of economic activity in New Brunswick.[27]

In effect, the degree of ideological autonomy of a newspaper depends on the goodwill of the owner. In a criticism of press concentration in 1969, Ryan insisted that Desmarais's personal qualities were not a sufficient safeguard that the huge power which he wielded over the press would always be used in the public interest.[31] In an attempt to defend the purchase of *Montréal-Matin* by *La Presse*, the latter's editorialist Vincent Prince claimed that Desmarais had allowed the setting up of an autonomous and "representative" board of directors at *La Presse*. [29] Here again, it was the goodwill of the owner which was the primary determinant of the degree of autonomy enjoyed by a newspaper. When the newspaper is part of a conglomerate which has extensive non-media interests, as in the case of Power Corporation, there is the additional problem of freedom of the newspaper to criticize the conglomerate or one of its subsidiaries. As Ryan put it, even if Desmarais wanted to administer *La Presse* totally independently of Power Corporation, there would always remain doubts concerning the liberty of that newspaper to treat on the same footing as any other topic the questions surrounding the commercial, financial, and industrial interests of Power Corporation. [30] Mintz and Cohen detailed many examples in the United States where media owners either intervened to influence the content of news or fired editors whose views were incompatible with theirs. [31]

The fact that owners name editors makes direct intervention both unnecessary and unlikely. If intervention should become necessary, however, Desmarais, for one, would not hesitate. On February 24, 1970, at a hearing of the Senate Committee on Mass Media, he claimed he would intervene if one of his dailies published a pro-PQ editorial. [32] Desmarais also said that he would prefer letting *La Presse* die than allow it to be controlled by journalists. [33]

La Presse made no pretence at neutrality in regard to the main political issues in Québec. In a statement on December 9, 1972, signed by editor Roger Lemelin and endorsed by Desmarais and the directors of the newspaper, *La Presse* outlined specifically its ideological orientation. The statement supported Canadian unity as well as private enterprise and limited state intervention:

> The newspaper *La Presse* believes in private enterprise such as it is practised and is evolving in the world, but approves limited intervention and planning by the state.
>
> The newspaper *La Presse* will follow with a vigilant eye any trend that could incite governmental leaders to go beyond the limits of healthy state intervention. [34]

The latter part of the statement makes it quite clear that *La Presse* will vigorously oppose any attempt by the state to significantly increase its role.

The second level of control over the orientation of a newspaper is at the managerial or editorial level. At this level, decisions governing the political orientations of a newspaper involve indirect rather than direct intervention. At *La Presse,* a manifesto put out by the journalists' union [35] claimed that the number of political reporters had declined steadily since the paper was acquired by Power Corporation in 1964. Under the editorship of Gérard Pelletier, *La Presse* used to have seven reporters in Québec City; in 1973 it had only three. Under its new ownership, *La Presse* also forced desk editors to drop out of the journalists' union because they had "showed too much autonomy." [36]

The manifesto complained that *La Presse* had attempted to avoid controversial political and social questions and that the reduction of personnel in key political areas had meant that the newspaper had often satisfied itself with transmitting the "official version" of the facts, that is, communiqués from government or corporate public relations departments. The budgetary decisions by management, for example, more money for features and sports as opposed to political news, the choice of journalists, and the distribution of journalists within issue-areas, for example, *La Presse* had 12 financial reporters and only one labour reporter,[37] all have a crucial impact on the political orientation of a newspaper. The manifesto concluded that the owners of *La Presse* had always had sufficient powers to orient news to a certain extent in the direction which suited them.[38]

Apart from ownership, there is another major source of dependence for the communication media on business: corporate advertising. According to the Senate Committee on Mass Media, 65% of the gross income of newspapers and 93% of the gross income of the private broadcasting industry came from advertising.[39] Although there was a good number of examples of individual corporations cancelling their advertising because of their displeasure with a specific newspaper story,[40] the Committee maintained that, in general, Canadian media did not bend before advertisers. It explained further:

> The point, of course, is that they do not have to; because broadly speaking the advertisers, their agencies, and the media owners are all the same kind of people, doing the same kind of thing, within the same kind of private-enterprise rationale. There is nothing sinister about it, nothing conspiratorial. Advertiser pressure is not necessary because the influence is there anyway — subtly and by implication.[41]

Desmond Morton expressed much the same views in *Canadian Forum:*

> It doesn't matter whether the *North Bay Nugget* belongs to Max Bell, Roy Thomson, or a local dry goods merchant. They are all, without a single exception, in the same kind of hands. They all belong to the Canadian business community and they all do what the business community wants . . . And if Canadian business assumes an automatic, infallible identity between their views and those of every right thinking Canadian, they are hardly unique among the oligarchy of history.[42]

It is likely that self-censorship plays a more important role than censorship as such. As Epstein put it: "Since the media are dependent on business advertising, they are often reluctant to publish or transmit criticism of corporate practices."[43] Meynaud reached the same conclusion in his study of political information on U.S. television.[44]

In the case of Québec, there was evidence that corporations were willing to use advertising for political purposes. Thirty-two point eight percent of the businessmen questionned felt that companies should refrain from advertising in "newspapers opposed to the present political system."[45] The lack of advertising revenue had also resulted in threatening the survival of "opposition" papers, be they separatist or socialist leaning.[46] *Québec-Presse* was created in 1968 with the help of the unions and other groups which felt that the regular press was not adequately presenting their viewpoints. The publication of the weekly newspaper was discontinued at the end of 1974 because of financial difficulties. The main problem was that *Québec-Presse* had not succeeded in attracting significant amounts of corporate advertising. According to editor Gérald Godin, the paper would have had no problem in being profitable and expanding if it had obtained a share of advertising revenue corresponding to its circulation.[47]

Le Jour, a Montréal daily created in February 1974, is another example. It was founded by the heads of the Parti Québécois after the provincial election of October 29, 1973. The PQ, although it obtained 30% of the vote in the election, received no editorial support from any of Québec's daily newspapers. Its leaders also felt that the party viewpoint had not always been adequately presented in the existing press. Although in 1974 and 1975 the circulation figures of Le Jour were on a par with those of Le Devoir — from 25,000 to 30,000 — Le Jour had not been able to attract the crucial big business and governmental advertising contracts which guaranteed the survival of Le Devoir. Thus, although circulation revenues have been much the same for both newspapers — $1.6 million for Le Jour in 1974 and $1.5 million for Le Devoir — the latter newspaper's advertising revenue was over three times that of the PQ supported daily — $1.7 million as opposed to $539,000. Commenting on an editorial by Le Jour in which editor-in-chief Yves Michaud criticized the government's refusal to advertise in his newspaper, the Montreal Star's Jim Stewart predicted that the Québec government and most large companies would continue to boycott the newspaper. He felt this attitude was justifiable since one should not give matches to a man who wanted to burn down your house.[48]

It would certainly be an exaggeration to claim that communications media are simply the mouthpiece of the business community. It is obvious from even a superficial examination of Canadian media that conflicting opinions, including criticisms of corporate behavior, are expressed. The point is rather that media depend on business, through ownership and advertising, much more than any other social group and that, at times, this can be used as a source of political power by business. It should also be remembered that the degree of pluralism within media depends to a large extent on the goodwill of the owners and advertisers. That the latter two groups have been generally discreet in their pressure does not alter the fact of media's dependence.

NOTES

(1) Miliband, chapters 7 and 8.

(2) A study of media concentration and of the various links between media and business in the United States can be found in chapter 2 of Cohen and Mintz.

(3) See Senate Committee on Mass Media, Report on Mass Media (Ottawa: Queen's Printer, 1970), and also Porter for detailed discussion of media concentration and ownership in Canada.

(4) If the six Canadian Broadcasting Corporation Stations were excluded, only six independent stations were left.

(5) Senate Committee on Mass Media, Report on Mass Media, vol. 1, p. 17.

(6) Ibid., p. 31.

(7) For more information concerning media groups and the economic interests of the heads of the media industry in Québec, see Jacques Guay, "Une Presse asservie: des faits," Socialisme 69, pp. 67-90.

(8) From Québecor Inc., 1972 Annual Report (Montréal: Québecor, 1973), and Ian Rodger, "Pierre Péladeau isn't a Publisher Like Other Newspaper Publishers," Financial Post, 14 October 1972.

(9) Another link was provided by a $23 million loan which Power Corporation granted to Gesca.

(10) The remaining 4.45% was owned by businessman Pierre Dansereau.

(11) Information is from the Senate Committee on Mass Media, vol. 1, pp. 28-39.

(12) See Lionel Desjardins, "Le Soleil acheté par M. Jacques Francoeur," La Presse, 12 January 1974. See also Gérald Leblanc, "Les Journalistes veulent des garanties contre la concentration," Le Devoir, 15 January 1974.

(13) Claude Ryan, "Que s'est-il passé entre Paul Desmarais, Jacques Francoeur et les frères Gilbert?" *Le Devoir*, 18 February 1974. See also Gérald Leblanc, "Une Abondante documentation révèle une action concertée de Francoeur et Desmarais dans l'achat du *Soleil*," *Le Devoir*, 30 January 1974.

(14) Gérald Leblanc, "Paul Desmarais n'a renoncé à son option que le jour de la vente à Jacques Francoeur," *Le Devoir*, 19 February 1974.

(15) Senate Committee on Mass Media, vol 1, p. 35.

(16) Key, p. 96.

(17) Epstein, p. 216.

(18) Senate Committee on Mass Media, vol. 3, p. 64. The corresponding figures for television and radio were 50% and 30% for Anglophones and 49% and 33% for Francophones.

(19) Ibid., pp. 27-28. The figures for French-speaking Quebecers were 62% in the case of big business and 45% in the case of the federal government (p. 49).

(20) Ibid., p. 30.

(21) The Confederation of National Trade Unions, for example, published a book entitled *La Grande Tricherie* (Montréal: Confederation of National Trade Unions, 1973) in which it denounced the anti-labor bias of the media and the collusion between political and economic power and the media.

(22) See, for example, the Greater Montreal Anti-Poverty Coordinating Committee, "Statement of Principles: Mass Media," *The Poor Peoples' Paper*, vol. 2, no. 9, February 1973.

(23) Some of the journalists who have written critical accounts of Québec media include Pierre Godin, *L'Information-opium* (Montréal: Parti Pris, 1973); François Béliveau, *Pogné* (Montréal: Editions Québécoises, 1971), *Pour une radio civilisée*; and Claude Jean Devirieux, *Manifeste pour la liberté de l'information* (Montréal: Editions du Jour, 1971).

(24) Pierre Vadeboncoeur, "L'Affaire Mackay: une sentence qui doit être dénoncée," *Le Devoir*, 3 November 1971.

(25) The film was screened for textile executives prior to its release. The executives then complained to Newman concerning the authenticity of certain facts on their industry (Sidney Newman, "Pourquoi l'ONF a interdit 'On est au coton,'" *Le Devoir*, 12 November 1971).

(26) Ibid. See also François Béliveau, "Blitz pour un beau Canada uni," *La Presse*, 6 January 1973.

(27) *Le Devoir*, "Le Monopole de K. C. Irving, une menace pour la démocratie," 7 November 1972.

(28) Claude Ryan, "Concentration et liberté dans les entreprises de presse," *Le Devoir*, 16 September 1969.

(29) Vincent Prince, "L'Achat de *Montréal-Matin*," editorial, *La Presse*, 11 August 1973.

(30) Ryan, "Concentration et liberté." According to Epstein, "It is highly improbable that a subsidiary would publicize views that are incompatible with the interests of its parent" (p. 213).

(31) Cohen and Mintz, pp. 109-162. For example, in 1965 William P. Steven, editor of the *Houston Chronicle*, was fired by the heads of the holding Houston Endowment "because he supported higher education, Lyndon Johnson, and civil rights" (p. 143).

(32) La Presse Canadienne, "Paul Desmarais interviendrait si l'un de ses journaux publiait un éditorial appuyant le PQ," *Le Soleil*, 25 February 1970.

(33) *Québec-Presse*, "L'Empire de presse de Paul Desmarais," 2 September 1973. Desmarais said: "Plutôt la mort du journal que le contrôle par les journalistes . . . Personne ne va contrôler ce damné journal, c'est mon journal . . ."

(34) Roger Lemelin, "Définition du journal *La Presse* et de son orientation idéologique," *La Presse*, 9 December 1972.

(35) Michel Lord, "La Censure a pris un tour carrément politique," *Le Devoir*, 27 October 1971.

(36) Ibid. The manifesto, which was published during the *La Presse* strike in 1971, outlined 14 alleged cases of censorship by the newspaper management. It also complained that many controversial political issues — e.g., the debate on school reorganization, strikes in French universities, activities of the federal government with regard to urban planning — were deliberately underplayed. An example of direct censorship by members of the board of directors of *La Presse* was outlined by Yves Bougie. He claimed that in June, 1968, after a violent St. Jean Baptiste Day demonstration, two members of the *La Presse* board of directors, M. Lafrance and Parisien, spent the night in the newsroom checking and cutting news copy as well as eliminating photographs. See "La Presse écrite au Québec: objet et agent de pression," research paper presented to Jean Meynaud's course on pressure groups at the Université de Montréal, 15 December 1969.

(37) The Confederation of National Trade Unions complained about the lack of labour news in Québec newspapers: ". . . Nous savons que le mouvement syndical qui touche directement plus de 500,000 travailleurs ne se voit pas accorder des pages syndicales dans les quotidiens alors que les financiers (qui sont peu nombreux) ont leurs pages financières (2, 3, 4, et même plus chaque jour)" (p. 17).

(38) Lord, "La Censure."

(39) Senate Committee on Mass Media, vol. 1, p. 243.

(40) According to the Senate Committee on Mass Media, vol. 3, an article by Sidney Katz in 1962 *Macleans* on over-medication led to the cancellation of $80,000 worth of advertising from drug companies. Similarly, a *Financial Post* article in 1962 which commented adversely on the take-over of Canadian Oil by Shell led to the president of Shell cancelling all the company's advertising in Maclean-Hunter publications. Although Maclean-Hunter stood its ground in this case, the Committee pointed out: "A struggling publisher, or one who puts profit before editorial liberty, might hesitate to risk the alienation of a major revenue source" (pp. 199-200).

Sonja Sinclair, in an article on the press in *Canadian Business*, January 1969, outlined two other cases of corporations attempting to use advertising for political purposes:

"John Harbron [former editor of *Executive* and one-time editor of *Business Week*] recalls a case where the Canadian subsidiary of an American duplicating firm cancelled its advertising program in retaliation for an editorial which expressed agreement with some of Walter Gordon's policies. Frank Oxley [a partner in Oxley, Dickens and Harper, previously of the *Financial Post*] was once told by a furious finger-pointing oil company executive: 'We are buying six full pages in your god-damned newpaper, and you write what I tell you to write'" (pp. 23-24).

(41) Senate Committee on Mass Media, vol. 1, p. 245.

(42) Desmond Morton, "Advertisers Don't Use Pressure," *Canadian Forum*, July 1969. According to Jerry Goodis, Toronto advertising agency president, advertising and the necessity to please the advertiser influenced the content of the media in favour of the affluent:

"What are the results of the necessity to build an audience of affluent consumers to serve up to the advertiser a more affluent or more efficient audience than the next man? Editorial content inevitably comes to serve this end. The measure of editorial acceptability becomes how does it fit, or will it interest the affluent. As a consequence, the mass media increasingly reflect the attitudes and deal with the concerns of the affluent. We don't have mass media, we have class media — media for the middle and upper classes.

"The poor, the old, the young, the Indian, the Eskimo, the blacks are virtually ignored. It is as if they didn't exist. More importantly, these minority groups are denied expression in the mass media because they cannot command attention . . ." (quoted by Senate Committee on Mass Media, vol. 1, p. 245.

(43) Epstein, p. 212.

(44) Jean Meynaud, "La Télévision américaine et l'information sur la politique," *Le Devoir*, 22 January 1972.

(45) The question read: "Some companies have been criticized for advertising in newspapers opposed to the present political and economic system. Do you feel companies should refrain from advertising in such newspapers?" The answers were 32.8% "yes" and 67.2% "no" (excluding the 8.4% who did not answer the question).

(46) According to Claude Jean Devirieux, ". . . Les organes d'information publiant des articles mettant en cause le système établi (et il n'y en a guère) attirent difficilement la publicité, sont rarement des entreprises rentables et, par voie de conséquence, peuvent difficilement améliorer leur présentation, s'assurer de vastes moyens de diffusion et élargir leur rayonnement. Je songe, entre autres, au journal *Vrai* publié par Jacques Hébert vers 1955, au *Nouveau Journal* de Jean-Louis Gagnon, en 1961; plus près de nous: les journaux étudiants, *Québec-Presse* . . ." (p. 56).

(47) Gérald Godin, "Les Amis de *Québec-Presse* et la censure," *Québec-Presse*, 7 November 1971.

(48) Jim Stewart, "*Le Jour* Wants Bourassa Ads," *Montreal Star*, 25 July 1974.

CHAPTER 7

COMPETITIVE POTENTIAL OF OTHER GROUPS: THE CASE OF LABOUR

HOW DOES THE POWER of business compare with that of other groups and which group or groups can be considered worthy competitors of business in the arena of power?

The questionnaire asked businessmen who they thought was "the most influential group in Québec politics". As can be seen in table 10, labour was judged to be the most influential by 32.0% of the respondents, followed by intellectuals (22.2%), business groups (16.9%), communications media (13.7%), nationalist groups (10.5%), other (4.6%), and religious groups (0%). Some significant differences appeared between the French and English respondents. The influence of business was perceived to be higher by the French (27.6%) than by the English executives (10.5%). On the other hand, the English respondents gave more credit for influence to nationalist groups and intellectuals. A possible explanation is that both the French and the English feared or were more likely to be awed by the groups in which they were under-represented; thus the intellectuals and nationalist groups were closer to and dominated by the French element whereas the business groups were more closely tied to the English community.[1]

Given that labour was perceived by business to be the most influential group in Québec politics, I will discuss briefly labour's strengths and weaknesses with a view to determining its overall power position vis-à-vis government.

The strength of organized labour stems from its mass membership, union dues, and more generally from its important role in production. In Québec, in 1972, 700,000 workers, representing about 35% of the labour force, were unionized.[2] They were divided into five groups: the Québec Federation of Labour (QFL), the Confederation of National Trade Unions (CNTU), the Centrale des Syndicats Démocratiques (CSD), the Québec Teachers Corporation (QTC), and the Union of Agricultural Producers (UAP).

In the nineteen sixties and early seventies, Québec unions had succeeded to some extent in overcoming many of the weaknesses which had undermined their political effectiveness previously. In the first place, the unions had greater success in achieving some unity within their ranks; they had more and more frequently joined together in forming "common fronts" and in submitting common briefs to the government. The *La Presse* strike in 1971 and the public service strike

TABLE 10

PERCENTAGE DISTRIBUTION OF RESPONSES OF QUÉBEC BUSINESS LEADERS REGARDING MOST INFLUENTIAL GROUP IN QUÉBEC POLITICS[a]

(Question III F: "Which group do you feel has the most influence on government policy in Québec?")

	All Respondents	English Respondents	French Respondents	Respondents From Large Companies	Respondents From Secondary Companies
Intellectuals	22.2	27.4	13.8	20.8	27.3
Religious Groups	0	0	0	0	0
Nationalist Groups	10.5	14.7	3.4	10.0	12.1
Labour Groups	32.0	30.5	34.5	31.6	33.3
Communications Media	13.7	12.6	15.5	15.8	6.1
Business Groups	16.9	10.5	27.6	15.8	21.2
Other	4.6	4.2	5.2	5.8	0

N = 139

(a) The figures exclude the 2.8% of respondents who did not answer the question.

in 1972 were good examples of joint action. Second, Québec unions had begun to move away from "market unionism" — exclusively oriented towards short-term gains in individual factories — in favour of a more politically-oriented "social movement unionism." The "manifestos" published by labour unions in the nineteen sixties had all emphasized that many of the problems facing labour could not be solved at the bargaining table.[3] Thus, the labour movement in Québec had devoted increasing attention to promoting socialism and to attempting to influence governmental policy in such fields as taxation, labour legislation, education, and language. The collective bargaining process itself had been more directed towards political issues. Some concrete examples were the attempt in 1970 to have French accepted as the working language at General Motors and the stress on issues related to "freedom of the press" during the *La Presse* strike.

Despite increasing unity in the Québec labour movement, and despite greater emphasis on attempts to wield political influence, labour unions were not on even terms with business in the power arena.[4] First, important divisions remained within the labour movement: the CSD was created in 1972 as a result of an ideological split within the CNTU, and bitter struggles between the QFL and CNTU concerning the affiliation of construction workers occurred in 1972 and 1973. Second, as Miliband argued, "Labour lacks a firm basis of economic power."[5] It does not play a crucial role in production, investment, expansion, and other key economic decisions. For that reason, labour has "much less pressure potential vis-à-vis the state," and, as a consequence, "governments are much less concerned to obtain the confidence of labour than of business."[6]

Third, the strike, which is labour's primary means of pressure, has become increasingly less effective, especially since the development of the multinational corporation. Thus, large companies with large stockpiles or inventories, or companies which have many plants in different countries producing the same product, can withstand strike action with minimum inconvenience. As an exemple, during the 1971 negotiations at Aluminum Company of Canada, the union decided not to strike because it was aware that the company had stockpiled 1,000,000 tons of aluminum in anticipation of a strike in the U.S. which never occurred. The union knew full well that Aluminum Company would not settle for months, or until its stockpile was almost depleted.[7]

Miliband and Porter also pointed out that strikes usually occur in a hostile environment; more often than not, unions lose the fight for public opinion during strike action. Part of the problem is that "labour, as a pressure group, always appears as a very much more sectional interest than business . . ." and that "the demands of business in contrast are always claimed to be in the national interest."[8] A related problem is that labour leaders are under substantial societal and media pressure. As Porter said: "The responsible labour leader is one who does not make too great demands on the system and whose activities do not interrupt the processes of production." [9]

Fourth, labour lacks important resources. It certainly cannot match the expenditures of business associations and individual corporations on public relations efforts. It has not been as successful as business in penetrating media and educational institutions. Overall, then, there remains an "imbalance between business and labour."[10] Even though business predominance is far from absolute, it is generally in a better position to further its interests than its most worthy competitor, labour. Speaking of the weakness of labour unionism, Hacker argued that this had resulted in "a serious blow to the doctrine of social pluralism, for organized labour has been traditionally counted upon as a source of countervailing force against the strength of corporate management," and that "insofar as they [the unions] are weakened, they deprive society of yet another check to the power of the corporation."[11]

The above analysis does not claim to be exhaustive. The discussion of concrete issues which follows in part II will be the real test of the power of business and other groups. Given that business perceives labour to be the most influential group in Québec politics, particular attention will be paid to a comparison between the effectiveness of labour and business groups.

NOTES

(1) The feeling that labour was the most influential group in politics was not shared by the Canadian population as a whole. According to a survey by the Canadian Institute of Public Opinion in 1960, big business was perceived by 58.2% of Canadian respondents to have "the most influence in Ottawa," compared with 23.3% for labour, 12.2% undecided, and 6.5% who felt there was no difference between labour and business.

The same survey asked who "should have the most influence in Ottawa." 38.6% replied labour, 20.2% opted for business, 27.2% chose neither, and 14.0% were undecided. See R. R. March, *Public Opinion and Industrial Relations* (Ottawa: Privy Council Office, 1968), p. 37.

(2) Louis Favreau, *Les Travailleurs face au pouvoir* (Montréal: Centre de Formation Populaire, 1972), p. 110.

(3) See, for example, the CNTU's *Ne Comptons que sur nos propres moyens* and the QFL's *Un Seul front* (Montréal: Québec Federation of Labor, 1971) and *L'Etat, rouage de notre exploitation* (Montréal: Québec Federation of Labour, 1971).

According to Fernand Daoust, secretary-general of the QFL, labour's "politicization" stemmed from the realization that "isolated battles did not produce what we expected they should produce." The problems of layoffs, unemployment, and plant closures could not be dealt with solely at the bargaining table, according to Daoust (quoted by Arnold Bennett, "Daoust Says Labour Is Now Militant," *McGill Daily*, 3 February 1972.).

(4) For detailed discussions of the power and weaknesses of labour, see Miliband, especially pp. 155-165, and Porter, pp. 328-36.

(5) Miliband, p. 155.

(6) Ibid.

(7) *Québec-Presse*, "Alcan-Québec affronte ses 8,000 syndiqués," 14 November 1971.

(8) Miliband, p. 162.

(9) Porter, p. 312.

(10) Miliband, p. 165.

(11) Hacker, p. 13.

PART II

MANIFESTATIONS OF BUSINESS POWER: ISSUE-AREAS

THE REMAINDER OF THIS STUDY will analyse governmental outputs in three issue-areas: education and language, labour and social matters, and economic development. In addition to attempting to determine the degree of success achieved by business vis-à-vis specific policies or legislation, the section will focus on the overall satisfaction of business within each issue-area and on the impact of governmental activity on the power of business in each sector. The focus will be not only specific decisions but also the general position of business vis-à-vis government in each issue area.

There will also be a concentrated effort to analyse business pressure tactics, that is, how business succeeded in obtaining favourable policy outputs from government. Until now I have studied the structural dominance; this part will examine how this structural dominance is used to pressure government. Several "persuasion techniques" can be identified, some of which may be specific to Québec: threats to move plants and head offices; threats not to invest or to export capital; pressure on governmental credit. The multinational corporations, because of their flexibility and mobility, were particularly prone to using these pressure tactics.

As will be seen with respect to each issue-area, these persuasion techniques were used frequently by business. At this point, it can be said that the "political climate" was a definite consideration in investment decisions, and that a government which wishes to attract investment must ensure a favourable or stable investment climate. Our data revealed that 52.4% of business respondents thought their company would invest more in Québec if the socio-political climate was more stable. According to a former senior executive, "Politics, over the last year, have done an unbelievable amount of harm to the economics of Québec. What you need most of all is the expectation of political stability."[1] The Fantus Report, prepared in 1972, made it abundantly clear that foreign investors were reticent to put money in Québec because of the political problems, including militant unions, the threat of separatism, and the uncertainty of the language situation.[2] The government was being told by business, in effect, that it would not get any funds for industrial development unless it stabilized the language situation, held militant unions in check, and minimized the possibilities of separatism.

113

Québec, of course, was not alone in being subjected to this kind of pressure activity. For example, at the federal level, the *Financial Post* had a front page headline in 1963 saying that foreign capital was ready to leave if one of the two parties, Liberal or Progressive Conservatives, did not get a working majority.[3] David Barrett, former NDP premier of British Columbia, was also put under pressure to "regain the trust of business," while he was in office. To quote the *Financial Post:* "The securities of British Columbia took a pounding on stock markets last week . . . The question now to be asked is whether Barrett can recover by deed and word a measure of the earlier acceptance or tolerance he seemed to enjoy . . . Can Barrett seriously believe that unyielding utterances such as he is making will encourage investment to come to British Columbia and companies to spend the necessary capital?"[4]

The problem for government is that it is very difficult, especially during the long run, to resist business pressure. Since government is "dependent upon private industry for the fulfillment of basic economic tasks,"[5] it cannot allow business to "lose confidence" in it. And, as Arnold Rose pointed out, "It is the threat that counts, not the exercise of the threat. As long as people think that business might move, their behaviour will, at least in part, be effectively controlled by business."[6]

I asked the businessmen in the interviews what they thought was the main governmental constraint on their operations. I was trying to get a general reflex reaction by senior businessmen towards governmental activity. By far the most frequently heard complaint was the amount of paperwork (reports, forms, questionnaires, and statistics) and the number of regulations imposed by government. To quote the president of a major bank: "It is costly and time-consuming to make sure that you follow all the petty little laws and fill out all the forms."[7] There were also complaints about governmental inefficiency, the level of government spending, and taxation. In general, however, it was felt that as long as constraints such as taxation were applied equally to all companies they would not be a major problem for business.

The overall reaction of the businessmen was one of satisfaction and sympathy for the government's position. According to the vice-president of a holding in the food and beverage section, "We can understand constraints put on us by government. They have to respond to political situations; we can understand why they do certain things."[8] A senior executive of a pulp and paper company said: "Government is good for the economy," and "we need long-term planning, export regulations, etc."[9]

NOTES

(1) Interview, May 1973.

(2) The Fantus Company, "Industrial Development in Québec," report prepared for the Québec department of industry and commerce, May 1972.

(3) Nevile Nankivell, "Foreign Capital Ready to Go, if Political Muddle Gets Worse," *Financial Post*, 23 February 1963. "If there is another political stalemate, or if the minor political parties get the balance of power, substantial withdrawals of foreign capital from Canada are almost certain . . . The experts conclude that a working majority by one of the major parties is the best guarantee of foreign confidence in the future of the Canadian economy."

(4) Hyman Solomon, "Can David Barrett Regain the Trust of Big Business?" *Financial Post*, 21 October 1972.

(5) Epstein, p. 209.

(6) A. Rose, p. 210.

(7) Interview, May 1973.

(8) Interview, May 1973.

(9) Interview, May 1973.

CHAPTER 8

LANGUAGE AND EDUCATION

EVEN THOUGH IT IS UNLIKELY that issues involving language and education could be considered objective threats to the economic system in Québec, it is undeniable that business has devoted considerable energy to obtaining favourable governmental outputs in this area. An analysis of language and education issues is particularly complex in the case of Québec because of overlapping socio-economic an cultural cleavages. Thus, because the English-Canadian community in Québec is in a generally more favoured socio-economic position, it is often difficult to distinguish between the interests of business, predominantly English dominated, from those of the English community as a whole. It will be seen, however, that the unity of French and English elements of business has been on the whole stronger than the cohesion within the English or French communities. In addition to studying education and language issues, I will examine briefly the related issue of Québec separatism.

Language in Québec

The language issue was probably the most controversial problem in Québec politics in the late nineteen sixties and early seventies. The government was faced with strong public pressure to pass legislation ensuring the survival and expansion of the French language. The primary concern of business, on the other hand, was to resist any governmental legislation that would force it to use French as the language of work in plants and head offices. Thus, according to the *Financial Times,* "The great fear in the business community has been that the government will resort to coercive legislation to impose French as a language of work."[1] Another concern of businessmen, particularly those who were English speaking, was to ensure the availability of English schools for their children.

Without attempting a detailed historical analysis of the language issue, one can say that business had been concerned with governmental outputs concerning language since 1969 at least. Thus, it was in October 1969 that Bill 63, the Québec government's first piece of legislation dealing with language, was passed.[2] The primary aim of the bill was to ensure that parents would be free to choose whether the language of instruction of their children was to be French or English. Although seemingly innocuous, this legislation was massively opposed by Québec's French-speaking population.[3] It was estimated that 286 groups expressed their disapproval of Bill 63: 54 teachers' associations, 63 student associations, 27 cultural associations, 36 worker organizations, 17 professional organizations, 60 miscellaneous groups, 11 parent associations, and 3 religious congregations.[4] This included all three labour federations, QFL, CNTU, QTC, the farm union, UPA, the Montréal Catholic School Commission, the Superior Council of Education, the Council of Universities, the Syndicat des Ecrivains, and some nationalist groups such as the Société St. Jean Baptiste.

The support for the legislation came primarily from business groups, including the Montréal Chambre de Commerce, the CMA, the Centre des Dirigeants d'Entreprise, the Conseil du Patronat, and the English education associations, including the Association of Catholic School Principals. The questionnaire demonstrated that 94.4% of the businessmen approved Bill 63.[5] The English respondents were unanimous in supporting the legislation, whereas the French element gave a 78.7% level of support. It is not surprising that there should be a minority element in the French business elite manifesting "nationalist" leanings.

There is little doubt that numerically the groups opposed to Bill 63 represented a substantially larger percentage of the Québec population than those who supported it. Although some have questioned the "representativeness" of labour unions and St. Jean Baptiste Society leaders in Québec, the executives of these associations were elected by over 650,000 people. One way or the other, a majority of the groups taking stands on Bill 63 opposed the legislation.

Beyond the group approach, there was substantial evidence of "mass opposition" to Bill 63. First, the bill led to the largest demonstrations in Québec history; at least 50,000 people participated. Second, a very large majority of the Québec press opposed the bill. This was not surprising for the French press in Montréal,[6] but the amount of regional press opposition was striking. As can be seen in table II, 25 weeklies were against the bill, 3 in favour, and 10 undecided. The dailies Le Nouvelliste and La Tribune also opposed the bill. The opposition was significant for two reasons. In the first place, the regional press, which by and large supported the Union Nationale, saw fit to break their traditional allegiances during Bill 63. In the second place, many editorialists claimed to have changed their minds during the debate and opposed the bill as a direct result of local opposition.

The extent of local opposition was one of the main themes developed by the regional press. To quote from an editorial in La Voix d'Alma: "Monday night at Alma 11 groups in the region declared themselves opposed to Bill 63. This is true of many regions in Québec. Thus the government cannot claim that the opposition comes only from students and a few professional agitators."[7] Similarly, a Le Nouvelliste editorial claimed: "It would be a serious mistake to believe that the opposition to Bill 63 is limited to a group of fanatics."[8] Le Progrès de Magog was even more categorical: "Politicians cannot insult our intelligence much longer by claiming that this vast protest movement is the work of terrorists."[9] Some of the editorialists also referred to the "financial angels" of the government:

> The bill could provoke a civil war if the heads of the provincial government continue to stubbornly defy public opinion and to believe that they are the only masters of the destiny of the population. They will have to accept that decisions concerning the future of the people should be made with the people, not only according to the goodwill of business or the whims of a certain class of society.[10]

It should be noted finally that most editorialists did not support unilingualism but rather the integration of new immigrants into the French school system. Most also asked for a Québec-wide referendum on the issue.

A third indication of the extent of opposition came from a poll conducted among the Montréal general public by the psychology department of the Université de Montréal. The poll, published in *Le Devoir,* gave the following results: 38% against, 33% in favour, and 17% undecided.[11] A further analysis of the data indicated that opposition increased as a function of knowledge. Thus, 64% of those having a "good knowledge" of Bill 63 opposed it, while the corresponding figure for those having an "inadequate understanding" of the legislation was 45%. Considering that over a third of the population in Montréal is English or immigrant, the degree of opposition was high.

One can wonder why the Union Nationale chose to alienate such a large element of the French population in Québec by passing Bill 63. More specifically, one can wonder why the UN went against the middle-class nationalist element in Québec which in the past had provided much of the basis of its power. Given that business or the economic elites, English as well as French, were the only major groups to support the legislation, it would seem a legitimate hypothesis to claim that the government responded to their pressures.[12]

Another key element which had to be studied in order to understand group behaviour vis-à-vis the language issue was the Gendron Commission. Named after its chairman Jean-Denis Gendron, this Commission was given a mandate in 1968 to examine the situation of the French language in Québec and to suggest measures to ensure its survival and development. The Commission submitted its recommendations to the Québec government in February 1973, almost five years after it had been created. The first phase of the Commission's work involved extensive public hearings in which individuals and groups were encouraged to submit policy statements or briefs.

The largest single group to participate in the public hearings was composed of corporations and business associations; in fact, some two-thirds of the briefs came from business. The main focus of the business offensive was to oppose any measure that would legislate French as the main language of work in Québec. Most briefs stressed the difficulties of using French at the upper and middle levels of business.[13] Another common theme was the implication that the standard of living would fall and that capital would leave Québec if legislation judged unfavorable to business was passed. The Board of Trade maintained: "A coercive approach to this matter [language policy] by government will adversely affect the economic environment . . ."[14] Imperial Oil warned: "Any attempts to restrict the use of English can jeopardize

TABLE 11

THE POSITION OF THE FRENCH-LANGUAGE QUÉBEC WEEKLY PRESS REGARDING BILL 63

Against

L'Avant Poste Gaspésien
  (Amqui)
Le Canada Français (Saint-Jean)
Le Clairon (Sainte-Hyacinthe)
L'Action Populaire (Joliette)
Joliette Journal (Joliette)
La Voix d'Alma (Alma)
Le Meilleur Journal
  (Port-Cartier)
Le Saint-Laurent
  (Rivière-du-Loup)
La Boussole (Nicolet)
L'Union (Victoriaville)
La Voix Métropolitaine (Sorel)
Le Nouveau Courrier Riviera
  (Sorel)
Avenir de L'Est (Montréal-Est)

Le Progrès (Valleyfield)
Le Saint-Lawrence Sun
  (Beauharnois)
La Voix des Mille-Îles
  (Sainte-Thérèse)
L'Écho du Nord (Saint-Jérôme)
L'Argenteuil (Lachute)
Le Dynamique de la Mauricie
  (Saint-Tite)
Beauce Nouvelle
  (Saint-Georges de Beauce)
Le Progrès-Chronique (Magog)
L'Écho du Saint-Maurice
  (Shawinigan)
Le Lac Saint-Jean (Alma)
L'Essor (Saint-Jean)
Le Citoyen (Asbestos)

In Favour

Le Bien Public (Trois-Rivières)
La Parole (Drummondville)[a]

L'Écho d'Abitibi Ouest
  (La Sarre)[a]

Undecided or Unclear

La Voix de Lévis et Lotbinière
  (Saint-Agapit)
L'Écho de Louiseville
  (Louiseville)
Le Réveil de Jonquière
  (Jonquière)
L'Éclaireur-Progrès
  (Saint-Georges de Beauce)

Le Richelieu (Saint-Jean)
Métro-Sun (Longueil)
La Voix Populaire
  (Hebdo-Montréal)
Progrès-Dimanche (Chicoutimi)
L'Avenir (Sept-Îles)
La Voix Gaspésienne (Matane)

(a) Were in favor in their October 29 editorials. However, their attitudes changed to "mildly against" in the following editorials.

economic progress in Québec."[15] The CMA spoke of "the adverse economic consequences which could result to the province and its citizens if anything resembling obligatory provisions were introduced in an attempt to legislate French as the sole language of usage in the Québec business and industrial community."[16] It also emphasized that head offices could leave if they were not given "the option to work in whatever languages are essential to its corporate needs:" "A province can ill afford to lose head offices. Unfortunately, if there is a serious deterioration in the business climate in which they are located, . . . that particular part of the corporate enterprise is most easily able to seek a new home."[17] Lever Brothers' brief stressed that by discouraging the use of English, Québec would risk provoking a fall in the standard of living and also a profound social malaise.[18] Noranda Mines insisted that bilingualism at all levels of business was impossible and that the state of uncertainty in Québec society had created an unhealthy economic climate in the province: "We are looking for a climate of social and economic stability, in the long run, and we have faith that the governmental authorities will restore and maintain such a climate."[19] Finally, Dominion Glass warned that it would move its head office out of Québec if the government established a policy of unilingualism."[20]

During the five-year period when the Gendron Commission was preparing its report, two other events of significance to the language issued occurred: Bourassa's attempts to have French accepted as the language of work by the Ste. Thérèse plant of General Motors and the publication of the Pantus Report.

During the 1970 election campaign, Opposition Leader Bourassa had put considerable stress on making French the language of work in Québec. Once elected, he seemed intent on realizing his election promise. In fact, during the first few months of his mandate, Bourassa was quite active in attempting to promote French as the language of work. Six weeks after his election, he met with 50 senior business leaders in Montréal and impressed upon them the necessity to act as quickly as possible on the language situation.[21] It was in this context that Bourassa intervened personally during the strike at General Motors at the end of 1970 in order to support the demands of the union for more French in the plant. Bourassa promised the government would intervene if the company did not accede to the legitimate demands of the workers. To quote the *Montreal Star:* "Premier Bourassa went out of his way to suggest that GM was the kind of test case from which his government would not remain aloof."[22]

Bourassa's private meetings with GM executives met with no success, however. After securing a few financial concessions, the unions called off the strike without having obtained satisfaction on the language question.[23] Bourassa did not intervene. He explained, a year later, that "GM représente quatre fois le budget du Québec, c'est David et Goliath."[24]

Bourassa's "activism" on the language issue, including his intervention in the GM strike, angered the business community. Barely a few weeks after the GM episode, G.A. Hart criticized Bourassa for being too aggressive on the language question and warned that the

French language, more than bombs, was frightening investors away from Québec.[25] In a later speech, he stated:

> Québec needs capital, it needs a constant flow of techniques and competent workers; and if it is true that money has no mother tongue, it is nonetheless certain that the uncertainties of the language situation weigh heavily on the decisions concerning capital flows.[26]

About the same time, the *Financial Post* published a story stating that companies were prepared to leave Québec if the language pressure was maintained:

> In the face of growing pressure [concerning the use of French] business hasn't forgotten that there are other alternatives besides resisting or acquiescing . . . Indeed, some companies in Montréal may be getting to a point where they feel it might be more responsible, and more considerate of Quebecers, to pack up and leave than it would be to stay.[27]

The impatience of the business community in regard to the uncertainties of the language situation, and, more specifically, the fear that the Québec government was about to legislate the increased use of French in the work place were quite evident in the Fantus Report. Indeed, the Report argued that language was "one of the major areas of discontent"[28] within the business community and "one of the most serious obstacles to the industrial expansion in Québec."[29] According to Fantus:

> Clearly there is a widespread fear that the Québec government may be planning to mandate the exclusive use of French as the language of business . . . There is no doubt that the imposition of stringent French language requirements would severely inhibit the ability of Québec to attract new industry either from the United States or the other provinces of Canada. It is also probable that many existing firms would choose to limit their expansion in Québec or even discontinue their operations in the province.[30]

The Report concluded: "Anxiety over the language issue could only be dispelled by a clear definition of provincial government policy in this area."[31]

The attitudes manifested by the companies surveyed in the Fantus Report were quite similar to those expressed during the Gendron Commission hearings. There was evidence, however, in the Fantus study that American companies were considerably less flustered by the language issue than Ontario or Québec businesses. For example, one American respondent said he believed that the business climate was quite sound in Québec and that he did "not believe that Quebecers' struggles to maintain their culture against the forces of the rest of North America, regardless of the outcome, will affect business investment or traditional business methods."[32] An American company, manufacturing precision equipment, stated that language was no serious problem, since the company operated in France and all over the world.[33]

Local and Ontario respondents, on the other hand, were sharply critical of language uncertainties.[34] Many companies claimed that they would not move into Québec or expand their operations if the language problem was not solved satisfactorily. A pharmaceutical company, for example, stated: "The decision to expand in Québec is, to a large extent, predicated on the attitude the Provincial Government takes towards the language problem.''[35] An electrical products company claimed the language problem would "discourage English-speaking people from investing in the province."[36] Finally, a consumer goods firm declared bluntly: "Tell the government not to get stupid on the language question . . . If handled wrong, companies or divisions will be forced to move. This is perhaps the most important cloud hanging over business in Québec."[37]

Meanwhile, the Gendron Commission was continuing the preparation of its report. My interviews confirmed that senior Québec businessmen benefitted from preferential treatment and privileged access at every stage of the drafting of the Gendron Report. First, Aimé Gagné, director of public relations at Aluminum Company of Canada, was selected as one of the five members of the commission. According to an executive of Aluminum Company, Gagné was considered the "representative from industry" within the commission, and "we made things easy for him by supplying him with extra staff in order to allow him to spend most of his time on the Gendron Report."[38] What is more important, however, is that Gagné was given the responsibility of writing the part of the Report concerning the language of work.

The interviews revealed that secret meetings between Gendron commissioners, especially Gagné, and small groups of senior businessmen were held throughout the preparation of the Report. According to a senior executive, "We met Gagné before the final draft [was made public]. We encouraged him in some areas and discouraged him in others. We worked directly with the commissioners."[39] The Conseil du Patronat and the Québec Chambre de Commerce also claimed that many private consultations took place involving government, senior businessmen, and the Gendron commissioners. The meetings usually involved only small groups of businessmen because "large meetings become public too easily."[40]

The Gendron recommendations were published in February 1973. They included mainly suggestions of a technical nature as to how to encourage immigrants to attend French schools and how to encourage business to use more French in the plants and head offices.[41] Not surprisingly, the business community expressed considerable satisfaction with the report.[42] The Conseil du Patronat told the *Montreal Star:* "It is easy to see that a large number of the conclusions and recommendations in the report are along the same lines of thought as our policies."[43] The CMA was also satisfied: "The commissioners found our recommendations worthwhile — they included in the report the same safeguards which we suggested. The positions of the commission and ours are in almost complete agreement."[44] Although the degree of satisfaction varied somewhat, all the businessmen interviewed expressed agreement with the main conclusions of the Gendron Commission. In fact, business and the English press took the recommendations so lightly — because by and large they felt the status quo was being maintained — that Gendron angrily criticized them for not taking the Report seriously.[45] Perrault went out of his way to insist that, contrary to media and public opinion, the Report went beyond the status quo. "The Gendron Report," he said, "implies changes, some of which are

122

profound, that are not simply the continuation of the present state of affairs."[46]

In contrast to the reaction of business, unions and nationalist groups sharply opposed the Gendron recommendations. For example, Fernand Daoust, secretary-general of the QFL and spokesman for the Mouvement pour un Québec Français,[47] criticized the Report for leaving the language of work problem almost entirely up to the goodwill of the private sector and accused the commission of acting as an extension of a government which was crawling in front of private enterprise.

In early April 1973, the members of the General Council of Industry asked Bourassa and several of his ministers to meet privately with them to discuss the Gendron Report and the legislative intentions of the government on the language question. Five of the businessmen interviewed were present at this meeting. According to them, Bourassa was questioned at length on specific points of the Gendron Report as well as on a draft of forthcoming legislation in the area of language. The chairman of the board of a trust company said: "Bourassa asked us to tell him what was workable in the legislation."[49] The businessmen left the meeting satisfied with the government's intentions.

The preferential treatment accorded to businessmen with regard to language policy also stemmed from the fact that many of them, including executives of the Royal Bank, Bank of Montreal, Royal Trust, Conseil du Patronat, and the CMA, were able to analyse and comment upon various drafts of the legislation. An executive of the Conseil du Patronat, for example, said that he was in possession of the next to last draft of the language of work section of the legislation.[50] When one considers that the Québec government made public its legislative intentions in May 1974 with the introduction of Bill 22, it is quite interesting that, more than a year earlier, senior Québec businessmen were already able to study and influence the content of the legislation.

The businessmen who had seen the legislation expressed considerable satisfaction. Even though businessmen were told by government to keep details of the forthcoming legislation secret,[51] the interviews revealed some of the main elements of the bill: no coercion on language of work, except for things like labelling; some measures to encourage companies financially and technically to use more French; and a statement of principle concerning French as the "official language in Québec."[52]

Most businessmen, of course, would have preferred the status quo and the complete *laisser faire* attitude which had prevailed until then. Some were annoyed by measures in the bill; overall, however, senior businessmen were in agreement with the legislation. According to one senior executive, "Bourassa told us we had to accept some legislation because of the need for him to be re-elected. We agreed to go along with a few crazy things [in the legislation] in order to achieve the larger result."[53] Similarly, a senior executive of the Royal Bank said: "The government had to legislate because of the 'political aspect.' At the GCI meeting, we told the government that we would not mind some legislation, as long as it concerns things that are already being done anyway."[54]

In the year between the publication of the Gendron Report and the introduction of Bill 22, business continued its pressure on government. A letter from J. Claude Hébert,[55] president of Warnock-Hersey International, to Bourassa warned that if the government used coercion to increase the use of French, many head offices, senior managers, and investors would leave Québec:

> The more Québec makes life difficult for big companies, the greater will be the risk to see it regressing compared to the rest of North America. This is a crucial argument for us, and it explains why all the measures taken by government should call upon persuasion rather than the law and should as much as possible avoid changing the present state of affairs.[56]

During the electoral campaign of October 1973, the government was discreet about its language plans. Bourassa, however, made "cultural sovereignty" one of the main themes of his campaign and vowed to act upon the language of work. In May 1974, Bill 22 was introduced. As regards the language of education, Bill 22's main provision was that any child who wanted to go to French or English schools must first pass a proficiency test indicating that he had a sufficient knowledge of the language. The immigrants who knew neither language would automatically be sent to French schools. As regards the language of business, chapter 4 of the bill specified that trade-names, most contracts, placards, and labels, among other things, should be in French at least. The legislation also contained some measures to help companies use more French if they so desired. Finally, chapter 3, dealing with the language of work, provided for the compulsory use of French in labour negotiations and grievances, collective agreements, and internal company notices and rules.

Bill 22 was passed on July 31, 1974, after several months of bitter controversy. Of the 74 groups which submitted briefs to the committee of the National Assembly, business was the only group to have indicated some support for the legislation.[57] Although for different reasons, all other groups, English and French, opposed the legislation. While some French groups argued for unilingualism, most of them argued in favour of the integration of the children of new immigrants into the French school system and in favour of more stringent regulations regarding the use of French as a language of work. The French groups which opposed the legislation included all the labour unions, the Montréal Catholic School Commission, several professional corporations (doctors, psychiatrists, school principals, university professors, engineers, and journalists), the Ligue des Droits de l'Homme, and the St. Jean Baptiste societies. Ryan, for one, claimed that, as regards the language of education, Bill 22 was simply a new edition of Bill 63.[58] Quoting studies to the effect that some 90% of immigrant children chose English rather than French schools, Ryan recommended that French be the language of education for all, except resident Anglophones who had acquired rights concerning English education.[59] English groups, particularly educational institutions such as the Protestant School Board of Greater Montréal, on the other hand, were critical of the bill because they said it interfered with the principle of freedom of parental choice of the language of education.

Business was also favourable to the specific regulations which guided the application of Bill 22. In August 1975, for example, the Government of Québec introduced the regulations on labelling and other guidelines. According to Lysiane Gagnon of *La Presse,* business leaders, including the Board of Trade, the Canadian Manufacturers' Association, and the Québec Chamber of Commerce, reacted serenely to the guidelines and considered that they did little more than consecrate what most companies were already doing.[60] This was confirmed in a meeting of 150 businessmen organized by the Business Linguistic Centre the following month.[61] On the education side, studies published in early 1976 indicated that Bill 22 had had little impact on the assimilation pattern of immigrants and had perhaps contributed to exacerbating tensions between the French and immigrant communities.

In October 1973, I published some of the research included in this chapter in Montréal area newspapers. Claude Ryan of *Le Devoir* reacted sharply in an editorial published on October 19. He argued that I had largely exaggerated the degree of business influence and that I had naively taken the "boasts" of businessmen at face value. In July 1974, Ryan came back to the issue. He published a private letter which Arnold Hart, the president of the Bank of Montreal, had sent to Premier Bourassa during the Bill 22 debates. Ryan indicated that many of the criticisms and suggestions made by Hart had not been taken into consideration by the legislators and that, therefore, the whole thesis of business influence in Québec politics was false.[62]

Ryan's argument is obviously ludicrous. I have never claimed that the government responded favourably and completely to every request, suggestion, or proposal made by individual business leaders. There are a sufficient number of shades of opinion and even contradictions among businessmen to make that impossible. My argument is that business, more than any other group, has managed to obtain a substantial degree of satisfaction in its dealings with the Québec government. On the language issue, business succeeded in its primary objective of avoiding any coercion with regards to increasing the use of French in plants and head offices. The evidence also suggests that the language legislation was almost entirely the product of a business-government dialogue, and that business received preferential treatment with regard to information and with regard to access to crucial decision-making centres.

The Education Issue:
School Reorganization in Montréal

The reform of the educational system was one of the main preoccupations of successive Québec governments in the nineteen sixties.
In the early sixties, business was by and large absent from the major
debates on the issue. The main cleavage was religious, as in the case
of Bill 60, for example,[61] and the main objective was to adapt the
French educational system to an advanced industrial society.

In the mid-sixties, however, business decided to get involved in
the controversy surrounding school reorganization in Montréal. It is
very doubtful whether this issue actually constituted a threat to business
in Québec, but several managers, particularly English Canadians
involved in business associations, felt strongly enough about the issue
to launch a pressure campaign to obtain the kind of legislation they
wanted.[65] The scale of this compaign, however, was not comparable
to the efforts put into the language arena or into the opposition to
separatism. Also, the highly technical nature of the legislation and the
complexity of the issues involved discouraged the kind of "politicization" and mass involvement which surrounded the language issue.
Finally, in the case of school reorganization, it was particularly difficult to distinguish between the intents of the English-speaking community as a whole and business. Business, in many ways, acted as the
vanguard or spearhead of the English-speaking community in Montréal.

The school reorganization debate began in 1966 with the publication of the fourth volume of the Parent Report on education. The commissioners noted substantial inequalities in the school services offered
by the 40 or so independent school commissions operating in Montréal.
By and large, rich socio-ecnomic areas were able to provide a much
better educational product than the poor ones — thus helping to perpet-
uate the "class structure" in Montréal. To remedy this situation, the
Parent Report suggested that the number of regional school commissions be reduced to seven and that these school commissions be "unified", that is, not divided as previously on the basis of religion or
language. It also recommended that an island council be set up to
coordinate the activities of the commissions. The island council would
be crucial in that it would have the responsibility to collect and redistribute all school taxes, as well as to pool all resources and equipment.
The Parent commissioners thought this would contribute to the elimination of regional disparities in school services.

Given that, in Montréal, socio-economic cleavages (rich/poor)
largely corresponded to ethnic cleavages (English/French), it was the
English-speaking community that potentially had the most to lose from
an equalization of school services. Spearheaded by its educational and
business elites, the English-speaking groups began their campaign
against school reorganization immediately after the publication of the
Parent Report. Although many of their arguments were couched in

terms of cultural survival, that is, autonomy of their school system, the main objectives of the English-speaking groups were three-fold: delaying the legislation as long as possible, given that the status quo was the most desirable alternative; the weakening of the island council, including the control over immovables at the local school board level; and linguistic rather than unified school boards. The strategy was thus to delay legislation as long as possible and, failing that, to amend the school reorganization bill according to their interests.

The English-speaking groups were successful in delaying the legislation. A definitive school structure for Montréal was not expected before the end of 1976. Here is the sequence of events which followed the publication of the Parent Report in 1966.

In 1968, the Union Nationale set up another commission to look into school reorganization once again. The Pagé Report recommended linguistic school boards. The government ignored the Report and, in 1969, introduced Bill 62, which was largely based on the recommendations of the Parent Report, that is, it favoured unified boards and a strong island council. With the exception of the Association des Parents Catholiques du Québec, which expressed a preference for maintaining "denominational" boards, all French or predominantly French groups supported the bill.[66] These included the Superior Council of Education, The Montréal Catholic School Commission (MCSC), the largest school board in the province, most major French newspapers, the Alliance des Professeurs, and labour unions.

Bill 62 also received some support in the English-speaking community, particularly among English Roman Catholics. Noel Herron, assistant regional director of the MCSC, English sector, stated that he was favourable to a unified system and a strong island council.[67] Earlier, MCSC executives John T. McIlhone and Kevin Quinn signed a minority report appended to the Pagé Report supporting the same objectives. Finally, Bill 62 was received sympathetically by the *Montreal Star*. After indicating that it felt that the existence of separate school systems helped foster inequalities, the *Star* expressed approval for the main objective of the bill: "The government's foremost objective in any new education legislation should be the removal of existing inequalities in facilities, taxation, and suffrage."[68]

The opposition to the legislation came mainly from Protestant English educational groups, the Protestant School Board of Greater Montréal, for example, and business groups, especially the Montreal Board of Trade.[69] These groups led an active campaign in the English-speaking community to stir up public opinion and also presented briefs to the committee of the National Assembly studying Bill 62. Both the PSBGM and the Board of Trade argued in favour of linguistic boards and a weaker school council. They also claimed that investment would leave the province if the legislation was approved. The PSBGM brief stated: "The passage of Bill 62 could be followed by a serious exodus of funds from the province . . ."[70] The Board of Trade brief was in the same vein:

To create a totally unified education system, at this time, would have a substantial retardant effect on the economic growth of Montréal and the province of

Québec . . . The educational structure which Bill 62, in its present format, proposes will not serve the economic needs of the business community.[71]

While it is unquestionable that most English-speaking groups remained opposed to the bill, the government could have relied on the support which it had in the French community and among the English Catholics to pass the legislation. Instead, the UN government decided to withdraw the legislation. Shortly thereafter it called an election.

The Liberals, who won the election in April 1970, had promised during the campaign to re-introduce the school reorganization legislation shortly after their election. It was not until July 1971, however, that Guy St. Pierre, then minister of education, introduced a new piece of legislation. Bill 28 represented substantial concessions to English business and education groups. Although maintaining unified school boards, the legislation weakened the island council, thereby jeopardizing the egalitarian aspects of the bill. Specifically, in accordance with the recommendation of the Board of Trade and contrary to the Parent Report and Bill 62, it transferred the property and administration of buildings and equipment to local school boards. This not only weakened the ability of the school council to ensure a rational and efficient use of school resources, but it also made it more difficult for the council to play an effective role in democratizing their use.[72] The school boards in the weaker socio-economic areas would, in effect, have as a starting point the same inferior buildings, equipment, and facilities they had previously.

It is not surprising that, in a letter to St. Pierre dated October 6, 1971, the Board of Trade expressed considerable satisfaction with Bill 28: "This Board commends those who drafted the legislation for the obvious efforts which have been made to incorporate into the bill certain of the suggestions advanced by many segments of the community in respect to the preceding draft legislation — Bill 62." [73] The Board, however, asked that the bill be further retarded to allow a study of its constitutionality. The PSBGM maintained its pressure for linguistic boards. Thus, although Bill 28 achieved the primary objectives of English educational and business groups, they decided to press for even more favourable legislation. On the French side, there was general opposition to the weakening of the island council, although the complexity of the issue discouraged militant opposition.

In December 1971, Bill 28 was withdrawn by the Québec government. The Liberals claimed that Parti Québécois opposition[74] had forced them to let the legislation die on the order paper. This is unlikely, given that the government had succeeded in passing many controversial bills despite heavy opposition, for example, the legislation dealing with the James Bay Corporation and, of course, Bill 22. A much more likely hypothesis would be that the bill was retarded because of the continuing pressures of English educational and business groups. According to the *Montreal Star,* it was "adverse feeling among some sections of the English community [that] obliged the government to postpone the presentation of the bill." [75] Lysiane Gagnon of *La Presse* was more specific:

> According to trustworthy sources, there are currently in the halls of government some strong pressures to amend this legislation again, even though it is already

drafted and even though it has already been submitted to the cabinet... These pressures, which come from the financial circles and from the upper levels of the English educational hierarchy, also originate from many cabinet ministers who represent constituencies in the west end of Montréal. The latter have apparently succeeded, in the cabinet, to further delay the presentation of the bill . . .[76]

The Bill 28 episode brought to light, as in the case of language, the privileged position of business and educational groups vis-à-vis the Québec government.[77] On April 14, 1971, K. D. Sheldrick, vice-president of Bailey Meter and president of the Lachine Protestant School Board, claimed that he had been given a copy of Bill 28, courtesy of St. Pierre. He added that the legislation was to be discussed at a secret meeting the following week with St. Pierre and education department officials. The legislation was made public some three months later, and the heads of the MCSC were not informed of its contents until that date.[78]

Finally, on December 18, 1972, a new piece of legislation on school reorganization was adopted by the National Assembly. Bill 71 provided for the regrouping of Montréal's 33 school boards into eight denominational boards — six Catholic and two Protestant. According to the bill, these structures were supposed to be temporary, and the school council was given the responsibility to submit a definite plan for school reorganization in Montréal to the department of education before December 31, 1975. The school council remained an essentially weak body as in the case of Bill 28. The property and administration of buildings and equipment remained vested with the local boards. What is more, the legislation made the school council a creation of the local boards. Indeed, of the 17-member council, 14 were to be chosen by the boards and three by the government. Rather than having the autonomy and power to deal with overall problems, such as the reduction of school inequalities in Montréal, the council seemed destined to be little more than the sum of the particular and specific interests of the local boards.[79]

Bill 71 provided no clear guidelines for the school council concerning regional disparities and the redistribution of wealth among the boards. In fact, the degree of egalitarianism in the school system would depend entirely on the goodwill of the council commissioners. Thus, according to Jules Leblanc of *La Presse:* "Les mesures spéciales pour assurer le rattrapage des zones défavorisées en matière d'enseignement ne seront possibles que si le conseil scolaire de l'île de Montréal adopte des règlements et des politiques efficaces en ce sens . . ."[80]

An added hurdle was that the weak socio-economic areas were under-represented in the school council; thus the MCSC which accounted for most of the poorer zones in Montréal had only a representation of 35% on the school council even though it was responsible for 56% of the population. The decisions concerning measures to eliminate school inequalities were then likely to be taken by a majority of "rich" school boards. The question became:

> To what extent will the latter [the rich] agree to slow down the progress of their schools to allow the disadvantaged areas to catch up . . .? To what extent will they accept to impose on themselves additional taxes in order to help those who are in need?[81]

Not surprisingly, the Protestant educational groups and business were the only ones to support the legislation. A PSBGM spokesman was quoted as saying: "We believe that this bill largely takes into account the demands of the Anglo-Protestant community."[82] Bill 71 was also approved by the Montréal and Québec chambers of commerce,[83] and by the Montreal Board of Trade. As for the business respondents to the questionnaire, 54.7% said they agreed with the bill. This is a lower degree of approval than for the other governmental measures that businessmen were asked to evaluate.[84] It could be noted also that 25.9% of the respondents did not answer the question or were not well enough informed on the legislation. This would seem to suggest that some senior level businessmen did not feel much concern towards the school reorganization issue.

All French groups, other than business, as well as the English Catholic groups, opposed the legislation. The latter groups were particularly vocal in their opposition; they wanted the same rights as the English Protestants, that is, their own school boards. However, even though the English Catholics (who include many immigrants) in the MCSC were more numerous than the English Protestants in the PSBGM, the government refused, in part, perhaps, because English Catholics were marginal in terms of economic power compared with the English Protestants.

On the French side, the unions and MCSC, among others, argued that Bill 71 would not be able to deal with the socio-economic disparities in the Montréal school system. They also claimed that religious boards, like linguistic boards, would lead to an inefficient use of school resources and would make it that much more difficult to deal with the problem of regional inequalities in school services.[85]

Even though the issue of school reorganization was probably not considered vital by the business community, and probably involved the middle levels of business more than it did the senior executives, it is nonetheless safe to conclude that business groups played an important supporting role in the successful pressure on the Québec government. The weakening of the school council and the creation of religious boards — which, from an English Protestant's point of view have the same effect as linguistic boards — were obtained against substantial opposition from most of the French community and the English Catholics.

The Issue of Separatism

In the sixties and early seventies, business was particularly active in its attempts to prevent the province of Québec from separating from the rest of Canada. As noted, 99.3% of the businessmen in the questionnaire declared themselves opposed to separatism. Even the French-Canadian managers who manifested some nationalist tendencies on the other issues, for example, language, were unanimously against separatism. Thus, it would seem that senior French-Canadian executives did not consider that separatism could be an opportunity for them to replace senior English-Canadian managers at the helms of Québec firms. Nonetheless, as will be seen, English-Canadian managers from Québec and Ontario were the most ardent opponents of Québec separatism.[86]

By contrast, there was some evidence that U.S. and other foreign investors or owners of Québec industry were much less concerned and felt much less threatened by the issue of separatism. An analysis by Laurier Cloutier in *La Presse*[87] revealed that in 1972 Toronto financial institutions sold only 2% of Québec bonds, amounting to some $10 million. On the other hand, $275 million worth of Québec bonds were sold on the New York market and $55 million on the European market. Cloutier reported that Toronto financial circles cited separatism and political strikes as the main causes for the lack of confidence of the Toronto market. New York investors, by contrast, according to the *La Presse* reporter, did not feel threatened by separatism and other political issues.[88] The Japanese investors seemed to agree. Claude Beauchamp, in his analysis of a transaction in which Québec obtained an important loan on Japanese financial markets, claimed: "The problem of Québec independence only raised minor questions... questions that did not shake the confidence of Japanese investors in the future of Québec:"

> "The political situation does not worry Japanese investors and the possibility of Québec separatism does not particularly bother them. Tokyo financial circles do not think Québec will go so far as to separate from the rest of Canada but, in the hypothesis that this were to occur, they do not foresee any "dangerous consequences' for themselves."[89]

In 1969, Yves Bernier of *Le Soleil* conducted a series of interviews with Bay Street and Wall Street financiers, particularly those who already had heavy investments in Québec. His conclusion was that U.S. financiers were not preoccupied by Québec political problems and invested their funds only according to economic criteria.[90] Bernier also quoted executives from Morgan Guaranty Trust and New York Life as saying that, whether or not Québec separated, its market would always be there, it would still need to borrow money, and "we will always be interested in a good deal."[91] Similarly, David Rockefeller, president of the Chase Manhattan Bank, stated: "Investors do not distinguish between Québec and Canada and are much more preoccupied by the proposals of the [federal] white paper on taxation, such as the capital gains tax, than with separatism."[92] He also said he did not think it was the business of foreign investors to dictate what kind of government Québec should have. Finally, James Roosevelt, president of Investors Overseas Services, one of the biggest international investment funds, was quoted as saying that American investments and those of his company would continue in an independent Québec.[93]

Even though foreign investors did not feel threatened by separatism, it remained unquestionable that an overwhelming majority of local French and English senior executives were opposed to Québec separatism. This opposition manifested itself throughout the nineteen sixties but became more intense in the later part of the decade. With the creation of the Parti Québécois in 1968, business began to feel that separation was a definite possibility.

Indeed, after René Lévesque announced his separatist option in September 1967, a major anti-separatist offensive by business began.

It will be remembered that, at that time, Johnson was himself manifesting some aggressive nationalism with his slogan "equality or independence" and with his demands on the federal government for largely increased taxation rights for Québec. In October 1967 while Johnson was in Hawaii, there began what can be considered a concerted effort by business to discredit separatism and to discourage the Union Nationale's militant nationalism.[94] A front page article in the *Globe and Mail*[95] on October 6 signalled the beginning of what Brunelle and Papineau called "a campaign of economic terrorism." The Toronto daily claimed that capital and companies were leaving Québec and that some firms were not expanding there because of the fear of separatism. It mentioned the case of Investor's Syndicate, a Winnipeg-based mutual fund, which had just sold 200,000 shares of Banque Canadienne Nationale,[96] the transfer of 300 Bell Telephone employees from Montréal to Ottawa, the decisions by the Québec-based companies Dominion Textiles and Crane Canada to expand in Ontario rather than Québec, and the difficulties of attracting financing for the Churchill Falls hydro-electric development. As regards the Churchill Falls financial problems, Kierans, then president of the Québec Liberal Federation, argued: "The company was having difficulty in getting financing because investors know a separate Québec would need less power than a province that was part of a Canadian confederation."[97] The *Globe and Mail* article also quoted several senior business executives from Montréal. Charles Neapole, president of the Montreal Stock Exchange, was reported to have said: "There is no doubt that the threat of a separate Québec has had a very noticeable impact in alarming investors."[98] Similarly, Jean Ostiguy, Montréal investment dealer, said: "I certainly believe that capital is being scared away from Québec by separatism. To restore confidence, French and English Canadians must finally arrive at a formula for working together."[99]

The next day, it was the turn of the *Financial Post* and the *Montreal Star*. R. G. Gibbens, financial editor of the *Star,* put it this way:

> Québec as a market has a big potential growth between now and 1975 — even faster growth than in Ontario because of basic population trends. But with a noisy constitutional debate superimposed above general Canadian economic worries, the immediate problem is whether Québec can exploit its potential, attract enough investment and prosper at least at the rate of Ontario and the west.[100]

Amy Booth of the *Financial Post* reported that although Québec stocks "haven't fallen to bargain basement level," many of them were losing ground in a week when "leading Québec politicians heated up the separatism debate."[101]

On October 14, Laurent Lauzier of *La Presse* said that, even though the exodus of capital from Québec was not tragic for the time being, this movement could become critical if the present political uncertainty continued to sap the confidence in Québec's economic and political stability.[102] He also claimed to have been told by senior business executives that if the exodus of capital increased, it would become extremely difficult to sell the bonds of the province at reasonable interest rates.[103] According to Parizeau, the rumours of the exodus of capital did in fact cause Québec bonds to slip, and the gap between Ontario and Québec interest rates widened considerably.[104]

Parizeau further maintained that during the "crisis," the department of finance had been "bombarded" with alarmist telephone calls by many senior financial executives, in particular from the Bank of Montreal, Royal Trust, and the Royal Bank.[105] He also claimed that two senior French-Canadian executives went to see Johnson in Hawaii to impress upon him the need to act rapidly.

On October 31, 1967, Johnson named Marcel Faribault, president of the Trust Général du Canada, to the post of economic and constitutional adviser and Jean-Guy Cardinal, also of the Trust General, to the Québec cabinet. He also announced the eventual creation of the General Council of Industry: "In the near future we will need a task force to coordinate all economic activities."[106]

The next day, Neapole, who only five days earlier told the English CBC that capital was leaving the province,[107] expressed satisfaction with the nomination of Faribault and stated that the exodus of capital had reached its peak and had been falling off in the last couple of days. [108] The Québec government was also successful in floating a $50 million bond issue at a reasonable interest rate.[109]

Ryan expressed scepticism towards the climate of panic created by the financial circles:

> Yesterday's events [i.e., the bond sale and the nomination of Faribault] makes us wonder about some of the elements of the climate of panic which seems to have propagated itself recently in financial circles . . . It seems, according to many observers, that this crisis has been exaggerated at will by many individuals more starved for profits than concerned for public welfare.[110]

The conclusion that the crisis had in many ways been provoked and exaggerated artificially for political purposes was strengthened in a speech delivered to the Montréal Chambre de Commerce by Otto Thür, former chairman of the department of economics at the Université de Montréal. Thür claimed that investments in Québec had been dropping at least since the beginning of 1967 and rejected the cause-effect relationship which some people had been trying to establish between "political turbulence" and the fall in investments in Québec.[111]

Writing in 1971, former Union nationale MNA Jérôme Proulx confirmed that Johnson had been subjected to heavy pressure from business and that the Faribault nomination was intended to reassure financial circles of the pro-business and pro-federalist orientation of the government:

> While in Hawaii, Mr. Johnson was being submitted to stiff pressures from the financial circles. He had his back against the wall. He had to borrow and the recent events [i.e., manifestations of nationalism] must have indisposed many . . . And it is without a doubt as a result of these kinds of pressures and of the multiple attacks concerning the exodus of capital, that Mr. Johnson invited into his cabinet Faribault and Cardinal, both businessmen occupying prestigious jobs. With a federalist reputation, Mr. Faribault would know how to restore the image of the party which had a too nationalist flavor for our natural enemies. The objective of his nomination was to reassure the top officials of the financial circles.[112]

The attempt by business to discredit Johnson's ultra-nationalism and the separatist proposals of the Parti Québécois continued uninterrupted until the 1970 election. The leaders of the opposition Liberal Party jumped on the business bandwagon, so to speak, and with increasing frequency predicted that Québec was losing investments because of the UN's ambiguous constitutional stands and would lose even more if Québec were to separate. Thus, to quote opposition leader Jean Lesage: "Let us not kid ourselves, the word independence in itself is enough to frighten capital from Québec. And I hold the present government responsible for the investors' fears, because of its ambiguous and ambivalent constitutional policies."[113]

William Tetley, Liberal MNA for Notre Dame de Grâce, similarly blamed nationalism and separatism for the economic difficulties of the province. Specifically, he argued that the French tire company Michelin had not settled in Québec because of the political uncertainties. He also said that Ford and Chrysler would not invest in Québec as long as the political situation remained unstable:

> In other words, bombs, our ultra-nationalism in Québec during these last years, the 'separatist' tendencies of the government, and the fact of presenting itself as an independent state during international educational conferences have led investors, even the French ones, to lose confidence in the province.[114]

As in the case of language, the threat of head offices leaving Québec was used. Tetley, in the article noted above, mentioned having helped three companies in 1969 move their head offices out of Québec in his capacity as a lawyer.[115] William Hall, former president of Domtar, argued in a lengthy article in *Le Devoir* that at least 500,000 people in Montréal owed their living to the presence of head offices. He warned that, even within the federal framework, Québec could not go beyond certain limits in the direction towards special status or French unilingualism without jeopardizing the jobs provided by the Montréal-based head offices of Canadian companies.[116]

Several business association studies were also published during that period. They defined the economic advantages of federalism and predicted that separatism or independence would lead to economic stagnation. Thus, the Québec Chambre de Commerce published a study entitled *Québec: le coût de l'indépendance:*

> Sovereignty-association and independence are abstract ideals in an economic sense and their objectives cannot withstand serious analysis. These two options would drag Québec society into stagnation and regression for many years to come, if not many generations.[117]

Although until 1970 senior business executives had always been closer to the Liberal Party than to the Union Nationale, they had made a point of contributing generously to both parties. In the 1970 election, however, the UN, because of its intransigent nationalism,[118] lost the confidence and thus the financial support of the business community. [119] From then on, business gave its support almost exclusively to the Liberal Party. The questionnaire revealed that 87.2% of the business respondents felt that the Liberals were "the provincial party most favourable to business." The UN and the Créditistes followed far behind with 6.7% and 6.0% respectively. The Parti Québécois received no support. This contrasts sharply with 23.9% and 30.1% levels of popular support for the PQ in the 1970 and 1973 elections respectively.

Business activities during the 1970 electoral campaign could be classified in two distinct phases. At first, there was an attempt to discredit the incumbent government, the Union Nationale. Then, when the polls made it obvious that the Parti Québécois was rising rapidly, business concentrated its attacks on the separatist party.

In early April 1970, Lafferty, Harwood and Company, Montréal stockbrokers, sent a confidential letter to their customers accusing the UN of having "statist" projects, that is, socialist tendencies, and suggesting that stocks and funds should be moved out of the province at least until the April 29 election. The letter was published in *La Presse* on April 4. Mario Beaulieu, minister of finance, reacted angrily to the letter and said that an inquiry would be held by the department of financial institutions. Two days later, Armand Maltais, another UN minister, while criticizing Lafferty for electionneering and partisanship, was prompt to reaffirm the government's faith in private enterprise:

> The minister, in his speech, made himself the ardent defender of private enterprise. He underlined the firm intention of his government not only to remain the faithful partner of private enterprise, but also its vigilant guardian and its most effective servant.[120]

On April 11, another "confidential" letter from Lafferty, Harwood and Company to its customers was published in the press. It predicted, among other things, that the province's credit rating would be seriously weakened on the international markets and the perspectives of the French-Canadian banks would be threatened if political parties tending towards separatism gained an influential position within the National Assembly. A few days earlier, Bourassa predicted that Bombardier would have to close down if the PQ took power because of the possible demise of the Canada-U.S. agreement on the exportation of ski-doos.[121]

By far the best-known episode of the 1970 electoral campaign was the Brink's-Royal Trust affair. On the morning of April 26, nine Brinks' trucks were parked in front of the Royal Trust offices on Dorchester Boulevard in Montréal. Royal Trust employees were carrying metal boxes later reported to contain stocks to be shipped to Toronto. Edward Church, a photographer for the *Gazette,* was on the spot, his newspaper having been warned the night before by an anonymous telephone call that securities would be shipped out of the province.[122] The next day, front page newspaper stories gave the event substantial coverage.[123]

Business also got involved more directly in the election campaign through the "Canada Committee." The committee was made up of some 100 prominent Canadian businessmen from all major cities. One of the committee's main objectives was to "support the federal system of government as the only means of assuring the country's future and the preservation of racial and cultural diversity."[124] In practice, however, since its formation in 1964, "The Canada Committee centered its efforts in Montréal, Trois-Rivières and Québec City in an effort to counteract the strong separatist element in those areas." The evidence also indicated that, although the committee pretended to operate throughout Canada, its focus was clearly on Québec; indeed, five out of six of its governors were from companies situated in Québec, namely the Royal Trust, Bell Canada, Banque Canadienne Nationale, Concordia

Estate Holdings, and Clarkson, Gordon and Company.[(125)] During the 1970 campaign, several days before the election, the Canada Committee distributed pamphlets from door to door throughout Québec. The pamphlet predicted economic chaos in the event of separatism, including the loss of federal pensions and other social benefits.

After the Liberal victory on April 29, Lafferty, Harwood and Company issued a release stating the publicity surrounding its confidential letters, although not desired, had had beneficial effects and that the election had shown that private capital had no intention of allowing itself to be intimidated by "those [i.e., the UN government and the PQ] who formulate these kinds of policies."[(126)] The communiqué also claimed that the funds and stocks transferred out of the province would come back as long as the new government respected the rights of the private property of capital.[(127)]

In an article entitled "When Will the Money Return," the *Financial Post* claimed that at least $1,000 million left the province prior to the election:

> It began as a trickle in 1966-67 when some of the late Daniel Johnson's cabinet ministers threatened separatism. It built to a crescendo when a sizeable convoy of Brinks Express Co. trucks left in convoy from Royal Trust Co. offices in Montréal laden with securities bound for Ontario only a few days before the April 29 election.[(128)]

After giving several examples of money having been moved out of the province during the campaign, the *Financial Post* concluded the funds "will come back, and will be joined by other funds, in direct proportion to the degree of political stability in the province."[(129)]

Following the 1970 election, despite numerous predictions from within the business community that separatism had been definitely rejected,[(130)] business maintained its offensive against independence. The prime targets, as before, were Québec's credit rating and the possibility of head offices leaving Montréal. In an analysis of Québec's credit difficulties, the *Financial Post* explained in 1971 that the province had not had any problems in the fifties and that "it was the issue of separatism and then Jean Lesage's defeat in 1966 that raised the first doubts about Québec bonds."[(131)] Further, according to the newspaper: "Dealers say Québec's lower credit rating is not due to any basic weakness of its economy or of its finances, but to investor uncertainty about the province's political stability and the strength of its links with the rest of Canada."[(132)]

In a series of articles on the benefits of head offices in Montréal, Robert Stewart of the *Montreal Star* predicted that separatism could have dire consequences for the city of Montréal:

> Imagine Montréal with no skyscrapers, no commuter trains, no Metro. Imagine it without its swarm of taxis, its multiplicity of restaurants and hotels. A large industrial city, maybe — but not a world-ranking metropolis. That is what it would be like if so many national and international companies did not have their head offices here . . .
> It is not alarmist to say that this could happen. The people who emphasize the prospect most are the very people who have it within their power to make it come true. They are the top executives who state unequivocally that they will be

gone — and their head offices with them — if Québec ever separates from the rest of Canada.[133]

Here again, the Liberal government felt it would derive political advantage from keeping the issue alive. On August 17, 1972, for example, Bourassa said he was very preoccupied by the fact that some head offices were de-emphasizing their Québec operations.[134] Interpreting Bourassa's motives, Patrick Finn of the *Montreal Star* argued it was likely the premier was "focussing attention on the subject for political reasons;" thus, "such talk is bound to cramp the style of René Lévesque and the Parti Québécois in the next provincial election."[135]

Before the 1970 election, business had focused its attacks more on the "threat of separatism" put in general terms. After the election, however, more energy was concentrated on discrediting or criticizing the Parti Québécois. In the first place, attempts were made to identify the PQ with terrorism. Ouimet, for example, when asked to comment about bombs which had exploded in Montréal in May 1970, said: "Some people are just poor losers. We had a democratic election and they lost."[136] A *Financial Post* editorial, commenting on the entry of Pierre Vallières[137] into the Parti Québécois, stated this was proof that the PQ was "infiltrated by Québec revolutionaries."[138]

A second example was the intervention of prominent businessman Marc Carrière in the October 12, 1972, by-election in the riding of Duplessis. Carrière, who was president of a large retail chain called Dupuis Frères, told an audience in the riding four days before the election that he intended to build a branch in Sept-Iles (which is part of the Duplessis riding), but that the election of the Parti Québécois candidate might compromise his project.[139]

Despite the defeat of the PQ candidate, Carrière changed his mind about building the store. According to Parizeau, the Liberal government rewarded Carrière a few weeks later by renting four floors for the department of justice in the newly-built Place Dupuis in Montréal. At the time, Dupuis Frères was experiencing financial problems in meeting bank loans and mortgage payments.[140]

In 1972 and 1973, the main brunt of business attacks was reserved for the economic manifesto which the PQ had prepared for the 1973 election.[141] Jean Brunelle of the Centre des Dirigeants d'Entreprise predicted the PQ's over-emphasis of the economic role of the state would result in a sharp drop of the standard of living in Québec.[142] Claude Hébert denounced the manifesto as "hypocritical," "utopian," and "intellectual prostitution."[143] Desmarais warned: "The business community must speak out and tell people of the enormous costs involved not only in separation but in the prolongation of its discussion with attendant uncertainties."[144] Finally, Perrault claimed the economic program of the PQ would signify the deathknell of private enterprise in Québec; he predicted increased taxes, a massive exodus of head offices and key personnel, and a slowdown in foreign investment.[145]

NOTES

(1) *Financial Times*, "Perspective on Québec," 19 November 1973.

(2) In 1968 the Québec government had introduced Bill 85, which dealt with the language issue but which was withdrawn after opposition from both French and English groups. Businessmen had expressed particular dissatis-

137

faction with the legislation. As a result, when they submitted briefs to the National Assembly committee, the CMA and the Board of Trade decided to back their "suggestions" for amendments by threats of economic retaliation. The CMA brief, for example, stated:

"Nous nous devons de souligner que quel que soit le niveau des normes de l'enseignement, l'industrie québécoise ne pourra donner du travail aux futurs diplômés que dans la mesure où les politiques gouvernementales favoriseront un climat qui inspirera confiance aux bailleurs de fonds" [Canadian Manufacturers' Association, *Brief to the Committee of the National Assembly on Bill 85* (Montréal: Canadian Manufacturers' Association, 1968), p. 7].

(3) The rationale for the opposition was the demographic threat which the assimilation pattern of immigrants (that is, 90% assimilate into the English community) posed to the French element in Québec.

(4) J. M. Provost, "Le Bill 63," *Sept Jours*, 8 November 1969.

(5) 12.9% of the respondents did not answer the question.

(6) *Montréal-Matin*, owned by the Union Nationale, was the only French daily in Montréal to support Bill 63.

(7) L. Tremblay, editorial on Bill 63, *La Voix d'Alma*, 5 November 1969.

(8) *Le Nouvelliste*, "Le Bill 63", editorial, 29 October 1969.

(9) E. Hains, editorial on Bill 63, *Le Progrès de Magog*, 12 November 1969.

(10) F. Berthiaume, editorial on Bill 63, *L'Argenteuil* (Lachute), 5 November 1969.

(11) Gilles Francoeur, "Les Montréalais et le bill 63," *Le Devoir*, 7 November 1969.

(12) Precisely how the economic groups succeeded in influencing the government is open to question. Some claimed that the UN needed money for the forthcoming election. Another theory maintained the UN offered to stabilize the language situation in return for a more receptive attitude of the financial markets towards Quebec bond issues. The evidence cited is that of a $50 million bond issue floated by the Québec government one week before Bill 63 was introduced. Sales were very slow until the day when Bill 63 was passed, when they were sold within hours. See Gérald Godin, "Une hypothèse: le bill 63 payable sur livraison," *Québec-Presse*, 7 December 1969.

(13) French business and state institutions, although expressing the same concerns as English companies concerning the maintenance of a political climate favorable to foreign investment, disagreed with their English couterparts as regards the use of French as a language of work. Briefs from Hydro-Québec, the Société Nationale de Fiducie, the Commission de Transports de Montréal, among others, all argued that it was possible to make money in French in Québec.

(14) Montreal Board of Trade, *Annual Report: 1970-1971* (Montréal: Board of Trade, 1971), p. 3.

(15) Lise Lachance, "Toute restriction imposée à l'anglais peut compromettre le progrès du Québec," *Le Soleil*, 13 March 1970.

(16) Canadian Manufacturers' Association, *An Industrial Policy For Québec* (Montréal: Canadian Manufacturers' Association, 1972), app. F, p. 1.

(17) Ibid., p. 2. Similarly, at the annual meeting of the stockholders of the Montreal Trust in 1971, President Frank Case stated that Québec's forthcoming language policy could force some companies to transfer their head offices out of the province (*Le Devoir*, "La Situation linguistique au Québec préoccupe les milieux financiers anglophones," 26 February 1971).

(18) *Montréal-Matin*, "L'usage de l'anglais lié au niveau de vie," 13 February 1970.

(19) François Barbeau, "Noranda Mines: le bilinguisme à tous les échelons ne serait pas pratique au Québec," *Le Devoir*, 12 December 1969.

(20) Francois Barbeau and Jean-Luc Duguay, "L'unilinguisme pousserait Dominion Glass à déménager son siège social hors du Québec," *Le Devoir*, 11 december 1969.

The only divergent voice in the business opinion on the language question was that of Sun Oil of Canada. This company claimed that it would stay in a unilingual Québec. See *Montréal-Matin*, "Nous resterons dans un Québec devenu unilingue français," 20 March 1970.

(21) Pierre O'Neil, "Les Chefs d'entreprises doivent faire vite; la situation presse," *Le Devoir*, 30 June 1970.

(22) David Waters, "Labor and the Language Issue," *Montreal Star*, 21 December 1971.

(23) Ibid. Waters explained the union's reticence to keep the strike going on the language issue by saying: "The workers were not going to be suckered into being the victimized vanguard of the struggle which would inevitably ensue . . ."

(24) Bourassa interviewed by Jacques Keable, "Notre marge de manoeuvre est très mince," *Québec-Presse*, 23 January 1972. "GM represents four times Québec's budget, it was David and Goliath."

(25) Quoted in Louis Fournier, "Qui est George Arnold Hart?" *Québec-Presse*, 3 January 1971.

(26) G. Arnold Hart, speech at Emanu-El Temple, Westmount, 25 January 1971.

(27) Amy Booth, "For Business, Pressure in Québec Goes Higher," *Financial Post*, 2 January 1971.

(28) Fantus Company, p. 89. The Report was ordered by the Québec department of industry and commerce from the Fantus Company, a Chicago-based consulting firm. Its aim was to examine the various factors affecting industrial development in Québec. The Report was never made public, but was leaked to the press. A copy was obtained by the author from a Montréal journalist.

(29) Ibid., p. 162.

(30) Ibid., pp. 162-63.

(31) Ibid., p. 171.

(32) Ibid., p. 86.

(33) Ibid., p. 83.

(34) Ibid., For attitudes of Ontario respondents, see pp. 43-55.

(35) Ibid., p. 18.

(36) Ibid., p. 25.

(37) Ibid.

(38) Interview, May 1973.

(39) Interview, May 1973.

(40) Interviews with executives of these associations, May 1973.

(41) A month before the publication of the Gendron Report, 72.2% of the respondents to the questionnaire felt that "the present government's attitude towards the language question [was] satisfactory" (Question IV J). At that time, some information concerning the Gendron recommendations had been leaked to the press, but the definite position of the commission was not yet known. It is likely that the degree of approval would have been higher had the questionnaire been sent after the publication of the report.

(42) On the other hand, according to an executive of a business association, the Gendron Report used much of the data supplied by the Business Linguistic Center. The latter group was created under the initiative of the CMA and 40 major companies: Aluminum Company of Canada, Eaton's, Steinberg's, etc. Among other things, it carried out an inquiry on the use of French in plants. The same executive claimed that many secret meetings were held between the Gendron commissioners and the center.

(43) *Montreal Star*, "Conseil Backs Gendron Proposals," 17 February 1973.

(44) Interview with an executive of the CMA, May 1973.

(45) Michel Guénard, "Déçu, M. Gendron critique la réaction des milieux anglophones à son rapport," *Le Devoir*, 10 March 1973.

(46) François Barbeau, "Le CPQ insiste sur l'urgence de donner suite au rapport Gendron," *Le Devoir*, 11 May 1973.

(47) The Mouvement pour un Québec Français is made up of all Québec unions, the St. Jean Baptiste societies, and several other nationalist groups.

(49) Interview, May 1973. The president of a chemical firm told the writer that Bourassa had promised that Bill 63 would stand (interview, May 1973). As will be seen later, Bill 63 was abolished with the passage of Bill 22 — although according to many observers the main principles or effects of Bill 63 were maintained. It is impossible to determine whether the Bourassa government later changed its mind on the question or whether the executive in question misunderstood the implication of Bourassa's statement.

(50) Interview, May 1973.

(51) Interview, May 1973.

(52) Bill 22 later confirmed that business had been properly informed concerning the contents of the forthcoming legislation.

(53) Interview, May 1973.

(54) Interview, May 1973. This statement was later confirmed by Pierre A. Fréchette, regional general manager of the Royal Bank. He made it clear that the language of work in the head office would continue to be English, and that, even though some regulations governing the application of Bill 22 had not yet been made public, there were no reasons to believe that the bank would have to modify its present practices with regard to language. See Gilles Gariépy, "L'Anglais gardera ses droits à la Banque Royale," *La Presse*, 11 January 1975.

(55) Pierre Godin, "Les Dix commandements de la Warnock à Robert Bourassa," *Québec-Presse*, 10 June 1973. The letter was confidential, but a copy was obtained by *Québec-Presse.*

(56) Ibid.

(57) See Lysiane Gagnon, "Les Libéraux clouent le bec des adversaires du bill 22," *La Presse*, 11 July 1974. Most French and English businesses supported the main thrust of the bill; these included Aluminum Company of Canada, Bell Canada, the Mines and Metals Association of Québec, the Centre des Dirigeants d'Entreprise, and the Chambre de Commerce de la Province de Québec. There was some opposition from the Montreal Board of Trade and the CMA, among others.

(58) Claude Ryan, "Un Projet sans épine dorsale," editorial, *Le Devoir*, 22 May 1974.

(59) Idem, "Le Projet de loi 22 et la langue d'enseignement," *Le Devoir*, 7 June 1974. An opinion poll conducted by the Institut Québécois d'Opinion Publique was published in *Le Devoir* ("Le Québec opte pour le français prioritaire," 8 June 1974). The institut surveyed a random sample of Québec residents of 18 years of age and over. The main conclusion of the poll was that 15.5% of the respondents favoured "French as the only official language," 40.5% opted for "French as an official language and English as a secondary language," 42.0% chose "French and English as the two official languages of Québec," and 2% favoured "other" alternatives. There were also some important findings with regard to the language of education which indicated clearly that Bill 22 did not go as far as the general population would have wanted. Thus, 61.5% expressed support for a law forcing new immigrants whose mother tongue was not English to send their children to French schools; 33% opposed the idea; and 5.5% did not know or did not answer. Also, 50.5% of the respondents said they favoured legislation that would force new immigrants whose mother tongue was English to send their children to French schools; 45.5% were opposed; and 4.5% did not know or did not answer.

(60) Lysiane Gagnon, "Les Milieux d'affaires réagissent sérieusement à la réglementation," *La Presse*, 21 August 1975.

(61) See Jean-Paul Soulié: "Les Hommes d'affaires ne sont pas inquiets," *La Presse*, 19 September 1975.

(62) Claude Ryan: "Un cas instructif: la lettre du président de la Banque de Montréal à Robert Bourassa," *Le Devoir*, 23 July 1974.

(63) See Pierre Fournier, "The Politics of School Reorganization in Montreal," MA thesis, McGill University, 1971.

(64) See Dion, *Le Bill 60 et la société québécoise.*

(65) As will be seen later, there is some evidence that some elements of big business were apathetic on the issue.

(66) This does not include the provision in Bill 62 that island council members would be named directly by the Québec government rather than elected or nominated by local school commissioners — which was opposed by all groups, French and English.

(67) Noel Herron quoted in Fournier, p. 72.

(68) *Montreal Star*, "School Reforms," editorial, 1 August 1970.

(69) There was substantial overlapping in the leadership positions of educational and business institutions in Montréal. For example, an analysis of the board of directors of the PSBGM illustrated some very close link with

the business community in general and with the Board of Trade in particular. Thus, the three main authors of the Board of Trade brief on school reorganization were also members of the board of the PSBGM: K. D. Sheldrick, vice-president of Bailey Meter and president of the Lachine Protestant School Board; Van B. Wight, member of the executive of Bell Telephone and president of the St. Laurent Protestant School Board; C. G. Southmayd, president of the Engineering Institute of Canada, former executive of Allis Chalmers, and president of the PSBGM education committee.

(70) Quoted by Derek Hill, "Bill 60 Confrontation Escalates Towards Impasse," *Montreal Gazette*, 10 March 1970.

(71) Montreal Board of Trade, *Memoir to the Standing Parliamentary Committee on Education* (Montréal: Board of Trade, 1970), p. 4. The brief specifically asked that local school boards be given "management responsibility for properties and equipment."

(72) Senator H. Carl Goldenberg, for one, in a study entitled *Report of the Royal Commission on Metropolitain Toronto* (Toronto: Queen's Printer, 1965), argued that a strong school council was a crucial element in any attempts to reduce socio-economic disparities between regions. His study documented with precision the inequalities in educational services between the various socio-economic areas in Toronto. His main recommendation was that the financial and administrative autonomy of the school boards should be reduced and that the school council should be strengthened.

(73) Quoted in David Allnutt, "Bill 28 Under the Microscope," *Montreal Star*, 12 April 1971.

(74) The Parti Québécois supported the principle of the bill but demanded that it contain a clear statement on language policy.

(75) Allnutt, "Bill 28 Under Microscope."

(76) Lysiane Gagnon, "Bill 28, la minorité aurait plus de garanties," *La Presse*, 12 May 1971.

(77) The English educational and business groups were probably helped in their pressure campaign by several spokesmen within the Québec government. After the 1970 election, the English community was better represented within the Québec cabinet and in the National Assembly. Victor Goldbloom, MNA for d'Arcy McGee, was appointed minister of state for education, second in command behind St. Pierre.

Also, two businessmen with no previous educational experience were named to key jobs in the education department. M. H. Dinsmore, formerly of General Electric, became assistant deputy minister, and J. N. Rutherford, of the Chambly Industrial Development Commission, became special adviser to the minister.

(78) K. D. Sheldrick quoted in Fournier. It was learned from Tilley that St. Pierre asked the PSBGM in the early months of 1971 to draft Bill 62 to its liking, while maintaining the principle of unified school boards. The government accepted most of the PSBGM proposals. See Fournier.

(79) According to Jules Leblanc, ("Des Miettes pour les défavorisées?" *La Presse*, 24 January 1973), "Le conseil scolaire régional sera étroitement contrôlé par l'ensemble des commissions scolaires. Le conseil régional ne pourra faire que ce que celles-ci voudront bien, par 'consensus,' qu'il fasse."

(80) Ibid. "The special provisions to ensure that zones which suffer from disadvantages in educational facilities will be able to catch up will only be possible if the school council of the island of Montréal endorses regulations and efficient policies to that effect . . ."

(81) Ibid.

(82) Lysiane Gagnon, "Seuls les anglo-protestants voient d'un bon oeil la nouvelle restructuration scolaire," *La Presse*, 16 November 1972

(83) *Le Devoir*, "La Chambre de Commerce appuie le principe du projet sur la restructuration scolaire," 8 December 1972.

(84) Of the French respondents, 66.6% were favourable to Bill 71. In contrast, 51.4% of the English respondents did not agree with the bill. A likely explanation is that (as indicated earlier) English businessmen and a substantial portion of the English community would have preferred the status quo. In addition, there was probably some insecurity concerning the possibility of modification in the school structures by 1975.

(85) Jules Leblanc, "Un Défi impossible à relever — Mme. Lavoie-Roux," *La Presse*, 26 January 1973. Also, idem, "Des Protestants contents, des francophones écoeurés," *La Presse*, 2 December 1972.

(86) According to Jean-Marc Piotte et al, [*Québec occupé* (Montréal: Parti Pris, 1971)], Québec separatism is against the interests of the Ontario industrial elite; this is so because the Parti Québécois's main economic objective is to create a network of manufacturing industries in the durable goods sector. Traditionally, Québec has been the main customer of Ontario's heavy industry. (pp. 61-63).

Ontario has a tendency to over-emphasize Québec's problems. This is understandable in that many of the decisions of foreign or U.S. investors express themselves in terms of Québec/Ontario alternatives. The *Financial Post*, for one, provides numerous examples of the often irrational insistence on Québec's instability.

(87) Laurier Cloutier, "Toronto a écoulé moins de 2 pour cent des $900 millions d'obligations du Québec," *La Presse*, 16 May 1972.

(88) Speaking of the difficulties of Québec bonds on the Toronto financial markets, Frédéric Wagnière noted that "Québec's credit has not slipped as much in foreign markets" and hypothesized that this was because "European and U.S. investors are more used to political and social unrest than Canadians" (quoted in "Québec Credit Still Feeling Effects of FLQ," *Financial Post*, 12 March 1971).

(89) Claude Beauchamp, "Encore beaucoup de gens pour le Québec!" *La Presse*, 7 November 1972.

(90) Yves Bernier, "Wall Street n'est aucunement influencé par les problèmes politiques actuels du Québec," *Le Soleil*, 6 November 1969. "La situation politique du Québec de nos jours n'affecte en rien le jugement de l'investisseur américain qui investit pour faire de l'argent, pas pour faire de la politique."

(91) Ibid.

(92) Quoted in Confederation of National Trade Unions, *Ne Comptons que sur nos propres moyens*, p. 25.

(93) Quoted in Parti Québécois, *La Question économique n'est pas un problème* (Montréal: Editions du Parti Québécois, 1970).

(94) See Brunelle and Papineau for details of this episode.

(95) Roger Newman, "Flight of Capital, Company Exodus, Project Changes Point to Québec Separatism Fear," *Toronto Globe and Mail*, 6 October 1967.

(96) C.A. Atchison, president of Investor's Syndicate, was quoted as saying: "If separatism keeps up, we might have to take another look at investment in Québec companies" (ibid.).

(97) Quoted ibid.

(98) Quoted ibid.

(99) Quoted ibid.

(100) R. G. Giddens, "Can Québec Keep Up its Growth Rate," *Montreal Star,* 7 October 1967.

(101) Amy Booth, "Some Money Likes Québec," *Financial Post,* 7 October 1967. She added: "Talk to almost any broker or banker, security analyst or real estate salesman and he will tell you that the price of the separation of Québec from the rest of Canada — if that is what lies ahead — is already being paid."

(102) Laurent Lauzier, "La Fuite des capitaux hors du Québec n'est pas tragique pour le moment," *La Presse,* 14 October 1967.

(103) Ibid.

(104) Jacques Parizeau, "De Certaines manoeuvres d'un syndicat financier en vue de conserver son empire au Québec," *Le Devoir,* 2 February 1970.

(105) Idem., "Le Terrorisme économique dégénère," *Québec-Presse,* 26 November 1972.

(106) Daniel Johnson quoted in Claude Beauchamp, "Faribault, un puissant conseiller auprès du cabinet," *La Presse,* 1 November 1967.

(107) Quoted by Claude Ryan, "Les Explications incomplètes de M. Neapole," editorial, *Le Devoir,* 26 October 1967.

(108) Michel Roy, "Le President de la Bourse se réjouit de la nomination de Faribault," *Le Devoir,* 2 November 1967.

Canadian Business was also enthusiastic about the Faribault nomination: "There was little doubt that prior to the appointment, the confidence placed in the Québec government by business was at a low ebb. The appointment, therefore, took on an added significance, for not only was Premier Johnson acquiring an acknowledged expert on constitutional matters and civil law, but a representative of the business world, a mogul of St. James Street, whose personal reputation within his own field is of the highest order" ("Faribault on Federalism," February 1968, pp. 58-59).

(109) Claude Ryan, "Un Frein à la panique," editorial, *Le Devoir,* 3 November 1967.

(110) Ibid.

(111) *Le Devoir,* "La Conjoncture politique québécoise," 25 January 1968. For further information, see Brunelle and Papineau, pp. 82-91.

(112) Proulx, p. 70.

(113) Pierre Godin, "Lesage prédit une très forte baisse des investissements," *La Presse,* 11 March 1968.

(114) William Tetley, "L'Affaire Michelin ou les raisons de la stagnation des investissements au Québec," *Le Devoir,* 4 September 1969.

(115) Ibid.

(116) William Hall, "La Place importante des bureaux-chefs canadiens dans l'économie de Montréal," *Le Devoir,* 3 December 1969.

(117) Chambre de Commerce de la Province de Québec, *Québec, le coût de l'indépendance* (Montréal: Editions du Jour, 1969), p. 93.

(118) The Union Nationale's intransigent attitude towards Ottawa, its emphasis on the possibilities of independence, and, to a lesser extent, the introduction of Bill 62, discussed previously, had angered the business community.

(119) See Proulx. Proulx also argued that the UN's flirtation with independence during the 1970 election alienated business (pp. 23-24).

(120) *La Presse,* April 6, 1972.

(121) Pierre Godin, "La Victoire de la peur," *Québec-Presse,* 3 May 1970.

(122) According to Gérald Godin ("Les Dessous de l'affaire Brink's-Royal Trust: des faits nouveaux," *Québec-Presse,* 17 May 1970), contrary to the normal procedures and to the customary security precautions, the Royal Trust loaded the Brinks' trucks in full view. Usually, the trucks were loaded in the basement of the CIL building where the Royal Trust had its offices. It should also be said that stock certificates were worthless per se and could easily be replaced if they were lost, burned, or otherwise destroyed.

(123) The *Montreal Star* titled "Securities Shipment Confirmed," *La Presse* headlined "Inquiétude face aux elections: des Québécois déménagent leurs valeurs mobilières en Ontario," and *Le Devoir* wrote "Des valeurs mobilières sont transférées à Toronto."

(124) Douglas Cunningham, "Corporate Group Accelerates its National Unity Effort," *Financial Post,* 6 May 1972.

(125) Ibid.

(126) Lafferty, Harwood and Company, Press Communiqué, 7 May 1970.

(127) Ibid.

(128) Amy Booth, "When Will the Money Return?" *Financial Post,* 9 May 1970.

(129) Ibid.

(130) For example, Louis Hébert, president of the Banque Canadienne Nationale, predicted at the European Institutional Investor's Conference in 1972 that the separatist movement had reached its apogee in 1970 (Claude Beauchamp, "Bourassa rassure les financiers européens sur le climat socio-économique du Québec," *La Presse,* 1 December 1972). Similarly, Ian Rodger ("Is the Handwriting on the Wall for Lévesque and the Parti Québécois?" *Financial Post,* 31 March 1973), speculated on the demise of the Parti Québécois.

(131) Frédéric Wagnière, "Québec Credit Still Feeling Effects of FLQ," *Financial Post,* 13 March 1971.

(132) Ibid.

(133) Robert Stewart, "The City's Forgotten Assets: Head Offices," *Montreal Star,* 25 May 1971.

Amy Booth stated: "The threat of secession is simply something the businessmen must do something about . . . They can move part of their head offices out to provide a base to operate from. Or they can set up in Ottawa, where they will be reasonable close by'' (''For Business, Pressure in Québec Goes Higher,'' *Financial Post*, 2 January 1971).

(134) Pierre Bellemare, ''L'Exode des sièges sociaux préoccupe le gouvernement,'' *Le Devoir*, 18 August 1972.

(135) Patrick Finn, ''Companies Still Sneaking Out of Québec,'' *Montreal Star*, 31 August 1972.

(136) Quoted in *Montreal Gazette*, ''City Businessmen Only Ruffled by Bombs,'' 2 June 1970.

(137) Pierre Vallières had openly identified with the socialist and separatist Front de Libération du Québec for several years.

(138) *Financial Post*, ''Fifth Column in Separatist Camp,'' editorial, 25 December 1971.

(139) Pierre-Paul Gagné, ''Carrière attend le vote dans Duplessis avant d'implanter Dupuis à Sept-Iles,'' *La Presse*, 9 October 1972.

(140) Jacques Parizeau, ''Le Terrorisme économique dégénère,'' *Québec-Presse*, 26 November 1972.

(141) Parti Québécois, *Quand nous serons vraiment maîtres chez nous* (Montréal: Editions du Parti Québécois, 1972).

(142) Quoted in Gilles Léveillée, ''Un Homme d'affaire rejette le caractère étatique de la société proposée par le PQ,'' *Le Devoir*, 5 May 1972.

(143) Quoted in *La Presse*, ''Le Manifeste économique du PQ: de l'inconscience ou de l'hypocrisie,'' 15 April 1972.

(144) Quoted in R. G. Gibbens, ''Canada Can't Go It Alone . . . Nor Quebec,'' *Montreal Star*, 31 May 1972.

(145) Charles Perrault, ''Le Programme du PQ, arrêt de mort de l'entreprise privée,'' *Le Devoir*, 22 March 1973.

CHAPTER 9

SOCIAL AND LABOUR ISSUES

RATHER THAN PRESENTING a detailed description and discussion of governmental policy in the social and labour fields, I intend to concentrate here on the attempts by groups other than business, e.g., labour, consumer groups, cooperatives, and tenants, to challenge the power of business and to obtain favourable outputs from the Quebec government. It is clear that these groups often overlap and seek the same objectives. Unions, for example, will often support and fight beside consumer groups on many issues. In the main, I will focus on those issues which were the least likely to be supported by business, such as consumer protection and the creation of worker cooperatives.

It would be incorrect to pretend that labour and social groups in the past few decades have not succeeded in making genuine gains. Unionization and various social programs such as unemployment insurance, pension plans, and health insurance programs have certainly improved the relative position of the work force. At the same time, it is important to keep an overall long-term perspective on these gains and improvements. Specifically, it is essential to measure the impact of social policies on income distribution and on the distribution of power within society.

As regards income distribution, there is substantial evidence that income inequality has fallen only slightly in the past decades in western countries. A study of the United States by Gabriel Kolko entitled *Wealth and Power in America* concluded: "The basic distribution of income and wealth in the United States is essentially the same now as it was in 1939, or even in 1910."[1] In fact, Kolko found that the five deciles with lowest income together received 27% of total national personal income in 1910, but only 23% in 1959. The two lowest deciles experienced particularly sharp declines: from 4.9 to 2.9% of total income for the ninth decile, and from 3.4 to 1.1% of total income for the last decile.[2]

The only deciles to make important gains were the second and third which climbed respectively from 12.3 to 15.8% and from 10.2 to 12.7% of total income, corresponding perhaps to the American middle class. The first decile dropped from 33.0% to 28.9%. According to Kolko, however, "this loss disappears when the 1950-59 figures are corrected to allow for their exclusion of all forms of income-in-kind and the very substantial understatement of income by the wealthy, both of which are consequences of the post 1941 expansion in income taxation" [3]

According to figures from Statistics Canada, no major redistribution of income occurred between 1951 and 1965. Thus the percentage distribution of total income by quintiles remained stable over the period; the position of the lowest quintile improved slightly, from 4.4% to 4.6% of total income, whereas the highest quintile accounted for 41.1% of total income in 1965 compared with 42.8% in 1951.[4] Further, the proportion of the Canadian GNP used for social welfare measures remained fairly stable during the period from 1959 to 1969, averaging 6.3%, peaking at 6.7% in 1961-62, and hitting a low of 5.7% in 1965-66.[5]

In Québec, a report published in 1972, popularly known as the Castonguay-Nepveu report for its two main authors who were respectively minister and deputy minister of the health and welfare department, found that social welfare benefits had only limited effects on the distribution of revenue. Thus, the report calculated that the net effect of the various welfare measures for the year 1965 was to redistribute 2.5% of the total revenue of people earning more than $5,500 a year in favour of the classes earning less than $4,000; for people earning between $4,000 and $5,500, no redistribution of income occurred.[6] Also, during the 1954 to 1969 period, despite the adoption of new measures, such as unemployment insurance, the lowering of the pension eligibility age, the increase in pension benefits, and family allowances, the proportion of the Québec GNP going toward social benefits increased from 4.4 to only 5.6%.[7] The report noted that the progression of welfare spending was "weaker than could have been expected during the period" and that "contrary to what is generally believed, the proportion of the wealth which is distributed in these ways [i.e., through welfare measures] shows almost no increase."[8] Thus, in social terms at least, the overall impact of the "quiet revolution" in Québec should not be overestimated.[9]

Considering that, as Birnbaum claimed, state welfare mechanisms had largely "effected a redistribution of the working class's own income,"[10] and that they had not substantially modified the distribution of wealth, it was not surprising that business had, on the whole, been favourable to the various social benefits devised by government. Thus, 93% of the business respondents to the questionnaire expressed support for unemployment insurance, and 97.1% approved of the Québec Pension Plan.[11] More generally, 80.1% of businessmen thought that government should take the initiative in resolving social problems, whereas 14.2% thought both business and government should take the initiative, and 5.7% opted for business alone.[12]

In addition, social reforms were granted not so much as a result of the pressure of organized labour, but rather as a the result of preventive, essentially defensive, measures on the part of business and government. Domhoff, in *The Higher Circles,* noted that the "fear of future troubles" had led to reforms. Besides, businessmen came to realize that "certain reforms were actually less expensive that the conditions that produced them;" "protective labour legislation," for example, "was just good business."[13] A speech by then minister of health and welfare, Claude Castonguay, to the St. Laurent Kiwanis Club in Montréal in 1971 made it clear that "social development" was necessary to stabilize the social climate and was, in fact, directly benificial to economic development:

> Social development must pursue realistic objectives without compromising economic development. Social development has a positive role to play vis-à-vis economic development; it must insure that the social climate does not deteriorate, that the changes which result from technological change do not result in too intense social tensions, that human resources be apt to contribute to economic development.[14]

Some of the more recent examples of attempts by groups to obtain favourable legislation from the Québec government will now be examined. The focus will be on issues in which business, to varying degrees, had chosen to get involved and which could therefore be assumed to challenge — even though, often, in a secondary way — the power of business.

Consumers Groups and Bill 45

In Québec, as in many other Canadian provinces and other parts of the world, consumer groups were active during the sixties and seventies. They focused mainly on the quality and safety of products, on credit institutions, and on the level of prices, The main consumer group in Québec was the Associations Coopératives d'Economie Familiale (ACEF).

The ACEF movement was founded in 1962. Its nine regional associations were regrouped in a Montréal-based federation in 1971. In 1972-73, the ACEFs had a full-time staff of 53 employees who were assisted by several hundred volunteers. The main thrust of the associations was educational and informational programs for consumers. They focussed particularly on offering budget consultation services for poor families and on the problems deriving from indebtedness. It was estimated that some 2,500 individuals received assistance from the ACEFs with regard to their involvement with finance companies. In 1968, the ACEFs founded a legal aid service; by 1973, the service had helped 431 families recover some $167,320 in damages or illegal interest. Finally, the consumer group organized courses on the development of cooperatives, providing assistance to several groups which were starting cooperatives in production, credit, and food distribution.[15]

As in the case of most consumer groups,[16] one of the ACEFs' main problems was financing. The main source of financial support came from the 389 member associations, including the labour unions, some citizens committees, credit unions, caisses populaires, and other social groups, and from grants obtained from private organizations and foundations, particularly the Fédération des Oeuvres de Montréal.[17] The remaining 30 to 40% of the revenue was usually provided by the federal and provincial governments.

In March 1972, however, William Tetley, minister of financial institutions, companies, and cooperatives, announced that the Québec government had decided to terminate its financial support of the ACEF movement.[18] In the three-year period from 1969 to 1972, the provincial government had given a total of $178,000 to the ACEFs — $41,000 in 1969, $57,000 in 1970, and $90,000 in 1971 — and had thus become a crucial source of revenue for the consumer group. The ACEFs had asked for $120,000 for the 1972-73 year, an amount which represented some 24% of the total revenue of the group.

Following Tetley's statement, the ACEFs launched a pressure campaign to inform the public of its financial difficulties and to attempt to reverse the government's decision. In September 1972, the government announced its decision to grant $25,000 to the group; this represented a 70% reduction from the 1971 grant.[19] As a result, the ACEFs had to reduce their activities in many Québec regions, in Thetford, Mauricie, and the North Shore, for example. The government gave no official reason for cutting the grant. ACEF executives, however, thought it was because they had been too aggressive vis-à-vis finance companies, particularly in regard to the 300 or so suits filed by its legal section.

In the 1972-73 period, the ACEFs lost more than $60,000, despite important budget cuts including staff layoffs. In 1973-74, the anticipated deficit was $160,000. Pierre Marois, executive director, said the survival of the group was in serious doubt unless governmental help was forthcoming.[20]

In 1971, the Québec government took its first initiative in the area of consumer protection by passing the Consumer Protection Act. Known as Bill 45, the act had several important weaknesses which limited its effectiveness. The first problem was that many areas were not touched by the legislation, such as house sales, collection agencies, the interest rates charged by finance companies, new car sales, and false advertising. Another weakness was that sanctions or penalties for a breach of the legislation were minimal; the fines imposed for first infractions ranged between $500 to $1,000, which, according to the ACEFs, provided no deterent, particularly for large companies.[21]

Along with the ACEFs, all Québec unions opposed Bill 45.[22] The opposition was, however, unsuccessful, and, according to Normand Caron, an executive of the ACEF, finance companies obtained more freedom of action than before as a result of the legislation.[23] The Board of Trade and the Québec Chambre de Commerce, on the other hand, supported the legislation.[24]

Once the law was passed, several other factors contributed to ✓ limiting its effectiveness even more. First, businessmen were given a ✓ dominant advisory role in the 15-member government-appointed ✓ Consumer Protection Council; the first president was Luc Laurin, president of Paula, a small pharmaceutical importing company.[25] In fact, seven of the 15 members of the council were businessmen — including Raymond Girardin, vice-president of Niagara Finance Company, and Perrault.[26] Thus, the council, instead of being oriented specifically towards consumer protection, was rather a forum for various groups involved in economic life to discuss the relation between industry and consumers.

Second, neither the Consumer Protection office nor the council were allocated enough funds to accomplish their tasks. In its first report, in September 1972, the council complained that it had insufficient physical and financial resources and also that the Québec population had not been informed on Bill 45.[27] The office, on the other hand, reported that, because of its limited jurisdiction, it was only able to follow up less than 20% of consumer complaints — which meant that more than 80% of the complaints were not covered by the law.[28] Of the 2,000 complaints lodged at the Montréal office in the first 12 months of operation, legal proceedings were taken in only one case.[29] On June 19 1975, the government approved Bill 18, a revised version of Bill 45. The legislation was opposed by some consumer groups, but it is too early to tell if it will be an improvement over its predecessor.

Cooperatives: Sogefor, Cabano, and Tembec

During the sixties, many plants were closed down by companies, usually because the machinery or the scale of production had become inefficient and because the company wanted to shift its production to larger units. These plant closures were particularly detrimental to the smaller towns where the plant was often the only or one of the few major employers. One of the responses by small towns to plant closures was the creation of "cooperatives" whose intent was to either start a new plant or re-activate one that had been shut down. Apart from creating employment and, in effect, insuring the survival of the town, one of the main motivating forces of many of these cooperative experiments was to ensure worker participation in the management of new plants. Embitterd by the unilateral decisions of companies to shut down plants, local elites and ex-workers pressed for representation, and sometimes control, in the decision-making centers of many of the newly-created plants.

The reaction of business to cooperative experiments was certainly not homogeneous or united. Thus, 47.1% of businessmen thought that production cooperatives were a "threat to the economic system," whereas 52.9% did not. Francophone and Anglophone respondents displayed divergent views; 61.1% of the English-speaking executives, compared with 20.8% for the French, felt that cooperatives were a threat, whereas 79.2% of the Francophone executives, compared with 38.9% of the Anglophones, answered in the negative. One possible explanation for the discrepancy, apart from the fairly large number of respondents from the cooperative sector in the French sample, e.g., from caisses populaires and agricultural distribution cooperatives, but not production cooperatives,[30] was that much of the economic power of the French-speaking community originated from the cooperatives, and Francophones had a much greater familiarity with cooperatives.

Faced with plant closures and often strong pressure from the local communities to contribute financially to the setting up of cooperatives, the Québec government displayed an ambivalent attitude.

On the one hand, supporting cooperatives was compatible with the government's efforts to create jobs. Also, as in the case of the Francophones executives, the Québec government did not feel that cooperatives were a threat to the economic system. Quite the contrary. In fact, St. Pierre argued in an interview with the *Financial Post* that encouraging cooperatives would contribute to saving capitalism: "I believe the way to save capitalism here, with its positive social role, will be to give special attention to French-Canadian capitalism, including cooperatives."[31] On the other hand, the Québec government, like business, was loath to set precedents with regard to full worker control of productive units or worker participation. Thus, if the government was often willing to assist cooperative projects financially, it attempted to discourage any attempts to institutionalize some form of worker control.

Even though cooperatives met with some success in the field of credit and agricultural distribution in Québec, production cooperatives were not likely to represent a threat to the supremacy of the large companies. If successful, of course, they could have a "nuisance value," in that every time a plant closed strong pressure would be exerted by the local population to start a cooperative; if too many local cooperatives were set up, this could begin to impinge on the markets of private companies. However, the important point is that it is unlikely, in the circumstances, that a production cooperative can be successful. A study by the Groupe de Recherche Economique[32] demonstrated that production cooperatives faced the same kind of problems as the small companies[33] in trying to compete with large companies. Inevitably, cooperatives in the field of production were small; this limited possibilities for economies of scale and access to reasonably cheap capital. Large companies, if they felt threatened, could easily make it difficult for the cooperative to obtain reasonably priced supplies and could make it impossible for the cooperative to distribute and sell its product.

In January 1971, in the town of Mont-Laurier, a broadly-based common front of the local population, including workers, small producers, and merchants, was organized to "save Sogefor,"[34] that is, to prevent the three local plants owned by Sogefor from being either sold or closed down. The Dupan and Dubé plants were in fact closed down in June 1971. This resulted in considerable local protest, including road blocks and demonstrations. On August 31, 1971, a mass rally involving the Mont-Laurier population, local elites, workers, and merchants, sought to pressure the government to re-open the plants and to create a board of directors where workers and managers would be represented evenly. In the face of the government's inaction, the local population decided to start a cooperative to buy back Dupan; it was decided that local wood cutters and workers would have full control of the newly-formed cooperative. The plan received support from the Québec unions, the caisses populaires, and other groups.

In november 1971, Dupan was reopened by the Québec government. The workers agreed to accept a salary freeze in exchange for two of the nine seats on the board of directors of the company. A year and a half later, the government decided to exclude the two union representatives from the board in order, according to St. Pierre, to "cleanse the board."[35] In June 1974, when it became obvious that attempts to buy back Dupan were in vain, the cooperative was dissolved.[36]

The case of Cabano was the best known attempt by a local population to set up a cooperative. As far as could be determined, it was also the only such case that provoked a comparatively strong reaction from some segments of the business community. On July 10, 1966, in Cabano, a pulp and paper mill owned by the K. C. Irving group, D'auteuil Lumber, burned down. The mill was comparatively small, employing some 200 workers and providing approximately 1,000 indirect jobs, but in a town of 3,000 inhabitants, it was crucial to the survival of the area. After the mill burned down. D'auteuil Lumber announced its intention to rebuild its plant. In 1970, however, the company changed its mind, claiming insufficient funding. The local population, with the help of the town council and a citizen's committee, then decided to attempt to set up its own cardboard producing plant. For this purpose, it created a cooperative called the Société Populaire des Pâtes et Papiers du Québec.

Two feasibility studies completed in 1971[37] concluded the project would be solvent financially in the middle and long terms and recommended the building of a plant. It suggested the mill produce corrugated medium cardboard and projected the new plant would provide 267 production jobs, in addition to several hundred forest jobs, mainly in wood cutting. The two studies argued that many factors put Cabano in a favourable competitive position, including the availability of specialized and experienced manpower, reasonable transportation costs, cheap electricity, and a good supply of raw materials, namely wood, at reasonable distances.

The total cost of the project was estimated at $31.5 million. The next move for the Société Populaire des Pâtes et Papiers was to raise capital. It succeeded in obtaining commitments for a loan of $16.5 million from its prospective European customers and for $5 million in capital stock, mainly from the local population, European investors, and various associations. The group also received guarantees for the sale of 75% of its production to Belgium and Spain. Sybetra, a large Belgian firm with assets of some $300 million, was to be the main buyer of the product as well as the main supplier of capital.

The next phase of the project is more complex to analyse. In its attempts to obtain the remaining $10 million of capital needed from the two levels of government, the Société Populaire opened up the avenues for increased governmental intervention in the project, particularly at the Québec provincial level. It should be noted also that the Cabano case had aroused substantial interest in the media and had, in many ways, become a test case of the government's willingness to create jobs and encourage local economic development.

At the same time, however, business, or perhaps more precisely some big pulp and paper producers, were applying pressure to block the project.[38] The questionnaire showed that 72.2% of senior business executives in Québec were opposed to government financing of the Cabano project. In November 1972, the Conseil des Producteurs des

Pâtes et Papiers, which included most of the Québec-based pulp and paper producers, argued in a brief submitted to the Québec government that the project was not economically feasible. Domtar, according to one of its executives,[39] also pressured the Québec government. Being a major producer of corrugated medium cardboard, Domtar stood to lose if a new plant came into production.

In the course of 1972, the Société Populaire des Pâtes et Papiers gradually abandoned its active efforts to set up a pulp and paper production cooperative. Government funds were slow in coming and, in any case, the Québec government had by now largely taken the initiative in the project. In October 1973, the Québec government broke off negotiations with Sybetra, thereby depriving the project of its main prospective customer and financial backer. The government claimed the Belgian company was "incompetent and not very serious."[40] This view conflicted with an earlier statement by André Déom, Liberal MNA responsible for the Sybetra negotiations,[41] to the effect that Sybetra's offer was serious and that the Société Populaire had been ineffective in its negotiations. It was also surprising that none of the studies done by the two levels of government and the Société Populaire during the two-year period of negotiations gave any indication that Sybetra was "not serious."

On June 14, 1974, it was announced that a cardboard producing mill would be built in Cabano at a cost of $17 million and would open in 1976.[42] The new plant would have only half the capacity (75,000 tons) of the original project and would create some 100 production jobs. Thirty per cent of the capital stock would be held by the Québec government through the Régie d'Exploration Forestière (Rexfor),[43] 30% by Les Papiers Cascades, a private pulp and paper producer, 20% by the caisses populaires, and 20% by the local population.[44]

Assuming the new mill goes ahead as planned, the Cabano case cannot be considered a complete failure for the local population; it did succeed against business opposition, although it is difficult to measure the intensity of business pressure, to have its projects for a new mill accepted and funded by the Québec government. The success, however, was limited. Not only will the plant be considerably smaller than originally planned, but, more important, the Société Populaire and the local population failed in their attempts to gain control of the new mill. Hence, while Cabano will produce some jobs in a town that badly needs them, it will certainly not set a precedent in terms of worker control.[45]

A situation very similar to that of Cabano developed in the town of Temiscaming in 1972. In January 1972, Canadian International Paper decided to close down its Kipawa plant, a sulphite pulp mill in Temiscaming. The plant was the only industry in this town of 2,500 inhabitants and the loss of 850 jobs which resulted from the closure threatened its continued existence.[46] The company's reasons for discontinuing production at Kipawa were insufficient demand and excessive competition. It cited the building of the Québec government-backed ITT-Rayonnier mill in Port Cartier[47] as one of the main factors in the weakening of its competitive position. As a result, International

150

Paper, the New York-based company which owns CIP, decided to concentrate its sulphite production in its Mississippi plant.

As in the case of Cabano, the population of Temiscaming reacted vigorously to the closure. Led by Charlie Carpenter, head of the Kipawa union, the Québec MNA, and the mayor, the citizens of Temiscaming decided to pressure the Québec government for financial support in order to buy back the CIP plant. Close to $1 million was raised, but CIP wanted $2.5 million for the mill.

At the end of 1972, three former CIP executives and the manager of the Kipawa plant decided to get involved in the efforts to put the plant back into production. The three included Georges Petty, former vice-president for international sales at International Paper, Jack Stevens, vice-president for corporate planning at the CIP head office in Montreal, and Jim Chantler, head of industrial relations, also of the Montreal office. The group decided to create Tembec (Temiscaming-Québec) Forest Products and suggested that a formula involving some financial assistance from Québec and Ottawa, some private investments, and participation of the local population and the workers of the Kipawa plant would be successful in reopening the plant.

After two separate feasibility studies, one by a Montréal consulting firm and another by a Toronto firm, indicated the market for sulphite pulp justified the continued operation of the plant, the two levels of government decided to give financial support to the project. When it became obvious that the attempts to reopen the plant were indeed serious, CIP asked for $6 million for its timber concessions in addition to the $2.5 million for the plant. On August 1, 1973, after lengthy negotiations with the Québec government, CIP accepted $2.4 million for its Kipawa mill and $5.9 million for the wood supplies and timber concessions.[48] In effect, the company had obtained almost complete satisfaction of its financial demands.[49]

In October 1973, the Kipawa mill return to operation employing some 500 workers in the plant and providing another 350 jobs in the forest; in its first three months of operation, from October to December, Tembec showed a profit. It required a $25 million investment to reopen the plant, including the purchasing of the plant and concessions, the modernization of machinery, and the setting-up of anti-pollution devices. Of this amount, $4.4 million was provided by Ottawa's department of regional and economic expansion, $3.5 million was provided by the Québec government, banks agreed to a $6 million loan, and $2.5 million was provided by a sale of bonds to private investors in Montréal. In addition, $400,000 was contributed by the workers of the plant, $200,000 by the Temiscaming population, and $100,000 by the former CIP executives.

With an investment of $100,000, however, the former CIP executives managed to obtain a dominant position in the control of the company. Thus, their investment gave them 38% of the capital share of the company, compared with 38% for the unions and local population, and 24% for the Québec government. This was because most of the money invested by the unions and Temiscaming population was channelled into bonds rather than stock. At the level of the board of directors, the former CIP executives were given four of the nine seats, compared with two each for the government and union, and one to a representative of the private investors.

As in the case of Cabano, the workers and local Temiscaming population ended up with minimal control over the new mill. Not only was their investment more substantial than that of the CIP heads, but the workers agreed to a three-year contract at wages much lower than the standards of the industry; Parizeau estimated that this represented an indirect subsidy of $2.7 million over the duration of the contract.[50] It should be pointed out also that the $2.5 million bond floated by Nesbitt Thomson in Montreal was "first mortgage," and thus the private investors were given more protection in the case of bankruptcy than the workers who were allocated "second mortgage" bonds.[51]

The above case studies show that results have been mixed in terms of business influence. The local population and the workers have enjoyed some success in keeping plants open despite pressure by private companies. Their attempts to obtain a significant degree of control over the plants were much less successful, however. Indeed, in many cases, the private sector managed to maintain an important degree of control over the new plants.

Tenants and Rent Control Legislation

In July 1972, the Québec government introduced its first rent control legislation since 1951. The 1951 law was inadequate in that, among other things, the province's rental review board had jurisdiction only over houses built before April 1951, and for which rents did not exceed $125 a month. The new law, Bill 59, would apply to all tenants. Its major provision was to put an absolute ceiling of 5% upon annual rent increases unless the owner could prove to a rent control board that he had carried out improvements or repairs justifying a higher increase.[52]

Tenant groups, such as the Association des Locataires du Montréal Métropolitain and the Fédération des Associations de Locataires du Québec, and the unions were generally favourable to Bill 59, even though they suggested several amendments to the projected legislation. Their main demands were a 3% rather than 5% ceiling in yearly rental increases, stiffer penalties in the case of racial or other forms of discrimination, and a clause preventing the destruction of low-cost housing.[53]

Business and apartment block owners, on the other hand, opposed the legislation vigorously. Dr. Perras, head of the Ligue des Propriétaires de Montréal, called Bill 59 "socialistic" and declared that the government had no more business intervening in property rentals than in other sectors of the economy.[54] The Québec Chambre de Commerce argued the government should not interfere in the supply and demand of housing and specifically rejected the 5% ceiling proposed by the law. The Chambre also predicted the legislation would result in an exodus of capital and a drop in the construction of new housing.[55]

In November 1972, the government decided to drop Bill 59 and introduced two new pieces of legislation: Bill 78, "an act respecting the lease of things," and Bill 79, setting up a rent control board. The main difference from Bill 59 was that the 5% ceiling on yearly rent increases was deleted and the burden of proving the unfairness of a rent increase was put on the tenant. Predictably, the tenant groups, the ACEFs, and the unions opposed the new version of the bill. In a joint press conference on November 30, they accused Jérôme Choquette, minister of justice, of giving in to the pressures of business and the owners, and of betraying the interests of the tenant population, which, in Montréal, was estimated at 80%. They also argued that the legislation had lost all its significance and potential impact because of the elimination of the ceiling.

Business and the owner associations, on the other hand, expressed considerable satisfaction with Bills 78 and 79. The Québec Chambre de Commerce, for one, was pleased to see that the new legislation contained "many of our own recommendations" and that the 5% ceiling had been eliminated.[56] At the National Assembly hearings on the legislation in May 1973, the Chambre reiterated its support of the new rental legislation:

> The Chambre de Commerce de la Province de Québec accepts without hesitation the necessity of permanent legislation conducive to better relations between tenants and landlords. In this respect, Bills 78 and 79 appear effective and realistic and reflect a search for equity and justice by maintaining a healthy equilibrium between the necessary intervention of the state and undue administrative control.[57]

There is little doubt that the Québec government responded to the pressures of owners and business in withdrawing Bill 59. According to the *Financial Post,* "The history of the rent control bill introduced last year [Bill 59] was marked by hasty visits to Québec City by real estate brokers, developers, the Montreal Board of Trade and the Chambre de Commerce," and "their extensive briefs contributed to the bill's withdrawal."[58]

In February 1973, the Québec government had to introduce emergency legislation "to stop landlords from raising their rents in an unsubtle flurry."[59] Indeed, after Bill 59 was dropped, and during the debates over Bills 78 and 79, landlords raised their rents in 1973 by an average of 15%. Montréal area tenants alone lodged 50,000 complaints to the Québec rent board during January and February 1973. The public outcry forced the department of justice to pass Bill 280, "a law to prevent abusive increase in rents in 1973." The emergency legislation, however, did not set any ceilings on rent increases; it merely provided for a procedure to allow tenants to appeal increases to the rent board.[60]

Since Bills 78 and 79 could not be passed before the end of the session in which they were introduced in the National Assembly, they were re-introduced at the beginning of the next session as Bills 2 and 3 and passed on December 22, 1973.[61]

Labour Unions, Business, and Government

Chapter 7 demonstrated that senior Québec business leaders were of the opinion that labour was the most influential group in Québec politics. The available evidence did not support this claim. Indeed, despite an unprecedented degree of activism and unity in the sixties and early seventies, Québec labour unions were unsuccessful in modifying the power structure in their favour. Government or business or both succeeded, by and large, in blocking the main demands of unions.

Before discussing in some detail the common front strike, a few examples will be given to show that the effectiveness of strikes has often been undermined because of the difficult atmosphere in which strikes take place. During strikes, unions almost always lose the public relations battle, whether the employer is the government or private enterprise.

In an interdependent economy, any strike in any industrial sector can be made to appear contrary to the public interest and detrimental to the economy as a whole. Most major strikes are usually accompanied by employers' claims that the economy of the area will suffer and jobs will be lost. During the strike at the port of Montreal during the summer of 1972, for example, "management spokesmen repeatedly pointed to the $204 million a year pumped into the Montréal economy by the port and 10,000 jobs which depended on its existence."[62] Jack Crighton, manager of the Shipping Federation of Canada, predicted the strike would have "lasting political and social effects on Montréal," and that layoffs were imminent in the port itself, the trucking industry, shipping firms, railways, and among river pilots. Crighton also raised the spectre of a "permanent move of the grain trade out of the Montréal area," which would "mean the loss of yet another 10,000 jobs in the region."[63]

The 10-month strike at Firestone Tire and Rubber Company in Joliette between March 1973 and January 1974 was another example of the tactics used by companies during strike action. Before the strike, Joliette's Firestone plant had the best record of worker productivity of the company's North American plants, but the salary levels averaged $3 an hour, about $1 less than in Ontario. Being a multinational corporation with 40 plants around the world, Firestone could well afford to support a long strike. In an effort to mobilize public opinion against the strike, the management of Firestone announced in September 1973 it would not go ahead with its $23 million expansion program because of the strike and that 400 new jobs would be lost as a result.[64] This announcement was made two weeks after Firestone's head office in Akron, Ohio, threatened to cancel the expansion program unless the strike ended immediately.[65]

In September 1973, Firestone also promised that major concessions would be made to the workers if they agreed to the firing of the more militant members of their union, who numbered about 30.[66] The workers refused the offer, and the determination of the union eventually won them some significant gains at the bargaining table. Describing the Firestone strike as one of the major victories of Québec labour, Marcel Pépin, president of the CNTU, criticized Québec's department of labour for having been incapable of bringing the company to the bargaining table despite the union's willingness to negotiate.[67]

Business and government agencies also often went out of their way to discredit labour unions vis-à-vis the rest of the population, which includes poorly-paid non-unionized labour, and to blame them for rising prices and other economic problems. After the settlement of the strike at Hydro-Québec in 1973, the *Financial Post* pointed out: "Hydro-Québec announced a stiff rate increase, the first in three years, on February 23, just a week after signing a contract with the Canadian Union of Public Employees on behalf of its 8,500 unionized workers," and that "the coincidence was not meant to go unnoticed."[68]

There was little doubt that the Québec government's attitude towards labour disputes had improved since the Duplessis years. The Union Nationale government in the late forties and fifties was notoriously opposed to labour unions and many examples of collusion between business and government to break strikes had been documented. Perhaps the best-known episode was the Asbestos strike in 1949 at the Johns Manville plant. Pierre Trudeau's *La Grève de l'amiante* described the repressive role played by the Duplessis government during that strike as well as collusion between company executives and government leaders.[69] The attitudes of the Duplessis regime towards strikes were documented in a more general way by H. F. Quinn in *The Union Nationale:*

> The tactics of the Union Nationale were to send a large number of provincial police into any town or area as soon as a strike broke out. On many occasions this action was taken, not at the request of the local municipal authorities, the only ones who legally had the right to ask for such assistance, but at the request of the company involved in the industrial dispute. More often than not, however, the police were used for the purpose of intimidating strikers, arresting their leaders, carrying strikebreakers through picket lines, and doing everything possible to break the strike.[70]

The former president of a pulp and paper company mentioned an episode in the fifties where, at his request, "Duplessis sent police and strongmen to keep the gates open and to make the strikers behave at the company's Laurentide plant in Shawinigan Falls." He said: "The Duplessis government was useful in keeping labour quiet."[71] This was not to say that the Québec government no longer intervenes directly to prevent strikes. An executive of the Aluminum Company of Canada said the government granted an injunction to his company forcing the workers back to work at the company's strike-bound plant in Arvida in May 1973. This was apparently done two days after the company had asked Jean Cournoyer to intervene by granting an injunction.[72] In general, the executive from Aluminum Company of Canada considered that the "Bourassa government is very good in standing up to the activists in the labour unions."[73]

The strike in the Québec public service sector by a common front composed of all civil servants, teachers, and other employees of state institutions was the best example of a concerted attempt by Québec labour unions to improve their relative power position. Superficially, the public service strike in April 1972 involved a "war of nerves" between the unions and the government. In reality, however, the issues were much broader. Business felt threatened because it knew that if the government gave in to the demand of the unions for a $100 a week minimum, the result would be substantial union pressure on the private sector to pay the same wages. Thus, in many ways, it was not just the wages and working conditions of 210,000 public employees and teachers that were involved, but also the overall wage structure and distribution of income in Québec.

In addition to wanting the government to hold the line on wage increases, business wanted the Bourassa administration to crack down on the growing militancy of the Québec unions. The businessmen interviewed in the Fantus Report, which was submitted to the Québec government a few weeks before the strike, pointed to the activism and politicization of labour unions as one of the main factors inhibiting the establishment of new plants in Québec or the expansion of existing facilities.[74] To quote the report: "The growing militancy of the leadership of major labour federations is a source of deep concern in the Québec business community."[75] The businessmen made it plain that they wanted the government to stabilize the labour situation. One of the executives of a beer company asked for "a tough attitude by the government towards solving labour problem;"[76] a large dairy producer also urged the government to "take a firm stand with the union element in Québec."[77]

The available evidence suggested that senior businessmen had an unjustified prejudice concerning the degree of activism or militancy of Québec labour unions. Thus, according to the Fantus Report, the negative attitudes of businessmen "are particularly unfortunate in view of the lack of any concrete evidence that labour disputes have been more frequent or more severe in Québec than elsewhere in Canada:"[78]

> In fact, the data available on strike activity strongly supports the opposite conclusion . . . In proportion to union membership, there was considerably less strike activity in Québec than in Canada as a whole. The time lost due to work stoppages in Canada during the 31-month period from January 1969 to July 1971 averages out to 7.6 days per union member. In Québec, the time lost per union member amounts to 4.9 days or about 50% below the Canadian average . . . During each of the past three years, the amount of time lost has been greater in Ontario both numerically and in proportion to the size of the work force.[79]

During the public service negotiations in 1972, 210,000 unionized government employees, including civil servants, nurses, liquor board personnel, teachers, Hydro-Québec employees, were negotiating collectively with the Québec government for the first time. The three main unions, the CNTU, QFL, and QTC, each of which represented certain categories of workers, had decided to bargain jointly with the government in an effort to obtain better and more uniform conditions for their members. They felt that their main demand of $100 weekly minimum as well as their desire to negotiate the government's overall wage policy could be more adequately dealt with at a central bargaining table. After several months of fruitless negotiations, the unions held a strike vote in March 1972, in which the membership voted overwhelmingly to strike. After several more weeks of negotiation, the common front called for a full-scale work stoppage by its members. The 11-day strike which followed was ended by the passage of a back-to-work law by the Québec National Assembly.

Bill 19, the back-to-work law, passed on April 21 after 24 hours of non-stop debate in the National Assembly, provided for one more month of negotiations but stipulated that the government could impose a settlement by simple decree, in the event no agreement had been reached with the unions within the period. Bill 19 also provided for fines of from $5,000 to $50,000 per day to be levied on unions and union officials who defied the back-to-work order.

The common front leaders decided to respect the law, even though a hastily-called vote on the night of April 21 showed that about 60% of the membership was prepared to defy the law by continuing the strike. In the following weeks, strikers who had defied earlier injunctions were brought to trial, fined, and jailed. The sentences were unusually heavy; several hospital workers were fined $5,000 in addition to being jailed for six months. This culminated in the indictments of the presidents of the three labour unions involved in the common front on charges of having urged their members to defy court injunctions.

The sentencing of each of the three labour leaders to one year in jail provoked the most massive labour walkouts in Québec history. The walkouts, which occurred between May 9 and May 17, involved not only the public service employees of the Québec government but also many workers from the private sector and the municipalities.[80] During the period, nine town halls as well as a dozen private radio stations, including in Joliette, Thetford Mines, and St. Jérôme, were occupied by unionized workers. After a week of strikes, union leaders called for a return to work. Several months later, pressured by the likelihood of a binding government decree, the unions agreed to a settlement with the Québec government. Although the settlement represented some significant gains over the government's original offers, "the common front," as the *Financial Times* put it, "failed to achieve its basic objectives."[81]

One of the conclusions that can be drawn from the common front experience is that even a unified labour movement is often weak. Largely because of financial limitations, the common front had to concentrate its publicity on maintaining solidarity within the front — an objective it largely achieved — and completely lost the battle for public opinion. The government, on the other hand, "launched a massive propaganda compaign extolling the generosity of its offers."[82] According to Nick Auf der Maur of the *Last Post:*

> The campaign was led by a well-paid force of recently-hired journalists pumping out the government side of the issue to the public. They [the government] spent a fortune on a glossy, multi-colored 32-page brochure entitled "L'Important" which was inserted in almost every paper in the province. They took on countless newspaper ads aimed at specific groups of workers, always implying they would be better off on their own.[83]

Once the strike was over, the Ligue des Droits de l'Homme (the Québec equivalent of the Civil Liberties Union) criticized the Québec government for not providing the population with adequate information on the *raison d'être* for the crisis and on the unfolding of its main episodes, and for thus forcing the population to judge the conflict without having been properly informed. The Ligue considered this was particularly serious in that social equilibrium was the ultimate stake in the common front strike.[84] There was also some evidence of a boycott of union publicity by private media. The board of directors of Montreal's channel 10, for example, decided to block a television message by the common front leaders which was scheduled for 11 p.m. on May 8. The action was taken even though the contract had already been signed and the time paid for by the common front. The director of the station gave no reason for the cancellation.[85]

Throughout the strike, the labour leaders argued that the government's main negotiating strategy was to hold the line on wages to protect private enterprise. The government at first denied the claim. During the negotiations, however, the common front offered to reduce substantially demands for the highest paid workers so that the acceptance of the $100 minimum would not cost the government any additional money. Garneau told the labour leaders the government could not accept such a demand because it would force private enterprise to pay the same minimum.[86] The credibility of the labour leaders' claim that the government was above all interested in protecting private enterprise was strengthened when a private government document concerning the governmental objectives in the negotiations was leaked to the press in July 1973. The 60-page report prepared before the negotiations by a group of Québec civil servants stated that one of the key principles underlying the government's wage policy and negotiating strategy should be to avoid setting any precedents prejudicial to the salary scale of private enterprise.[87]

Similarly, the Fantus Report confirmed the labour leaders' suspicions that the government had been told by business to crack down on union militancy and that the common front crisis had been a test case. According to Claude Girard, vice-president of the CNTU:

> The [Fantus] Report confirms . . . that the Bourassa government is manipulated by large companies and that the decisions are taken according to the interests of economic power rather than according to those of the Québec collectivity . . . We now understand why this government has passed laws such as Bill 19, why it has imposed severe penalties on labour leaders, why it has put the presidents of the unions in jail and why it is now preparing to pass Bill 89.[88]

Bourassa's statement to the *Financial Post* concerning the common front strike that "the unions learned a lesson last year"[89] lends credence to the hypothesis that the government was out to put a damper on union activism.

Predictably, business was very satisfied with Bill 19 and the government's attitude during the common front strike. Thus, 99.3% of the businessmen who responded to the questionnaire expressed support for Bill 19. The Québec Chambre de Commerce, for one, congratulated the government for the "firmness with which it protected the health and security of citizens,"[90] and transmitted to the government "the general satisfaction of the Chambre's membership regarding the way the government handled negotiations with public employees in recent months."[91] The CMA urged the government to "maintain its no-nonsense attitude;; and to "carry it through even after the present crisis is resolved."[92]

Following the common front crisis, the Québec government maintained its hard line against the unions. For example, in May 1972, it introduced amendments to Bill 64, a piece of legislation which had been introduced in July 1971, to make it more difficult for farmers to unionize. The original version of Bill 64 required that 60% of all farmers had to vote, and that 60% of those who voted had to be favourable to unionization in order for the union to be accredited or officially recognized. The new version required a cumulative majority of two-thirds;[93] most observers considered it would be next to impossible to obtain these majorities, especially considering the geographical dispersion of farmers. Ryan sharply criticized the amendment, claiming it set up too stringent requirements; in fact, he argued, the require-ments, were harsher than those ensuring the government's own legitimacy, which, he estimated, was based on the consent of some 30% of the total electorate.[94]

Bill 73, which forced Hydro-Québec employees back to work in November 1973 was another example. The government claimed the law was passed to ensure essential services. The strike, however, had caused no major inconvenience to Hydro customers, and the employees themselves had promised to maintain essential services. Further, the government's legislation forced *all* Hydro employees back to work, regardless of whether they were essential to the maintenance of the service. *Le Devoir* editorialist Laurent Laplante put it this way:

> By forcing back to work only those workers who repair breakdowns, the government would have satisfied the legitimate concerns of the public. It was not necessary to go further. By going beyond the limits in such a scandalous manner, the government sought to achieve results which have nothing to do with the needs of the public. It permitted the administration of Hydro-Québec to avoid economic pressures.[95]

To conclude this discussion of social and labour legislation, it should be repeated that labour and other social groups had made some gains in the 1960-1974 period. Consumer protection and environmental legislation, however limited in scope and ineffectual, were better than no legislation at all. It remained true, nonetheless, that groups other than business found it particularly difficult to obtain satisfactory governmental outputs. Business, on the other hand, even if often impatient with the activism of labour, had, by and large, expressed considerable satisfaction with most governmental initiatives in the labour and social arenas. Much of the government legislation in these areas seemed designed primarily not to offend the susceptibilities of business.

NOTES

(1) Gabriel Kolko, *Wealth and Power in America: An Analysis of Social Class and Income Distribution* (New York: Praeger Books, 1962), p. 3.

(2) Ibid., p. 15. See table 1: "Percentage of National Personal Income Received by Each Income-Tenth."

(3) Ibid., p. 15. Kolko backed up his point by a detailed statistical discussion (pp. 15-29). He estimated that undeclared income would add an additional 3 to 5% to the highest deciles' total income, and that corporate expense accounts would add at least another 1%.

(4) Dominion Bureau of Statistics, *Income Distribution 1951-65*, catalogue no. 13-529 (occasional) (Ottawa: Queen's Printer, 1969), table 12, p. 78. Figures included unattached individuals as well as families.

(5) Commission d'Enquête sur la Santé et le Bien-être, *Rapport de la Commission d'Enquête sur la Santé et le Bien-être*, vol. 4 (Québec: Editeur Officiel du Québec, 1972), p. 30.

(6) Ibid., vol. 5, p. 48.

(7) Ibid., p. 43. The social benefits reached a peak of 6.0% in the 1960-63 period and then declined somewhat.

(8) Ibid., pp. 42-43. The report noted that in 1969, fully 52% of social benefits were in the form of universal plans, such as family allowances and pension plans, applying equally to all citizens. (pp. 22-23). It revealed that 36% of the Québec population could be considered "poor," i.e., did not have the "vital minimum," and that 70% of the poor were not welfare recipients but wage earners (pp. 11-12).

(9) Léon Dion, in a speech delivered at the Conseil du Patronat annual meeting on May 26, 1972, entitled "L'Entreprise et la société québécoise," stated: ". . . On sait que, malgré tous les efforts des gouvernements et ceux, beaucoup plus timides, des grandes entreprises elles-mêmes, les écarts dans la répartition des biens économiques entre les couches sociales sont demeurés substantiellement aussi grands qu'il y a cinquante ans et que dans certains cas, ils se sont même accrus: malgré certaines apparences, les riches deviennent toujours plus riches, et la situation des pauvres, si elle ne s'aggrave généralement pas, reste stationnaire" (p. 1).

(10) Birnbaum, p. 78.

(11) The same seemed to be true in the case of the Québec Health Insurance Plan which began in 1970. Most of the businessmen interviewed by *La Presse* reporter Rhéal Bercier said they favoured the plan ("Bourassa un an après," *La Presse*, 30 April 1971).

(12) Here again, major companies seemed less reticent vis-à-vis state intervention than secondary companies. Thus, 84.2% of the senior company executives, compared with 63.0% of the secondary company executives, favoured government initiative in resolving social problems.

(13) Domhoff, *The Higher Circles*, p. 178.

(14) Claude Castonguay, speech at St. Laurent Kiwanis Club, 1970.

(15) Information from Rhéal Bercier, "La Guerre est déclarée entre les ACEFs et Québec," *La Presse*, 21 March 1972, and "Faute de fonds, les ACEFs menacent de se saborder à leur prochain congrès," *La Presse*, 30 June 1973.

(16) Ellen Roseman of the *Financial Post* told how the 90,000-member Consumers Association of Canada (CAC) could not intervene at the Canadian Transport Commission hearings in Ottawa in 1972 because they did not have the $20,000 necessary to pay for lawyers, research, transcripts, and transportation to Ottawa. An executive of the CAC was quoted as saying that "the regulatory agencies are set up to be guardians of the public interest," but that, in fact, "they never speak to the public; they only speak to the people they regulate" (Do Consumers Have a Fighting Change?" *Financial Post*, 24 February 1973).

(17) In 1972-73, the ACEFs received $92,000 from the Fédération des Oeuvres. According to Pierre Godin, the federation was under heavy pressure from finance companies to stop "financing the revolution" ("Fédération: la rue Saint-Jacques devra partager son pouvoir avec les syndicats," *Québec-Presse*, 29 April 1973).

(18) Rhéal Bercier, "La Guerre est déclarée." The CNTU, for one, was sharply critical of the governmental decision. It claimed the government was trying to prevent citizens from organizing themselves as consumers because of pressure from the finance companies (*La Presse*, "La Réforme des structures aura la priorité," 16 March 1972).

(19) Clément Trudel, "L'ACEF devra réduire ses activités, Québec ayant coupé ses subventions," *Le Devoir*, 22 September 1972.

(20) Ibid.

(21) Maurice Roy, "La Situation du consommateur québécois est dramatique," *Québec-Presse*, 25 October 1970.

(22) See, for example, the position of the QFL, *Un Seul Front*, p. 31.

(23) Louis-Bernard Robitaille, "Les ACEFs en ont assez de faire du patchage," *Québec-Presse*, 7 November 1971.

(24) Montreal Board of Trade, *Annual Report: 1970-1971* (Montréal: Board of Trade, 1971), p. 5; and La Chambre de Commerce de la Province de Québec, *Bulletin sur la législation provinciale* (Montréal: Chambre de Commerce de la Province de Québec, June 1972), p. 4.

(25) The nomination was criticized by the ACEFs and unions. See Roy, "La Situation du consommateur."

(26) In a speech at the Richelieu Club in Montreal, Perrault said he was sceptical about the role of the state in the area of consumer protection. This attitude was surely unusual, coming from a member of the Consumer Protection Council. See Renée Rowan, "Le Président du CPQ est sceptique quant au rôle de l'état dans le secteur de la consommation," *Le Devoir*, 9 November 1972.

(27) La Presse Canadienne, "Le Conseil de la protection du consommateur se dit incapable de remplir son rôle," *La Presse*, 26 September 1972.

(28) Gérald Leblanc, "Le Premier rapport de l'Office de protection du consommateur: un pas dans la bonne voie," *Le Devoir*, 11 April 1973.

(29) Louise Tassé, "Une Poursuite en un an," *Québec-Presse*, 1 October 1972.

(30) It is important to keep in mind the distinction between credit (caisses populaires, for example) and agricultural cooperatives (Coopérative Agricole de Granby, for example) on the one hand — where workers are simply the employees of the cooperative which is owned jointly by many individuals or groups — and production cooperatives on the other hand — where workers are owners or partners.

(31) Guy St. Pierre quoted in Ian Rodger, "How Guy St. Pierre Hopes to Save Québec Capitalism," *Financial Post*, 18 March 1972.

(32) Groupe de Recherche Economique, *Coopératives de production, usines populaires et pouvoir ouvrier* (Montréal: Editions Québécoises, 1973).

(33) See chapter 2.

(34) Sogefor was wholly-owned by the General Investment Corporation, which in turn, was wholly-owned by the Québec government.

(35) Réal Pelletier, "Saint-Pierre: La SGF a assaini le Conseil de Dupan en excluant deux employés syndiqués" *La Presse*, 20 May 1973.

(36) Pierre Vallières, "Les Travailleurs renoncent à la coop pour reprendre l'action militante," *Le Devoir*, 18 June 1974.

(37) The studies were done by two consulting firms — Morelli, Gaudette and Laporte Ltd. and Monarque Ltd.

(38) According to Joseph Landry, mayor of Cabano, "While we were talking with them [Sybetra], big paper companies were lobbying in Ottawa and Québec to discourage governments from giving us financial aid on the grounds that world markets were already saturated with cardboard" (quoted in Claude Arpin, "Cabano's Long Struggle Nears Happy Ending," *Montreal Star*, 27 December 1974).

Further, *Québec-Presse* (25 June 1972) claimed that Maurice Sauvé, former Liberal cabinet minister and vice-president of Consolidated-Bathurst, lobbied against the project in Ottawa, and that Walter Lavigne, associate deputy minister of regional economic expansion and a friend of Sauvé's was responsible for delaying the government subsidy.

(39) Interview, May 1973.

(40) *Le Devoir*, "Dès avril Québec voulait rompre toute négociation avec la Sybetra jugée peu sérieuse et incompétente," 26 July 1973.

(41) André Déom was also the former president of the Centre des Dirigeants d'Entreprise.

(42) Canadian Press, "Cabano Mill to Open in 1976," *Montreal Star*, 14 June 1974.

(43) See chapter 10 for discussion of this economic institution.

(44) See Claude Arpin, "Cabano's Long Struggle." The board of directors of the Cabano mill will be made up of two members from each of the four partners — two each from Papiers Cascades, Rexfor, the caisses populaires, and the local population.

(45) As Landry put it: "What we wanted was a company which would have been 100 per cent owned by the people and workers, but as we negotiated we soon realized that this can't be done without more sympathetic governments who are willing to buy this kind of notion and who want to back the people" (quoted by Claude Arpin, "Cabano's Long Struggle").

(46) For information, see Jacques Forget, "Tembec," *Perspectives*, 10 August 1974, and Tim Dickson, "Tembec: A Dream Comes True for Québec Town," *Financial Post*, 15 September 1973.

(47) See chapter 10 for discussion of the Québec government's subsidy to ITT-Rayonnier to build a multi-million dollar plant in Port-Cartier.

(48) During the negotiations, a flareup occurred between CIP and the unemployed mill workers. The company had decided to float 150,000 cords of pulp wood which had been lying idle for more than a year, downriver to the CIP mill in Gatineau. The workers decided to block the operation for over a week. Without the wood, Tembec could not have started production for at least another year because the cutting season was already past. See Dickson, "A Dream Comes True." According to Carpenter, CIP wanted to move its wood in an effort to blackmail the Québec government in the negotiations. See Louis Fournier, "Qui mène le Québec? International Paper ou le Premier Ministre Robert Bourassa?" *Québec-Presse*, 22 July 1973.

(49) According to Parizeau and Carpenter, the plant was worth at the most $800,000; the timber concessions, which CIP leased from the Québec government at a moderate price, were also considered overpriced. Ibid.

(50) Jacques Parizeau, "Les Bizarreries de Tembec," *Québec-Presse*, 17 March 1974.

(51) Ibid.

(52) A confidential report submitted to the department of justice by Gaston Massé, vice-president of the rent board, indicated that 56% of apartment building owners in Montréal were making net profits exceeding 15%. See Pierre Paul Gagné, "Louer des appartements, un commerce qui rapporte bien," *La Presse*, 25 January 1973.

(53) The brief submitted to the Québec government by the Québec Teachers' Corporation was typical. It manifested no enthusiasm but accepted the legislation as a step in the right direction: "Nous constatons avec intérêt que le gouvernement a fait des pas en avant dans la protection des locataires" [Québec Teachers Corporation, *Mémoire sur le projet de code des loyers présenté à la commission parlementaire permanente de la justice* (Québec City: Québec Teachers Corporation, 1972).

(54) Quoted in Claude Gravel, "Les Locataires et le Bill 59," *La Presse*, 8 September 1972.

(55) Chambre de Commerce de la Province de Québec, *La Législation provinciale*, vol. 10, no. 5, (Montréal: Chambre de Commerce de la Province de Québec, August 1973), p. 23.

(56) Chambre de Commerce de la Province de Québec, *La Législation Provinciale*, vol. 11, no. 2 (Montréal: Chambre de Commerce de la Province de Québec, January 1973), p. 9.

(57) Chambre de Commerce de la Province de Québec, *La Législation Provinciale*, vol. 11, no. 4 (Montréal: Chambre de Commerce de la province de Québec, May 1973), p. 3.

(58) Jane Davidson, "Rent Controls: Will They Really Work," *Financial Post*, 10 March 1973.

(59) Ibid.

(60) Ibid.

(61) It should be pointed out that, even though the Québec government was responsive to the wishes of the owners in the case of its rent control legislation, several provinces — including Ontario — had no rent control legislation at all.

(62) Kendal Windeyer, "Port Strike: What We Have Lost is Going to Stay Lost," *Montreal Gazette*, 14 June 1972.

(63) Quoted ibid.

(64) Pierre Richard, "Firestone réglerait contre la tête des chefs syndicaux," *Le Devoir*, 21 September 1973.

The *Montreal Gazette*, which is generally considered a probusiness newspaper, accused Firestone in an editorial of "multinational arrogance" ("Multinational Arrogance," 21 September 1973). The newspaper argued that the demands of the union were reasonable (i.e., wages closer to but still not equalling those paid to their counterparts in Ontario, notice of technological changes, guarantees that these changes would not eliminate existing jobs, and help in adapting to such changes) and that Firestone's cancellation announcement looked "like nothing so much as the spoiled child taking his marbles home when his playmates won't abide by his rules."

(65) Similarly, during a strike at United Aircraft's Longueuil plant, the company took out full page ads in Montréal daily newspapers saying the 5,300 jobs provided by the company would be in jeopardy if the union did not accept the company's offers quickly. The advertisement, which was entitled "Les Emplois sont en jeu" (jobs are in jeopardy), was published on February 22, 1974, the same day the United Aircraft workers were voting on the company's latest offers. Despite the intimidation, the workers rejected the offers.

(66) Richard, "Firestone réglerait."

(67) Marcel Pépin, "Le Conflit de Firestone a marqué la fin du 'cheap labor' québécois pour multinationales," *La Presse*, 19 January 1974.

(68) *Financial Post*, "Labor Settlement Pushes Up Québec Power Rates," 28 April 1973.

(69) See Pierre E. Trudeau, ed., *La Grève de l'amiante* (Montréal: Editions Cité Libre, 1956).

(70) H. F. Quinn, *The Union Nationale* (Toronto: University of Toronto Press, 1963), p. 94.

(71) Interview, May 1973.

(72) Interview, May 1973.

(73) Interview, May 1973.

(74) The Fantus Company. One of the executives of a large construction company stated he would not locate in Québec bacause of the "irresponsibility of organized labour" (p. 17). The head of a large mining firm claimed his company "would consider expansion outside Québec, due to the attitudes of Messrs. Pépin, Laberge, Chartrand, etc." (p. 16).

(75) Ibid., p. 112. The Fantus Report, however, found that the availability and relatively low cost of labour in Québec (as opposed to Ontario or the U.S.) as well as the quality of the work force were the main "industrial location advantages of Québec" (p. 4). As the head of a U.S. petroleum firm put it, "Québec has the highest unemployment and generally lowest wages than any other province in Canada. This is a strong competitive factor" (p. 70).

(76) Ibid., p. 45.

(77) Ibid., p. 31.

(78) Ibid., p. 112.

(79) Ibid., p. 112. The data presented by the *Financial Times* ("Perspectives on Québec," 19 November 1973) supported the conclusion that the time lost through strike and lockouts had been substantially lower in Québec than in the rest of Canada.

(80) They included, among others, workers from Domtar, CIP, General Motors, ITT, Carnation Foods, Weston, Aluminum Company of Canada, Canadair, Montreal and Québec City daily newspapers, Steinberg's, Dominion Stores, Imperial Tobacco, Firestone, Robin Hood Multifoods, Christie, mining companies in Thetford, Gaspé, and Asbestos, Regent Knitting, Davies Shipbuilding, Canadian Reynolds Aluminum, Quebec North Shore Paper, and Continental Can. Blue-collar workers from the cities of Montréal and Québec, most construction workers, and French CBC employees were also involved.

(81) *Financial Times*, "Perspectives on Québec." For a detailed history of the common front strike, see Nick Auf der Maur, "The May Revolt," *Last Post*, vol. 2, no. 6, July 1972.

(82) Auf der Maur, "The May Revolt," p. 14.

(83) Ibid.

(84) Ligue des Droits de l'Homme, "La Responsabilité de l'état dans la crise actuelle," *Le Devoir*, 17 May 1972.

(85) See François Trépanier, Le Front dénonce le réseau TVA pour son refus de diffuser un de ses messages," *La Presse*, 9 May 1972.

(86) Don MacPherson, "Front Leaders Attack Garneau," *Montreal Star*, 25 April 1972. Previously, the government was saying it could not accept the $100 weekly minimum because it would cost too much.

(87) *Le Devoir*, "Marcel Pépin révèle une stratégie du gouvernement," 4 July 1973. In July 1973, Auf der Maur claimed that in asking for the $100 minimum, "labour had clashed head on with the very real interests of business," and that "what might have been an ordinary collective bargaining struggle was transformed into a political confrontation with a government pledged to safeguard a system based on profit" ("The May Revolt," p. 13).

(88) Quoted in *La Presse*, "Le Rapport Fantus: du chantage, " 26 March 1973.

(89) Quoted in Amy Booth, "Capital Spending Signals New Buoyancy in Québec," *Financial Post*, 31 March 1973.

(90) It should be noted that the Chambre de Commerce supported the doctors in their strike when the Québec government introduced its health insurance scheme in 1970. The "Health and security of citizens" seemed to be a secondary consideration for the Chambre when dealing with the doctors' strike.

(91) Chambre de Commerce de la Province de Québec, *Législation Provinciale*, vol. 10, no. 3 (Montréal: Chambre de Commerce de la Province de Québec, May 1972), p. 3.

(92) Canadian Manufacturers' Association, *An Industrial Policy for Quebec* (Montréal: Canadian Manufacturers' Association, August 1972), app. G. p. 2.

(93) The Conseil du Patronat and the Coopérative Fédérée, among others, had asked for harsher accreditation mechanisms for the farmers' union in the briefs which they submitted after Bill 64 was introduced.

(94) Claude Ryan, "Le Volte-face du gouvernement sur le bill 64," editorial, *Le Devoir*, 6 May 1972. A La Presse Canadienne report (Les Libéraux craignent que l'UCC ne devienne une nouvelle force syndicale."

La Presse, 23 May 1972) noted that the requirements set up by the Bourassa government to allow the Union des Producteurs Agricoles to become the official spokesman for 50,000 farmers became more stringent at the same time as the unions were accentuating their protest against Bill 19. Despite the harsh requirements, however, the farmers succeeded in obtaining the necessary double two-thirds majority to obtain recognition for their union.

(95) Laurent Laplante, "Une Loi simpliste et abusive," editorial, *Le Devoir*, 16 November 1973.

CHAPTER 10

ECONOMIC POLICY

IN RECENT DECADES, the state has become increasingly involved in the economy of advanced industrial societies. It has intervened on a permanent basis in the planning of the economy and in performing, as Birnbaum put it, the "coordinating and steering functions."[1] The economic role of the state has taken on many facets: through monetary and fiscal policies, governments have attempted to stabilize economic cycles; through infrastructural spending (building roads and railways, providing cheap electricity, and setting up national communications networks), governments have sought to stimulate economic growth and encourage investment from the private sector; and through subsidies, tariffs, tax exemptions, and other measures, governments have also provided assistance to specific companies or industrial sectors.

By and large, the increasing participation of the state in the economy has been more a response to the needs of business than a manifestation of the desire to develop an economic power base autonomous from the private sector. The idea of economic planning, for example, has taken shape because of business rather than government initiative. Allen Fenton of *Canadian Business* argued in 1963: "Many of the pleas for a more rational approach to economic development have come from the ranks of management."[2] In Britain, the "initiative came from the Federation of British Industries, representing mainly the biggish businessman and upwards."[3] Similarly, in Canada, Fenton found growing pressure from the business community "for some form of planning program and with it a rationalization of our economic affairs." The need for planning arose from the "slow rate of growth in recent years which has created problems of relatively high unemployment, unused production facilities, balance of payments problems, government deficits."[4] More recently, the CMA, in a brief to the Québec government, clarified the attitude of business towards government intervention in the economy:

> . . . We recognize that some degree of direct government involvement is a prerequisite of the normal operations of the contemporary mixed private-public economic system which has evolved in Canada, as well as in most Western countries. Overall government responsibility for economic management and supplementary direct government action through the market place is recognized by the majority of Canadian businessmen as essential and desirable.[5]

The discussion of business ideology in chapter 4 demonstrated that the overwhelming majority of senior businessmen had moved away from *laisser-faire* capitalism. It also showed that business had a precise idea of what the economic role of the state should be. Thus, approximately 85% of the respondents to the questionnaire thought the government's main economic function should be to create conditions favourable to the growth of the private sector. A study by Laurent Bélanger of the ideology of business in Québec, which was sponsored by the Privy Council Office in Ottawa, arrived at a similar conclusion:

> The government intervention which business leaders find acceptable is closely linked to the principle of free enterprise. The desired intervention consists in the creation and maintenance by the state of an infrastructure which will lead to profitable operations; in the promotion of monetary and fiscal policies seeking to maintain an adequate level of demand for goods and services, to encourage full employment of human and physical resources, to keep inflation within acceptable limits . . .[6]

In short, business had shed its traditional negative attitude towards the state and sought instead to use the state to its advantage. In the process, however, business had continued to reject any governmental attempts to control or limit its economic power. As evident in the discussion of business ideology, an overwhelming majority of businessmen were opposed to "price fixing to control monopoly power," and to any "governmental initiative to regulate profits."[7]

One can now ask what attitude the government took towards these "demands" of business and to what extent the government's behaviour in the economic field was compatible with and responsive to the expressed needs of business. In his analysis of the Canadian state in *Our Generation,* Rick Deaton argued that the public sector played a predominantly supportive role towards private enterprise:

> Historically the public sector in Canada developed to complement and meet the needs of the private profit-making sector of the economy. The public sector of the economy developed to build the necessary technical infrastructure (supportive services) for the corporate sector, to generate investment to encourage profitable business activity and opportunities, to meet the social overhead costs of private profit-making production, and to socialize (make public) the private costs and risks of production, thereby protecting and expanding profits. The public sector of the economy has developed in such a way as to directly and indirectly support and meet corporate needs so that there are public costs and private benefits of production in the private profit-making sector.[8]

This study of Québec did not attempt to verify Deaton's ambitious hypothesis. It sought rather to determine, on the basis of the government's economic activities in the last decade, what orientation the Québec government's policies towards business had taken and what interests had been served by its economic initiatives. Particular emphasis was placed on the economic institutions created by the Québec government since 1962, that is, Hydro-Québec, Québec Deposit and Investment Fund, and General Investment Corporation. An attempt was made to determine if, as was often claimed, these institutions represented an economic power base for the government, and Québec's population, or if they were, rather, primarily conceived as adjuncts to private enterprise. The general hypothesis in the discussion that follows was that, despite increased government spending and intervention in economic affairs, the Québec government had played primarily a service role towards business and had not significantly increased its own power. Put another way, the increasing economic activities of the Québec state in the last decade did not provide a serious challenge to the economic power of private enterprise.

The first indicator of the Québec government's economic role was the way the members of the government themselves conceived that role. Most of the statements of Québec politicians in the 1960-1974 period supported the conception of government as a "stabilizer," a regulator, and an adjunct to business. To quote Johnson, "The role of the state is not to substitute itself for private enterprise, but to help it, sustain it, orient it, surround it with a climate of confidence and stability, stimulate it . . ."[9] In 1972, St. Pierre wrote in *Le Devoir:*

> The basis of the doctrine of neo-liberalism includes the necessity for the state to intervene in the unfolding of industrial activity without going as far as the compulsory planning feared by private enterprise . . . The Québec government remains convinced that private enterprise, operating in the framework of progressive legislation, remains the best alternative to develop Québec's industrial potential.[10]

St. Pierre went on to define some of the economic priorities of the Québec government: the defense and protection of its companies' markets, the creation of a system to provide risk capital for Québec businessmen, a program to develop high technology industry, and measures to encourage and facilitate exports. In the end, however, the Québec government would continue to rely on the goodwill of private enterprise for the improvement of its industrial structure:

> The Québec government . . . calls upon the private sector to develop a secondary sector, particularly manufacturing, which must double in Québec in the coming years. For too long Québec has been a land dominated by primary industry and has delivered its natural resources without transforming them.[11]

As can be seen from the above statements, there was a substantial degree of compatibility between business expectations and governmental intentions with regards to economic policy. In fact, many government leaders readily admitted that, because of the economic system of private enterprise, the potential impact of the economic policies of the state was limited. Hence St. Pierre said:

> The nature of our economic system limits the impact of state policies in the industrial and commercial domains. In large part, the key decisions in industry and commerce are taken in the private sector and are dependent on the market mechanism. Furthermore, multinational corporations have a process of decision-making which can be completely independent of the industrial and commercial policies of the countries in which they have settled.[12]

Similarly, in an interview in *Québec-Presse,* Bourassa stated that his government's "operating margin" was "very thin."[13]

As in the case of language and social and labour policy, business continually reminded the Québec government that future economic development and investments depended on economic policies favourable to business and on the maintenance of a good investment climate. In a 1970 study, the General Council of Industry told the government it would "be futile — and, ultimately, self-defeating — for Québec to adopt a course involving nationalization of the means of production or an undue expansion of the public sector of its economy." The GCI also told the government: "An unequivocal declaration by the provincial authorities of the principles which will guide Québec's economic policies in the future would go a long way towards creating a climate conducive to increased private investment."[14] R. B. MacPherson, chief economist of Du Pont, was even blunter; he told the Canadian and Québec governments that the Canadian textile industry could create 12% of the total jobs needed in Canada, and 20% in the case of Québec, if it was provided with favourable incentive measures by the governments.[15]

Before analysing some of the Québec government's concrete economic policies in specific areas, including legislation dealing with the pulp and paper industry, the budget, services to industry, and state economic institutions, I will examine briefly how the economic power of the corporations made it very difficult for the government to have a significant impact in the development of the province.

As regards regional development and plant close-downs, for example, the government's capacity to intervene effectively was limited. As demonstrated in the previous chapter, the government was powerless to prevent a company from closing or moving one of its plants. At best, and usually under exceptional circumstances, it could subsidize a plant to keep it open or it could finance an attempt by a new group, cooperative or otherwise, to reopen a plant. As the president of a chemical company put it: "When we phase out a plant, we do not negotiate with the government; we keep them informed."[16] Similarly, the government was powerless to prevent layoffs; the government could do nothing to stop key companies (Domtar, General Motors, Regent Knitting, and Northern Electric, among others) from cutting down the size of their work forces in the early seventies.

The government was, in many ways, at the mercy of the companies as regards regional development. A study of the St. Henri district of Montréal showed how corporate decision-making transformed a relatively prosperous area of the city into an impoverished slum area.[17] Thus, between 1900 and World War II, many important companies, such as RCA Victor, Stelco, Johnson Wire, and Imperial Tobacco, built plants in St. Henri and provided the local population with better than average incomes and working conditions. After the war, a large number of key companies left the district and were replaced by smaller companies paying lower wages. After 1960, important layoffs by many companies further contributed to its economic decay. It is estimated that since 1966, a total of 30 companies either left St. Henri or transferred important parts of their operations. Throughout this process, the government was a passive observer, contenting itself with providing unemployment insurance or social welfare to an increasingly large proportion of the population.

As a result of the crucial importance of corporations to the welfare of the population, particularly in areas where one or a few companies are responsible for most of the industrial activity, governments are often put in a position of a deferential suitor, courting business for its favours. In a full page advertisement in the *Financial Post* in 1961, for example, the Québec government described the investment climate of the province to potential investors:

> A richly endowed province, Québec provides power, labour and raw materials in abundance . . .
> Its people are noted for their ready adaptability to technological advances . . .
> Soundness of its government is a guarantee of freedom of enterprise, harmonious social conditions, equal opportunities for all.[18]

A March 1971 ad in the *Institutional Investor*, entitled "Here We Talk Profits," explained to investors how Québec was "incredibly rich in natural resources and enjoyed an abundance of vital hydro-electric power," and how it "offered unique profit opportunities for the investor."[19]

Another indicator of the Québec government's limited power in the economic arena was that financial institutions which operated in Québec and obtained their funds in the province, such as bank deposits, insurance policies, and trust funds, were under no obligation to reinvest those funds in Québec. In a speech to the Chambre de Commerce, St. Pierre stated that from 1968 to 1971, internal savings in Québec had been higher than total investments, but that Québec had nonetheless been forced to rely on substantial amounts of foreign capital, because much of the savings were being transferred out of the province by financial institutions and companies.[20]

Attempts by the Québec government to influence the direction of the investments by financial institutions encountered the wall of corporate secrecy. One of the executives of the Canadian Bankers' Association said that William Tetley, minister of financial institutions and cooperatives, had attempted repeatedly to get information on the Québec operations of the major banks but that this had been refused. Said the CBA executive: "We went through a long period of discussion with him, and after a few months he eventually gave up."[21] The absence of precise figures with regard to the financial activities of banks and other financial institutions made it almost impossible for the Québec government to set up any kind of controls or guidelines with respect to private investments.[22]

The Bell Tlephone hearings at the Canadian Transport Commission in 1972 and 1973 were another example of the negative effects of corporate secrecy. The Québec government was opposed to the rate increases asked by Bell and accused the telephone monopoly of transferring its earnings to its subsidiaries, mainly Northern Electric, and of not making an adequate regional distribution of its investments. Bell Telephone refused to furnish detailed data on its investments, even though more than 50% of its revenue went into investments each year, and refused a request to give financial information on the operations of its subsidiaries.[23] The CTC granted Bell's request for a rate increase, but one can seriously wonder whether this decision was based on sufficient information.

The government was also largely powerless to orient the exploitation of Québec's natural resources to the advantage of the citizens of the province. Chapter 3 examined Iron Ore's very limited contribution to the economic development of Québec. A secret governmental report prepared by the department of natural resources and leaked to the press in 1972 confirmed that this was also true in the case of the asbestos industry. Written by Yves Fortier of the Québec planning and development office and dated March 26, 1972, the report concluded: "The asbestos industry is far from constituting a positive factor for economic expansion — in Québec",[24] and that the government of Québec should take it over in part.

Québec was responsible for 40% of the total world production of asbestos and 83% of the Canadian total. Québec satisfied 85% of the United States demand for asbestos, thus putting the province in a quasi-monopolistic position as a source of asbestos vis-à-vis the U.S. market. Asbestos production was controlled by eight U.S.-based companies, the largest being the Canadian Johns-Manville. Québec derived 6,000 jobs from the mining of asbestos but only 1,225 at the manufacturing level. In the U.S., on the other hand, 22,000 manufacturing jobs and 2,000 research jobs resulted from the processing of asbestos. Johns-Manville, for example, had only one manufacturing plant in Québec, employing about 425 workers, but had 46 plants in the U.S. It is estimated that only 2% of Québec asbestos was transformed into finished products by local firms. The net result was that, in 1971, Canada, the world's largest asbestos producer, bought $14.5 million worth of finished asbestos products from external sources but sold only $5.7 million worth.[25]

The white paper on the asbestos industry, which was part of a larger report on the development of the Estrie region, was eventually made public on January 25, 1973. However, the harsh conclusions on the asbestos industry and on the government's inactivity were eliminated from the "corrected version" of the report. According to Maurice Tessier, minister of municipal affairs, some excerpts were deleted as a result of the intervention of Paul A. Filtreau, director general of the Québec Association of Asbestos Producers. Tessier attributed the deletions to "consultations" with the asbestos industry rather than "pressures." Rather than criticizing the asbestos industry and recommending government intervention, the new version of the report suggested that "the department of natural resources should study ways to increase the economic effects of the asbestos industry in Québec."[26]

Finally, even in those cases where they provided conditional subsidies to corporations, governments were largely incapable of making sure that these conditions were met. In the 1972 federal campaign, David Lewis, head of the New Democratic Party, published some revealing data on the job-creation effects of the subsidies which the department of regional and economic expansion provided to corporations. Lewis noted, among other things, that 3,100 jobs were lost at Northern Electric, despite a $26 million subsidy; that 420 jobs were lost at Canadian Celanese despite a $500,000 subsidy; and that 30 jobs were created at Aluminium Company of Canada's Arvida plant in February 1972 as a result of a $495,300 subsidy from the department of regional and economic expansion, but that 206 workers were laid off at the same plant a month later.[27]

Québec Government Services to Industry

In the nineteen forties and fifties, economic relations between the government and industry in the province were handled on an *ad hoc* basis and chiefly involved direct bargaining between company executives and cabinet ministers. According to the *Financial Post* in 1962, "It is fair to say that prior to the advent of the present administration there was no national economic planning in the province . . . Deals between the province and industrial concerns were most often arranged personally as favours, by MPP's, or by the late Premier Duplessis himself."[28]

One such example was contained in a letter of March 4, 1946, from R. E. Powell, then president of Aluminum Company of Canada, to Duplessis. In the letter, Powell explained to the premier that his company must be able to continue to count on cheap electricity rates and that the taxes must be kept low to maintain the company's international competitive positions. [29] Powell concluded his letter by preying on Duplessis's well-publicized anti-communist obsession: "There are reasons to suspect that our bitterest competition in international trade may come from Russia and her communistic satellites, including Yugoslavia, which have large quantities of bauxite as well as a lot of water power."[30]

After 1960, with the election of a Liberal government, planning and a more systematic promotion of industry began, largely under the initiative of the department of industry and commerce. The Industrial Funds Act, or Bill 65, which was approved by the National Assembly on May 24, 1961, was one of the first governmental measures providing direct assistance to industry. The act permitted municipalities to set up "industrial funds" with governmental money. The aim of these funds was to finance the purchase of land to develop industrial parks, or the purchase and erection of industrial buildings. These were then resold or leased for a 20-to 25-year period to manufacturing companies on favourable terms. In effect, the main objective of the act was to provide loans to companies wishing to build new plants in certain Québec locations.[31]

Throughout the sixties and early seventies, the government continued to build and expand its services to industry. The department of industry and commerce provided a wide range of services to corporations. These included a division of research and investigation, which, among other things, provided market surveys for companies; a trading practices division, which kept business up to date on commercial methods; a retail trade promotion division; an external trade service, which organized trade missions abroad, coordinated participation in international trade fairs, provided an export techniques services, and organized visits by prospective buyers. The department's industry section included a statistics bureau; an industrial research center, which participated with industrial and commercial enterprises in the development of industrial products, processes, and machinery, which carried out research in applied sciences, and which disseminated technical and industrial information; an industrial expansion council, which facilitated establishment of new industries in Montréal; an industrial park corporation, which concentrated its activities in setting up an industrial park at Bécancour; a regional development section, which assisted companies wishing to expand their facilities; and an industrial development corporation, which will be discussed in detail below.[32]

Other governmental departments also provided services to industry. Thus, the department of lands and forests furnished data on wood availability and allocation, had a mapping and forest inventory service, and provided assistance with forest conservation and the building of forest roads. The department of natural resources provided data on mineral deposits and exploration, built roads, and had a research center on mining techniques.[33]

As regards tax incentives, the government passed "An Act to Amend the Corporation Tax Act to Stimulate Industrial Development" (Bill 24) on April 1, 1971, making manufacturing enterprises investing in new plants and equipment anywhere in Québec eligible for a 30% tax credit on their annual investments in excess of $50,000.[34]

Perhaps the most important element of the Québec government's industrial assistance program was the Québec Industrial Development Corporation. The Corporation was created on April 8, 1971, by the National Assembly's enactment of Bill 20. One of its purposes was to replace the Québec Industrial Credit Bureau. The Bureau, created in August 1967 by Bill 60, had, during its four-year existence, played exclusively the role of an industrial bank — providing term loans to new or existing manufacturing enterprises for modernization of productive facilities in the province. It concentrated its efforts on small and medium-sized Québec-owned companies. In 1971, for example, 95% of the Bureau's customers involved companies which were owned by Quebecers. It should be noted that the Industrial Credit Bureau did not compete with financial institutions or private lenders. It provided loans only to those companies which had been refused by private financial institutions, in effect absorbing the risks of the more hazardous ventures.[35]

In creating the Québec Industrial Development Corporation, it was the government's intention to play a more active role vis-à-vis Québec's industrial structure than that of lender or provider of loans to industry. Bill 20's stated objectives were to create employment and to transform and strengthen Québec's industrial structure by encouraging financially those manufacturers making use of advanced technology. More concretely, the Corporation , according to article 2 of the legislation, was prepared to make loans at a preferential rate of interest, market or lower, to provide assistance on interest payments of up to 50% of total costs, and to purchase up to 30% of the capital stock issued;[36] the investment in capital stock could not represent more than 10% of the total assets of the corporation. To be eligible, companies were required to make a new investment in Québec of at least

171

$150,000, to use advanced technology, or to be involved in the manufacturing of new products or products offering potential for long-term growth. Bill 20 also provided financial and technical assistance for companies wishing to merge or regroup and several tax concessions schemes of from 30% to 100% depending on the region. In effect, the Québec Industrial Development Corporation became the umbrella under which most of the Québec government's assistance programs to companies were regrouped.[37]

The creation of the Québec Industrial Development Corporation was welcomed by business. The CMA, speaking of Bill 20, said: "The Québec government is to be strongly commended for these enlightened financial and tax incentives to manufacurers making use of advanced technology."[38] What is more, the Conseil du Patronat and the Centre des Dirigeants d'Entreprise suggested in August 1972 that the powers of the Industrial Development Corporation should be broadened so as to make it "a powerful instrument for the transformation of Québec's industrial structure."[39] Finally, the evidence suggested that Bill 20 was approved largely as a response to business demands. Thus, in May 1970, the General Council of Industry made the following recommendations to the Québec government: "A major aim of provincial economic policies must be to encourage the expansion of high-productivity industries and give Québec a more dynamic industrial structure . . ."[40] The GCI recommended several measures; among them:

> . . . the creation of a separate corporation to facilitate mergers among small and medium-sized companies in Québec, . . . the creation of fiscal incentives, in the form of tax credits, for industrial research and development in the province, . . . [the establishment by the provincial government of] a corporation to assist new industries to locate in Québec by supplying loans as well as equity capital. Only companies planning to set up a manufacturing operation not already carried out in the province would qualify for such assistance. (As an alternative to the creation of a new corporation for this purpose, the government could assign this as an exclusive function to an existing organization, such as the General Investment Corporation or a re-structured Industrial Credit Bureau).[41]

As can be readily seen, the GCI's recommendations were very similar to the provisions included in Bill 20.

In the first two years of its operation, the Québec Industrial Development Corporation provided some $53 million of assistance to 201 companies; $34 of the $53 million in grants were spent on the three high technology sectors of transportation, metals, and electrical equipment. The biggest grant involved a $4.4 million subsidy to Union Carbide for the building of a $26.5 million petrochemical plant.[42]

In practice, the Québec Industrial Development Corporation remained largely an industrial bank, even though it was oriented towards medium-sized high technology industries rather than the more traditional small companies which had been supported by the Industrial Credit Bureau. The Corporation's goals of creating employment and transforming the industrial structure were too ambitious in relation to the means provided by Bill 20. Indeed, the corporation maintained an essentially passive stance, waiting for the demands for financial assistance to emerge from the private sector, rather than attempting to actively orient the evolution of the industrial structure. Thus, rather than promoting new initiatives and concrete projects of its own, it merely sought to provide assistance to the companies making investments in the best economic interests of Québec.[43]

The questionnaire data demonstrated a high degree of satisfaction on the part of senior Québec businessmen with the Bourassa government's economic policies; thus, 81.1% of the business respondents expressed agreement with the government's economic policies. There was, however, less satisfaction with regard to "the recent economic initiatives of the Québec government (including the providing of incentives and the creation of the Industrial Development Corporation)" which received a 63.1% degree of support. The probable explanation for the relative lukewarmness of the larger corporations was that, as seen above, most of the services and assistance programs provided by the department of industry and commerce were more likely to be beneficial to small or medium-sized companies than to the large companies. Indeed, large companies were not likely to have any difficulty obtaining private funds for expansion or building a new plant; in addition, services such as market surveys, statistics bureaus, trade information, etc., were not needed by the larger firms.

Government Policy Towards the Pulp and Paper Industry

As seen in chapter 3, the pulp and paper industry is vital to the economy of Québec. It is the province's most important industrial sector in terms of employment and exports; many Québec regions are wholly dependent on the industry for survival. In the Eastern Townships, for example, Domtar employs between 70 and 75% of the workers in Windsor and East Angus, and Kruger Pulp and Paper gives jobs to some 85% of the workers in Bromptonville.

Thus, when the industry began experiencing severe economic difficulties leading to thousands of employee layoffs between 1969 and 1972,[44] the Ottawa and Québec governments decided to intervene.[45] The federal government reduced taxes on pulp and paper profits from 49 to 40%, effective January 1973. Québec dropped its 8% sales tax on pulp and paper machinery.[46] It also decided to assume the costs for the construction and maintenance of forest roads and to create a state institution, Rexfor, to conserve wood resources.[47] Finally, in September 1971, the Québec government announced special measures to provide financial assistance to companies installing anti-pollution devices. However, despite substantial financial support of the pulp and paper industry, the two levels of government did not acquire any decision-making power over the future of the industry.

The same was true of the subsidies provided by the Québec and Ottawa governments to major individual pulp and paper producers. The best-known case was that of ITT-Rayonnier in northern Québec. The company, which was a wholly-owned subsidiary of International Telephone and Telegraph, was building a pulp mill in Port-Cartier,

350 miles northeast of Québec City. The estimated cost of the mill, and the access roads and facilities to service it, was set at $165 million. Of this, $57.3 million was to be provided by both levels of government.[48] The government of Canada granted $20.8 million — $13.8 million from the department of regional and economic expansion and $7 million for the construction of roads and other infrastructures. The Québec government, for its part, promised to build $17.5 million of access roads and to provide $19 million worth of wood-harvesting machinery through the Crown timber corporation, Rexfor.[49]

In addition, and perhaps most important, the Québec government gave ITT-Rayonnier almost exclusive cutting rights over 51,000 square miles of domanial forest. This was done through the creation of a "Crown reserve forest." According to Walter Stewart of the *Toronto Star:*

> In theory that means that instead of selling concessions to industry as in the past, the province would control the reserve and sell timber rights to all comers at the best price it could get . . .
> In practice, Québec has reserved the heart of the forest, a 26,000 square-mile block, for the exclusive use of Rayonnier, and has given the company a virtual veto on other timber operations in the entire reserve.[50]

Through Rexfor, ITT-Rayonnier was also awarded generous wood-harvesting incentives. In fact, the agreement between Rexfor and the company, a copy of which was obtained by the *Toronto Star,*[51] stipulated that Rayonnier would pay only 50 cents a cord in royalties, compared with the normal charge of between $2.50 and $3, and that Québec would assume all responsibility for reforesting and silviculture.[52] The agreement allowed Rayonnier to harvest 600,000 cords annually until 1987, and then up to 2 million cords annually. Finally, a proviso was included in the contract to the effect that "if wood supplies do not prove adequate on the allotments ceded to Rayonnier, the province is required to deliver enough wood to make up the difference to Rayonnier's mill at the average price of Rayonnier's own harvesting operations."[53] The agreement ran for 40 years, with an option to renew for an additional 40 years, and "its effect is to give Rayonnier control over the forest reserves in an area twice the size of New Brunswick for most of a century."[54]

The project was estimated to create only 459 permanent mill jobs and 1,330 seasonal wood cutting jobs. This meant an investment of $359,477 for every permanent mill job created, or of $92,174 per job if the temporary jobs were taken into account. Here again, most of the jobs created would be outside Québec, mainly in western Europe. The ITT-Rayonnier plant would produce dissolved pulp, "a fairly crude material which will be shipped to western Europe to be turned into rayon fibre for use in fabrics, rubber tires, and other finished goods which Canadiens will buy back at much higher price."[55]

The agreement between ITT and the Québec government was signed in January 1972. The negotiator for ITT was Québec lawyer Marcel Piché, who sat on several boards of directors of key companies operating in the province. The government negotiator was Lesage, who, as noted earlier, was also a member of several key boards of private companies. In fact, both Lesage and Piché sat on the board of directors of Reynolds Aluminum Company.

Several senior businessmen expressed reservations about the government's deal with ITT-Rayonnier. Large pulp and paper producers in particular objected to the preferential treatment given to ITT. The chairman of the board of a large pulp and paper company complained that existing pulp and paper producers could not get the kind of concessions that the new companies were getting and that ITT would enjoy an unfair competitive advantage because the government subsidies would help it get its wood supplies at a lower cost.[56] Another pulp and paper executive complained that his company had received nothing when it built a $100 million plant in northern Québec.[57] Finally, the president of a bank thought that the employment gains would be offset because some of the older mills would have to close down because of their inability to compete on equal terms with ITT.[58]

The most significant indicator of the Québec government's attitude towards the pulp and paper industry was provided by the government's attempts to reform the forest concession system. The case was important because it represented an effort by the government to regain a measure of decision-making power over the use of the province's forest reserves.

In 1972, seven pulp and paper companies shared 163,000 square miles of forest concessions, representing some 80% of the total land conceded by the government. Unlike the United States, Québec had not passed legislation regarding the rational use of forest concessions. As a result, many pulp and paper companies had used bulldozers to cut the wood; while this was by far the easiest and cheapest method of obtaining the wood, it was wasteful and slowed down considerably the process of reforestation.[59] Another difficulty under the system was that forest concessions were not allocated rationally among the companies which used them. Thus, some company plants were located far away from their concessions, while others were located near concessions belonging to other companies.

As early as the beginning of 1963, the Québec government set up a committee "to look into the allocation of the province's forest resources and to suggest methods for their more efficient use."[60] According to Amy Booth of the *Financial Post,* one of the plans being considered by the committee called for "all limits to be taken away from the companies."[61] According to Parizeau, then economic advisor to the Québec government, the government had decided to introduce major forest reforms as early as 1966. The government's intention to redistribute timber concessions had, however, been blocked under the pressure of CIP, which itself controlled some 25,000 square miles of concessions.[62]

In April 1972, the Québec government finally made public the proposals of its white paper on forest reform. The main objective of the department of lands and forests, according to the report, should be to contribute to "the rectification, growth and development of the forest industry by helping to reduce the cost of wood fibre."[63] The principal recommendation of the white paper was the abolition of all timberland concessions within 10 years and government management of all forest developments through a "société de gestion forestière." Concessions would be replaced by 20- to 40-year contracts, available exclusively to the pulp and paper producers.

In addition to planning, orienting the development, and administering forest lands, and guaranteeing the supply of wood, the white paper suggested other ways by which the Québec government could help reduce the costs of pulp and paper producers. These included the creation of several applied research centers on the problems of forestry, the financing of the construction and maintenance of access roads, and participation in forest protection and conservation costs. [64]

After it was published, the white paper was criticized by several individuals and groups for not having gone far enough towards ensuring state control over forest lands. Yvon Valcin, CNTU economist, argued that the government was afraid to compete with private enterprise, that, to a large extent, the abolition of forest concessions was a smokescreen, and that the new system would make the exploitation of the forests even more profitable for the pulp and paper producers. [65] Parizeau maintained the concessions had been abolished in name only. and that the 20- to 40- year contracts would give the companies even better conditions than before. [66]

The pulp and paper producers, however, maintained their opposition to the white paper. This was confirmed in briefs submitted to the government by the Conseil des Pâtes et Papiers, the Association des Industries Forestières du Québec, Domtar, CIP, and Consolidated-Bathurst. [67] The two latter companies asked Kevin Drummond, minister of lands and forests, to prepare a new white paper. The major pulp and paper producers were not, however, unalterably opposed to the abolition of forest concessions. Their main concerns were that adequate compensation [68] be provided for the concessions and that "the basic system of management of the Province's timberlands continue to be entrusted to private enterprise." [69] Several of the briefs warned the government that serious economic consequences would result from the adoption of the proposals contained in the white paper; thus, the Association des Industries Forestières stated: "We affirm, without hesitation, that if the socialist measures governing wood supply are adopted, we will unfortunately not have to wait long to witness the end of any growth in Québec's forest sector." [70]. Similarly, Domtar claimed that many pulp and paper mills would probably close down if the white paper became law. [71]

The forest reform project was delayed, and, by June 1974, the government had given no clear indication of whether it would introduce legislation on this matter. This was all the more surprising in that the government had given every indication that it intended to introduce legislation on forest reform within a few months of the publication of the white paper. Thus, as early as July 8, 1972, Ian Rodger of the *Financial Post* could write: "Necessary legislation is being prepared for presentation this fall, and funds have been allocated in next year's budget." [72] Also, during the hearings on the white paper, Drummond adopted an aggressive and critical attitude towards the pulp and paper companies. Reacting to the briefs of the pulp and paper industry's trade associations, Drummond called the attitude of the large companies "reactionary and disgusting." He also stated that it was not in the "status quo" that one could hope to find a forest policy oriented towards the public good rather than the interests of a privileged group.[73] Later on in the hearings, Drummond was even blunter:

> Making laws is the job of the government, and neither CIP nor any other company will tell us what to do. Maybe there was a time when concession owners could tell the government what to do, but this is certainly no longer the case to day . . . We know that the companies would like to maintain the status quo: but a reform responding to the needs of the population is essential, and it will occur.[74]

On October 29, 1972, Drummond announced that the forest reform project would be delayed and also that the government no longer intended to set up a state corporation to manage the province's timberlands, that is, the société de gestion forestière. According to La Presse Canadienne, this action was taken as a result of the pressure of the pulp and paper companies.[75] As early as September 7, during the heated debates at the parliamentary commission, senior pulp and paper executives were predicting that the legislation on forest reform was "not for tomorrow."[76]

In May 1973, Drummond announced he would introduce a bill abolishing forest concessions before the summer recess.[77] This was not done. Then, in January 1974, Drummond said the government had decided not to abolish forest concessions all at once; instead, the department of lands and forests would negotiate terms with individual companies in each Québec region.

It is too early to determine the precise outcome of the government's attempts to reform forest concessions, but it is reasonably obvious that the pulp and paper companies have won several major concessions, and that their opposition and pressure were the main factors in the dealy of the legislation. Here again, the questionnaire data showed a considerable degree of satisfaction among senior businessmen with the Québec government. Thus, 82.4% of businessmen supported the government's decision to defer the forest reform legislation. Finally, an interview with a pulp and paper executive revealed that during the past two or three years, meetings averaging once a month were held between senior pulp and paper executives and a group of ministers, including the premier at times. According to the same executive, these meetings were "very helpful," and there were "no meetings in the last four months or so because we obtained what we wanted."[78] He also noted that the government had told the pulp and paper executives "not to broadcast the fact of the meetings because there could be criticism that they are favouring our industry."[79]

The Québec Budget

For the fiscal year 1972-1973, the Conseil du Patronat began a policy of submitting detailed recommendations to the Québec government about the content of the budget. These recommendations were submitted several months before the publication of the budget by the government.

Before examining the degree of success which the Conseil's proposals met in the 1972-73 budget, one can make a few general observations about the budgetary process. First, according to a study by the QFL, the fiscal revenues of the Québec government in the 1961-1970 period were increasingly derived from income taxes and less and less from corporate taxes. Thus, in this period, income tax increased from 16.5% to 41.7% of total fiscal revenue, while corporate taxes declined from 27.0% to 10.8%.[80] Sales taxes decreased from 51.2% to 44.6%. It is fair to say that the increased government spending during the period of the "quiet revolution" was shouldered mainly by individuals.[81] Second, according to the same study, it is incorrect to claim that the quiet revolution was the occasion for dramatic increases in the areas of social affairs and educational spending. Thus, from 1961 to 1970, educational spending dropped slightly from 25.93% to 24.04%, while health and welfare spending fell from 28.86% to 25.42% of the government's total budget.[82]

In regard to the 1972-73 budget, a Conseil du Patronat delegation headed by Perrault met Bourassa and Garneau on January 24, 1972. At that meeting, the Conseil formally presented and discussed its budget proposals with governmental officials.[83] The evidence indicates that the Conseil was quite successful in getting the government to incorporate some of its suggestions in the budget.

Thus, the Conseil recommended that total government spending not increase by more than 5%. The 1972-73 budget provided for an 8.1% increase, which represented a sharp decrease from the three previous fiscal years, in each of which the rate of increase had exceeded 15%. The second recommendation involved increasing governmental investments in sectors which contributed directly to the production of wealth. The 1972-73 budget included a 23% increase in para-public investments, mainly through Hydro-Québec and school construction. Public and para-public investments totalled $1.5 billion. The third recommendation involved slowing down the rate of increase in educational and health and welfare spending. The rate of increase in the case of education fell from 15% the previous year to 5.6%, whereas it dropped from 12.5% to 8% in the case of social affairs. [84]

Several other of the Conseil's demands were met in the budget, including the opening of a Québec delegation in Brussels to facilitate access to the European Economic Community; the appointment of a trade mission to visit the Far East (which was done by the GCI in 1973); the suspension of the sales tax on industrial machinery; a decrease in succession duties; and an increase in the budget of the Industrial Research Center.[85] Finally, the Conseil's budget proposals contained a general recommendation with regard to the government's wage policy in the forthcoming negotiations with the public employees.[86] As noted in the previous chapter, the government was responsive to the expressed needs of business during the common front strike.

The 1972-73 budget was received with considerable satisfaction by the business community in Québec. The Conseil du Patronat, the Québec Chambre de Commerce, the Centre des Dirigeants d'Entreprise, and the CMA all expressed their public support for the Québec budget.[87] Brunelle of the Conseil congratulated the government for cutting down the rate of increase of public expenditures "in conformity with the wishes expressed by business."[88] The Conseil noted that the government had recognized in its budget "the difficult situation facing Québec industry;" it was particularly pleased with the abolition of the sales tax on industrial equipment, the gradual elimination of succession duties, and the elimination of the tax on stock transfers.[89]

When interviewed, an executive of the Conseil expressed considerable satisfaction with the success of the pre-budget submission. He explained that the budgetary proposals required almost a full year of work and extensive meetings with ministers and civil servants. He claimed that the Conseil was "very encouraged and satisfied" with the impact of its proposals, and that "the government listens to us even with regard to details."[90] He also noted that Bourassa's public reactions towards the proposals were moderate, because he was afraid that public opinion would think that business ran the government.[91] The *Financial Post*, finally, quoted government officials as saying that the Conseil's budget proposal "is the most important document we have in assisting us with our budgeting."[92]

State Economic Institutions in Québec

The most important element of Québec's economic policies in the 1960-1975 period was unquestionably the creation of a network of state enterprises operating in several industrial sectors. The main enterprises were Hydro-Québec, which was established following the nationalization of private electricity companies in 1963; the General Investment Corporation; the Québec Deposit and Investment Fund; the Québec Petroleum Operations Company; the Québec Mining Exploration Company; and the Québec Steel Corporation.

Most of the state enterprises were created by the Liberal government of Lesage between 1960 and 1966. Although the objectives varied somewhat depending on the enterprise, the main avowed intention of the government in setting up state enterprises was to contribute to the "economic liberation" of Québec, in conformity with the Liberal election slogan "maîtres chez nous." In effect, this meant that the Québec government wanted to play an active role in creating an economic power base for the French-Canadian element. The Québec government considered that it was only through the use of the state that French Canadians could gain some participation in economic decision-making, which had heretofore been almost entirely in the hands of English Canadians or foreigners. To quote Parizeau:

> In Québec, the state must intervene. It is inevitable. It is what gives the people the impression that we are more to the left. If we had, in Québec, 25 companies like Bombardier, and if we had very important banks, the situation might be different. We have no large institutions, so we must create them.[93]

Parizeau's message was clear. The motives for state intervention did not derive from any social goals, but rather from a desire to put French Canadians in a better position vis-à-vis the "economic balance of power" in Québec. This opinion was shared by Dion: "It is to create a specifically Québécois economic base that, during the period of the quiet revolution, such enterprises as the General Investment Corporation, Soquem, Soguip, Rexfor, and Sogefor were created." [94]

Even if the nationalist impulse was the dominant motive behind the creation of a network of state institutions, in practice, the various state institutions assumed many other functions. These included the bailing out of companies with financial difficulties, which have been chiefly smaller or medium-sized companies, the taking-over by the government of economic sectors that were no longer profitable for private enterprises, and the providing of direct or indirect assistance to specific companies or industrial sectors.

This section will examine the relative importance of these various functions for each state enterprise and the discrepancies, if any, between the stated objectives and the actual performance of these enterprises. In addition, it will attempt to determine which interests the individual state economic institutions served, what economic impact, in terms of power and decision-making, it had on the industrial sector in which it was operating, and what kinds of links it had with the private sector. The main objectives will be to determine if the state enterprises gave the Québec government a significant degree of leverage and economic power vis-à-vis the private sector.

With few exceptions, the state enterprises had a marginal impact on the economy of Québec, even though they were involved in many crucial areas of economic activity, for example, pulp and paper, steel, oil, mining, and even though they were often granted broad powers by law. The main concrete function of the state institutions have been to support private enterprise, rather than challenge the economic power of business or develop an independent economic power base for the Québec government. Some of the factors which impeded the operation of state enterprises included inadequate budgets, structural weaknesses, legally limited spheres of activity, and the numerous affinities with private industry.

Hydro-Québec

The nationalization of the private electricity companies in 1963 was heralded as a major victory of the Québec government over the economic power of corporations and as the assumption by the state of an essential economic sector in the interests of the Québec population.

The economic importance of Hydro-Québec cannot be doubted. In 1975, it owned some $6 billion worth of assets, had annual sales of more than $800 million, and employed more than 12,000 workers. [95] The evidence indicated, however, that the private sector had been the main beneficiary of the operations of Hydro-Québec. In the first place, the private electric companies could not have afforded to risk enormous amounts of capital in multi-billion dollar hydro-electric projects such as Manic-Outardes, Gentilly, and, more recently, James Bay. According to Jean-Paul Gignac, commissioner of Hydro-Québec from 1961 to 1969 and then president of Sidbec, Québec's state-owned steel complex:

> I do not believe that a private company could have taken the risk to develop the Manic-Outardes complex and to transport electricity at a voltage of 735,000 volts. It must be realized that this calculated risk allowed Hydro-Québec to save hundreds of millions of dollars in addition to providing a cheap energy source.[96]

Second, nationalization resulted in a consolidation and rationalization of the market for electricity.[97] Hydro-Québec's pricing system was particularly advantageous to the industrial users. Thus, in 1973, the average cost of electricity to industrial users in Montreal was $1.92 per 1 million BTUs, while commercial users paid $4.19 per 1 million BTUs, and domestic users $4.34.[98] In addition, between 1961 and the end of 1972, the price of electricity in Québec went up by only 3.5%, while the general consumer price index rose from 100 to 146.3[99] Since private industry was the main consumer of electricity and since electricity was a vital raw material in most industrial sectors, the stabilization of prices and the preferential rates accorded to industrial users were primarily beneficial to the private sector.

The available evidence also suggested that the eight private electric companies received generous compensation from the Québec government when they were nationalized in 1963. According to the *Financial Post,* the Québec government's price offer to buy the stocks of the companies was in every case higher than the recent price of the stock, and in most cases higher than the stocks' "high" since September 1962.[100] In total, it cost the Québec government $604 million to nationalize the private electric companies. Finally, there were some indications that some of the owners of electricity companies were anxious to recoup some of the capital they had invested in order to re-invest it in more profitable ventures.[101] Power Corporation, for one, developed and diversified rapidly after 1963, largely as a result of the cash flow obtained from the nationalization of its subsidiary, Shawinigan Light and Power Corporation.[102]

It is not surprising that business expressed a considerable degree of support for the nationalization of electricity. The questionnaire data showed that 72.3% of businessmen, and 80% of executives of major companies, were favourable to the nationalization.[103] Even though Hydro-Québec had the economic potential to be an instrument of independent economic power for the Québec state, it limited its role to providing the private sector in Québec with a comparatively cheap and stable supply of electricity.

General Investment Corporation

The General Investment Corporation was created by the Québec government on July 6, 1962. Its overall objective, according to Bill

50, was to accelerate industrial development in Québec by promoting, financing, and assisting Québec enterprises. More specifically, the GIC's field of operations included:

> Lending money to undertakings which are in need of debt capital and which do not have access to long term credit sources.
> Acquiring a minority or controlling interest in undertakings in need of risk capital to develop.
> Participating in the creation and growth of new industries engaged in the development and transformation of Québec natural resources or in industrial projects offering employment to a large number of workers.
> Provinding technical, administrative and research services to undertakings whose margin of profit can be increased by the introduction of new techniques or the installation of administrative reforms.[104]

It should be noted that the GIC was created as a "mixed society." Rather than being wholly-owned by the state, it distributed its capital among the government, caisses populaires, the private sector, and the public. In fact, one of the secondary objectives of the bill was to encourage Quebecers to invest in the economy of the province. [105]

It is clear from a reading of Bill 50, article 8, that the GIC was to acquire a minority or controlling interest in a company only with a view of absorbing risks and salvaging threatened industries. Once the critical phase had passed and once the enterprise had become profitable, the GIC would withdraw its participation and restore it to private enterprise. Thus, according to industrialist Gérard Filion, the first director of the GIC: "The GIC will take over control of an enterprise only if it is for the common good; then it will attempt to sell it back to private interests."[106]

Gérard R. Ryan, one of the members of the committee which drafted Bill 50, confirmed the temporary character of the GIC's projected incursions in the private sector:

> "The GIC is a benevolent industrial bank which aims to provide all or an important part of the permanent capital of a new enterprise, to participate in its administration . . . up until the day when its shares can be sold to the general public with much less risk involved."[107]

In its actual operations, the GIC became primarily a holding company, made up mainly of family enterprises on the verge of bankruptcy or experiencing severe financial difficulties. It assumed as its main function the rescue of unprofitable companies. It placed particular emphasis on assisting French-Canadian enterprises; in fact, the GIC was a prime example of government attempts to improve the relative position of French-Canadian entreprise in the economic structure of Québec. René Paré, first president of the GIC and head of the committee which drafted Bill 50, made this obvious in an article which he wrote for *Revue Commerce:*

> Through our own fault, we (the French Canadians) occupy a secondary position in the economy of our province. This must change! We must have a network of institutions that belong to us. We must develop more than half-measures for our development . . .[108]

Even though it was the majority shareholder,[109] the government named only four of the 16 directors of the GIC. Another eight were chosen by the stockholders and the remaining four by the caisses populaires, In 1971, a majority of GIC directors were businessmen. These included several senior executives: Paul Leman, president of Aluminium Company of Canada, Pierre Salbaing, president of Canadian Liquid Air, Gérard Filion, president of Marine Industries, William Bennet, president of Iron Ore, and Marcel Faribault, president of the General Trust of Canada.

Since the GIC's subsidiaries were mainly companies with financial problems, it was not surprising that the GIC's own financial performance was less than brilliant. In 1971, the corporation lost $8 million on investments of some $50 million. The GIC's most important subsidiary by far was Marine Industries, the Simard family's construction company. Sixty per cent of Marine's capital stock was acquired in October 1965 at a cost of $12.5 million; at the time, this represented 43% of total GIC investments. It seems that the Simard family got rid of Marine Industries just in time; profits of $2.1 million in 1965 declined into a loss of $3.2 million in 1971. After substantial GIC investments in the modernization of the company, Marine showed a $3.8 million profit in 1972.

Most of the GIC's other investments were small French-Canadian companies employing not more than a few hundred workers. These included Forano, Volcano, Bonnex, Cégelec Industries, LaSalle Tricot, David Lord,[110] Soma, and Sogefor. Even though it attempted to reorganize and regroup many of its subsidiaries, the main effect of the GIC intervention was to ensure the survival of companies with financial problems by subsidizing them. In the case of Soma and Sogefor, the GIC got involved in setting up new industries. Both were financial failures. Soma was a car assembly plan created in February 1965 as a result of an agreement between the Régie Renault, and the GIC. Under the agreement, Soma assembled cars from parts furnished by Renault; the GIC put $4 million into the plant and hired 545 workers. As a result of a decision by Renault to stop assembling cars in North America, Soma closed down in February 1973.[111] It reopened in December 1973 to assemble buses for the German company Mann; the transformation of the plant cost the GIC an additional $3 million.[112]

Sogefor was created in 1963 by the GIC and was intended to act as a holding company in the pulp and paper sector. It was given the ambitious objective of becoming "an important industrial complex."[113] In practice, Sogefor bought three plants, Albert Gigaire, the Dubé sawmill, and Maki, and built another one, Dupan. In accordance with GIC practice, the three plants that were purchased were small, family-owned, financially unstable, and used inefficient technology. As with the other GIC experiences, the regrouping of small, inefficient plants did not prove a successful profit-making strategy. All four Sogefor plants incurred losses. Dupan and Dubé were closed down in June 1971. Dupan was reopened in November 1971. Maki was sold to Les Produits Forestiers Maniwaki in 1972, and Albert Gigaire was sold to Multigrade.

One of the main problems faced by the Sogefor plants was access to wood supply. Maki, for example, operated in an area where all forest concessions were controlled by CIP, and it was forced to buy its wood from that company at a high price. Despite repeated attempts by the GIC to obtain concessions for its Sogefor plants, the Québec government refused to make any modifications in the forest concession system. In fact, when Parizeau resigned from the board of directors of Sogefor on March 9, 1971, he attributed its failure to the "inaction of government vis-à-vis the forest concession regime . . . which is dominated by CIP and Consolidated-Bathurst." He went on to argue that a modification of the concession system would have been "the only imaginable solution to Sogefor's difficulties."[114]

In September 1972, the GIC became a state enterprise; through Bill 75, the government became its only shareholder. In December 1973, an additional $25 million in capital was pumped into the GIC, and its functions were clarified with the passage of Bill 20. By 1975, the GIC controlled assets of $59.4 million and its subsidiaries had total sales of $382.5 million. The "new" GIC has played the role of a holding, either financing medium and large companies directly by purchasing their capital stock or encouraging the merger of small firms in the same sector. The GIC has defined its objective as "intensifying its intervention in the economy of the province to create strong industrial sectors in Québec through an association between state capital and private enterprise."[115]

In practice, then, the GIC has conceived its role mainly in terms of assisting troubled companies and providing capital for risky ventures. Thus far, its main achievement has been to save jobs, often temporarily, by helping some companies to survive. This was a far cry from its original objective of accelerating economic growth in Québec by modifying the province's economic structure.

Québec Deposit and Investment Fund

The Québec Deposit and Investment Fund was created on July 15, 1965. It was a government-owned corporation which managed the funds collected by the Québec Pension Plan and also those of several other bodies, such as the Québec Health Insurance Board and the Québec Deposit Insurance Board. With a capital of some $4.3 billion in 1975, the Fund was potentially the most important economic instrument of the government. In fact, René Lévesque, then minister of natural resources in the Liberal government of Premier Lesage, claimed in 1966 that the Fund was the only state institution created by the Québec government which challenged somewhat the economic and political dominance of the English majority in Québec.[116]

As in the case of most of the other state economic institutions, the creation of the Fund was accompanied by high expectations. Lesage predicted: "The Fund is called upon to become the most important and the most powerful financial instrument that we have ever had in Québec."[117] The Fund also generated expectations with regard to greater governmental and French-Canadian control of economic dicision-making centers. An interdepartmental committee which was set up by Lesage to study the Québec Pension Plan reported in 1963 that the creation of the Fund would put in the hands of its administrators decision-making centers which were then located mainly outside Québec.[118]

On the positive side, there is little doubt that the Québec Deposit and Investment Fund was successful, at least in part, in reducing the dependence of the Québec government on the financial "cartel." Thus, during difficult situations when Québec bonds were not selling, the Fund often picked up the slack by purchasing substantial amounts.[119] Parizeau claimed that such a situation occurred in 1966 when Johnson was elected to power with the slogan "equality or independence."[120] Alarmed by Johnson's nationalism, the financial markets had been particularly unreceptive to Quebec bond issues. The Fund then stepped in and managed to sustain their value by buying up large amounts of the outstanding bonds. According to Alain Pinard of the *Montreal Star*, "The policy has literally saved the Québec government, in some cases, from falling flat on its financial face, because it couldn't sell its bonds through other channels."[121]

As regards the expectation that it would provide a major instrument through which the Québec government could exercise leverage in the major decision-making centers, the Québec Deposit and Investment Fund was much less successful. First, the Fund's capital of $4.3 billion remained relatively small compared to the vast pools of capital vested in the major private financial institutions. The Royal Bank of Canada, for example, had holdings of $18.5 billion in 1973. Second, and more important, the Fund has locked up over 70% of its capital in governmental and corporate bonds[122]. The remainder of the portfolio was made up of investments in mortgages and property.[123]

The potential impact, in terms of economic decision-making power, of the Fund's investments in company stock was substantially reduced by the law setting up the Fund. Thus, the Fund was prevented by law from holding more than 30% of a company's stock and was also forbidden from investing more than 30% of its total capital in stock.[124] The aim of the government was to provide capital to private enterprise, through the purchase of bonds or stock, but not to exercise a significant degree of control over the companies involved. Claude Prieur, who was chairman of the Fund from 1966 to 1973, had no hesitation in describing it as "above all a reservoir of capital." With regard to investments in stock, Prieur noted:

> In 1967, the Fund began to purchase stock. The objective was to make the Fund participate in industrial development through the stock market. This was another means by which the Fund could provide companies with an easier access to capital markets, by helping to create a better market for stocks.[125]

The Fund's essentially passive and supportive role vis-à-vis the industrial structure was also evident in another provision of its charter. Thus, the law setting up the Fund prohibited investments in companies which were not at least five years old; this essentially prevented the Fund from helping to create new industries or from helping to launch new public enterprises. Here again, Prieur underlined the Fund's role as defined by the law: "The Fund cannot substitute itself for private enterprise or even the state in the launching of new projects, because of the management conditions imposed on it."[126]

Another source of the weakness of the Fund was the expected long-term drain of its capital reserves. Prieur revealed in the 1972 annual report that an actuarial study of the Québec Pension Plan had predicted that the Fund would peak at some $5.5 billion in 1990, but would rapidly decline from there on and be completely dry by 1998.[127]

The businessmen interviewed were satisfied with the operations of the Fund. The vice-president of a bank maintained that the Fund had a "very important role" to play and that "its main function, apart from buying government bonds, was to encourage Québec companies by buying their stock."[128] The chairman of the board of a trust company noted, however, that the Fund had been "created for political reasons, rather than purely economic ones," and that "the job could have been done by private enterprise."[129] This view was shared by an executive from another trust company.[130] The latter statements indicated that some senior executives were somewhat sceptical with regard to the Québec government's attempts to become "maîtres chez nous" and to create a French-Canadian economic power base through state institutions.

Briefly, the Québec Deposit and Investment Fund provided the government with an excellent outlet for its bonds; this was found particularly useful at times when the financial markets — for political or other reasons — were lukewarm towards Québec bond issues. Its main function, however, was to support existing Québec companies by providing them with capital. Contrary to earlier expectations, the Fund did not bring about any significant increase in the government's economic decision-making power, nor did it have a significant impact on Québec's industrial structure.

Québec Steel Corporation (Sidbec)[131]

Sidbec was created on November 18, 1964, by the initiative of René Lévesque. It was given a broad mandate and wide powers. It was permitted to get involved in every phase of steel production, including mining, research, processing, and the distribution and sale of finished products. The main objective underlying the creation of Sidbec was to make steel available to Québec industry at competitive prices. St. Pierre, minister of industry and commerce, was quoted as saying: "Many companies had decided not to locate or expand here [in Québec] because of the high cost and unavailability of steel."[132] In 1973, Québec accounted for only 8% of total Canadian steel production, compared with 80% in the case of Ontario. Since the creation of Sidbec was intended to make Québec industry more competitive by remedying a flaw in Québec's industrial structure, business, including, for example, the Québec Chambre de Commerce, supported the government initiative.

Even though Sidbec was created officially in 1964, with an authorized capital of $25 million, it was not until July 1968, when

Québec agreed to the purchase of the private steel producer, Dosco, that Sidbec got off the ground. The purchase of Dosco's facilities at a cost of some $60 million followed two years of negotiations with the British firm Hawker-Siddeley, Dosco's majority shareholder. Due to outmoded technology and machinery, Dosco had been incurring major financial losses during the several years that preceded the purchase. Sidbec spent some $125 million in the next few years following the acquisition of Dosco in modernizing the company's old facilities and in building new installations.

During its first seven years of operation, the Québec Steel Corporation incurred substantial financial losses, including a deficit of close to $20 million in 1975. The Québec government, however, was willing to absorb these losses since its objectives were, according to St. Pierre, to "make steel available at cheaper prices," to "increase the value added of manufacturing in the province," and to "attract companies using steel to the province." Thus, St. Pierre said, "It is not essential that Sidbec achieves the same degree of profitability as other steel firms."[133] Assuming that Sidbec eventually made a profit, the indications were that the Québec government would turn it over to private enterprise. According to Jean-Paul Gignac, president of Sidbec, the Québec government gave the steel corporation the status of a stock company, with the government as the only stockholder in the early phases, rather than a Crown corporation or state enterprise, "with the idea of putting Sidbec's stock back on the market when it becomes profitable."[134] Gignac went on to say that it was "not normal for a government to run a steel company."[135] Gignac seemed to rule out the possibility that a state company could be run with a different set of objectives and in accordance with different interests than a private corporation.

Even though the government was the only stockholder of Sidbec, it was not represented on the original board of directors of the company, which was elected on March 20, 1965. Apart from Gérard Filion, who occupied the presidency at the outset, the other board members included Pierre Gendron, president of Dow Breweries, Gérald Plourde, president of United Auto Parts, Peter N. Thomson, an executive of Power Corporation, and René Paré. The situation was corrected somewhat on August 17, 1965, when the government named two civil servants to the board: Jean Deschamps, deputy minister of industry and commerce, and Michel Bélanger of the department of natural resources, who was later to become the president of the Montréal and Canadian stock exchanges.

The Québec government further undermined the position of Sidbec by subsidizing some of its competitors. Thus, the government subsidized Stelco's new $14.5 million plant in Contrecoeur as well as Québec Steel's new $24 million manufacturing facilities in Longueuil. In the latter case, federal and provincial subsidies covered almost half the costs of building the new plant.[136]

Thus, the Québec Steel Corporation was run by businessmen in the interests of business. It was successful in creating jobs, but its main objective was to provide cheaper and more plentiful steel to Québec industry. In effect, the Québec government agreed to picking up the losses of a non-profitable industrial sector in order to reduce the costs incurred by companies using steel. It also implied that this sector would be returned to private enterprise if and when it became profitable.

Québec Mining Exploration Company (Soquem)

The Québec Mining Exploration Company was created by the Québec government on July 15, 1965. Its main function was to carry out mining exploration. Lévesque justified the creation of Soquem by arguing that mining exploration and production were in need of greater rationalization in order to adequately meet Québec needs. He maintained that mining development since the beginning of the century had taken place with the capital and for the benefit of U.S. companies, and that exploitation exclusively for profit had had a negative effect on regional development, that is, the companies had skimmed each region by mining only the most accessible deposits and had not carried out really systematic exploration. Lévesque further argued that this had a detrimental impact on the long term viability of regions as well as on the government's efforts to rationalize and maximize the use of its infrastructural expenditures, for example, the building of roads, in each region. [137]

The objectives of Soquem as set in its charter were the following:

a) to carry out mining exploration by all methods;
b) to participate in the development of discoveries, including those made by others, with power to purchase and to sell properties at various stages of development, and to associate itself with others for such purposes;
c) to participate in the bringing into production of mineral deposits, either by selling them outright or transferring them in return for a participation. [138]

The essential element was that Soquem could not develop mineral deposits alone but had to seek a partner. In practice, this meant that, in most cases, Soquem played the role of junior partner to private mining companies.

As for financing, Soquem was given a $15 million budget over a period of ten years, at the rate of $1.5 million a year. According to Côme Charbonneau, formerly vice-president of St. Lawrence Columbium and Metals and then president of Soquem, this budget was inadequate and did not come close to the exploration budgets of the larger mining companies: "We have seen that business accepts an average cost of $35 million per discovery and that specialized technical firms accept an average cost going from $10 to $20 million." [139]

At the end of 1970, Soquem controlled assets of some $8.4 million. Because of a slowdown in private mining exploration and the closing down of several mines, the Québec government decided to increase Soquem's budget in 1971 and again in 1973. The company's total capital was expected to reach $45 million by 1980. This remained modest compared with some of Soquem's private partners. In 1970, for example, Falconbridge Nickel announced a $200 million investment to mine copper and nickel deposits in the Ungava region; the same year, Noranda Mines announced a $123 million expansion program to increase the copper output of its Québec installations.

Soquem's main activities since 1966 included the search for mineral deposits, the development of discoveries, and research on mining techniques. In regard to the search for mineral deposits, the company launched 16 programs of mining exploration in 1966-1967; of these, nine were unshared and seven were carried out jointly with private mining companies. Given the success of many of Soquem's projects, joint programs increased to 20 in 1970-71, while unshared ventures declines to only two.[140] Soquem's partners in the joint programs included many major private mining companies, such as New Jersey Zinc, Rio Tinto Exploration, Asbestos Corporation, Quebec Cartier Mining, and Falconbridge Nickel Mines.

Soquem conceived its exploration role in terms of subsidizing and diminishing the risks of private mining companies. When it achieved successful preliminary results in its exploration projects and when it made a discovery with potential for commercial exploitation, Soquem called for tenders in order to find a partner in the private sector. Even though it provided most of the capital in the joint exploration projects,[141] Soquem held only minority interests in most joint ventures. With one exception, private corporations had controlling interests of from 50% to 85% in the joint exploration projects. In effect, private companies were allowed to take over exploration ventures when they had showed signs of being profitable.

As regards the development of discoveries, the tendency for joint projects to increase relative to unshared projects was also noticeable. Thus, in 1966-67, there were 12 unshared and 11 joint projects, whereas in 1970-71, there was only one unshared project and six joint ones. Chart 6 demonstrates the evolution in the number and nature of exploration projects from April 1, 1966, to 1971. It includes all exploration projects, that is, the search for deposits and the development of discoveries.[142] Of the six joint projects in the development of discoveries, five were controlled by private companies which had interests ranging from 50% to 60%. The only exception was a uranium drilling venture in the Eastern Townships, which was controlled by Soquem to the tune of 90% and by Rio Tinto Exploration Company to the tune of 10%.[143]

Soquem did not participate in any producing companies except for the Louvem Mining Company and Niobec. The latter was set up jointly with Copperfields Mining and was expected to begin exploiting columbium deposits in the Lac St. Jean area by 1976. Copperfields Mining and Soquem each held a 50% interest in Niobec.

Louvem was wholly-owned by Soquem and was the only exception to the provision in Soquem's charter that the company had to participate with private enterprise in bringing mineral deposits into production. Louvem was created in 1967 after Soquem entered into a partnership with the Nemrod Mining Group to mine copper deposits which Soquem discovered near Val d'Or. After a complex two-year

CHART 6
EVOLUTION IN NUMBER AND NATURE OF EXPLORATION
PROJECTS FROM 1966-1967 to 1970-1971[a]

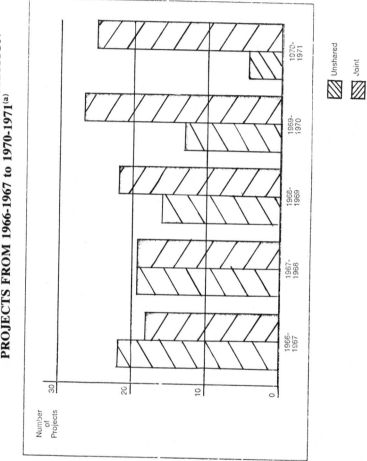

(a) Québec Mining Exploration Company, *1971 Annual Report* (Québec: Québec Mining Exploration Company, 1971), p. 9.

ownership dispute in Superior Court between Soquem and Nemrod, Soquem, in 1971, eventually purchased Nemrod's share of the Louvem stock. Louvem started production in 1970 and was expected to remain open until 1976. It provided 290 jobs.

As for research, Soquem had "paid particular attention to the improvement of exploration methods."[144] In 1971, $400,000 of its budget went into research. One of Soquem's major achievements in the research field was the development of an airborne electro-magnetic instrument. Called Emal-19, this instrument, which was put into service in June 1971, resulted in substantial savings in aerial surveys; it was estimated that this instrument reduced explorations costs from $25 to $35 to $3 to $4 a mile. Soquem allowed Aerophoto Inc. to commercialize Emal-19, permitting the private sector to reap the profits from an invention made in the public sector. In May 1970, Soquem began participating in a study with several private mining companies, including Cominco and New Jersey Zinc, to develop a strategy for the exploration of sulphide deposits.[145]

According to Claude Genest, vice-president of Soquem, private industry was initially lukewarm towards the state-owned company: there was some fear that Soquem would compete with the private mining companies. However, he claimed, "When we showed ourselves ready to participate with the companies and to integrate ourselves in the economic system, the attitude of the companies changed."[146]

When it is considered that Soquem financed the costs of mining exploration but in most cases did not seek to acquire control, it is not surprising that mining companies were willing partners.[147] Because of lack of funds, Soquem did not significantly involve itself in exploitation.[148] In effect, the most profitable phase of mining was being left to private enterprise. What is more, private companies continued to develop mineral resources according to their priorities, that is, according to the best possible rate of return. Overall, Soquem had a marginal impact on mining in Québec, and it had not significantly progressed towards the achievement of the objectives set for it when it was created. More specifically, since the initiative for mining production remained with the companies, Soquem was not a contributing factor in rationalizing mining exploitation and infrastructural use in Québec regions.

Québec Petroleum Operations Company (Soquip)

The Québec Petroleum Operations Company was set up by the Québec government on November 28, 1969. It was a "joint stock company with the attributes of a private company,"[149] but all issued shares were held by the government. The rationale for the creation of Soquip lay in the insecurity of supply and costs of petroleum towards the end of the sixties. Not only were 75% of Québec energy needs met by oil, but 80% of the oil consumed was imported from Venezuela and the Middle East. The dangers of depending too much on imported oil were made obvious during the 1957 and 1967 Suez crises, and also when the Organization of Petroleum Exporting Countries decided to increase oil prices. Finally, the Québec government anticipated that the Portland-Montreal pipeline, which brought in the oil from the Middle East and Venezuela, would not be able to satisfy oil demands by the end of the seventies. So that, as Bernard Cloutier, president of Soquip, said: "The creation of Soquip reflects the awareness by the government of the vital importance of the security of supply and the cost of energy for the economic development of Québec."[150]

In accordance with this objective, Soquip was given a broad mandate in its charter — covering, in fact, all phases of petroleum activity: production, refining, and distribution. The objects of the company were described in section 3 of the charter as:

> a) to explore for, produce, store, transport and sell crude hydrocarbons in liquid or gaseous forms;
> b) to participate in the refining of crude hydrocarbons in liquid or gaseous forms, in the storage, transport and sale of refined hydrocarbons, and in the development of discoveries of hydrocarbons made by others. It should also associate itself with any person, partnership or corporation for such purposes.[151]

As in the case of Soquem, the government made it clear that Soquip would only get involved in the refining and sale of petroleum in conjunction or association with the private sector. The government's intent to insure that Soquip give priority to exploration and not get involved in refining and sales was made obvious by section 14 of the charter which stated that Soquip could not "exercise its powers respecting the objects contemplated in sub-paragraph b of section 3 . . . without the authorization of the Lieutenant-Governor in Council."[152] Cloutier, for one, had little doubt that the government had chosen to limit Soquip's role to exploration:

> Amongst this spread of possible activities, Soquip's shareholder has chosen to give priority to the development of the petroleum potential of Québec's sedimentary basins through their systematic exploration, in partnership with private companies when possible.[153]

Thus, since 1969, Soquip limited itself to exploration. It acquired holdings of 39 million acres, 10 million of which were being explored in partnership with 10 private companies, including Shell, Texaco, and Gulf. It conducted many land-based and marine seismic surveys and participated with private companies in drilling eight wildcat wells. The main regions where it concentrated its exploration were the Gulf of St. Lawrence basin, the Baie des Chaleurs, the Anticosti basin, and the Taconic Complex.[154] In effect, then, Soquip's main function was to subsidize the exploration efforts of private industry. This was in line with Cloutier's conception of Soquip's role as an adjunct to private enterprise: "In the free-enterprise context of North America, the role of Soquip is to welcome, initiate and promote any industrial and commercial operations which can increase the security of Québec's oil supply . . ."[155]

As regards financing, Soquip was originally granted $15 million for a 10-year period. This was certainly insufficient to get involved in production, but is was hardly adequate for Soquip to carry out major exploration activities. As David Oancia of the *Montreal Star* put it: "Anyone in the oil business knows that not many wells can be drilled when the total investment is held down to $1.5 million a year."[156] Further, according to the *Financial Post,* drilling costs can easily reach $3 million per hole, and "some 200 holes were drilled in the North Sea's chilly waters before a commercial gas find was brought in."[157] The main effect of Soquip's low budget was to force it to seek partnership with private oil companies.

In 1974, the Québec government granted $7.5 million to Soquip for the 1974-75 year and made a long-term commitment of $92.5 million. Although no offical stipulation was made with regards to the time span over which the province would make its expenditures, this was certainly an improvement.[158] The main function of Soquip was to pay part of the costs in order to encourage private companies to invest in oil exploration:

> Québec's $100-million funding of Soquip (the figure includes funds spent to date) is seed money aimed to attract joint ventures with private corporations.
> The record so far is strong. Soquip is now seeing $4.50 spent by private interests for every $1 put into joint ventures, vs, a $1.30: $1 ratio two years ago.[159]

As in the case of Soquem, private companies were prepared to get involved in joint ventures when the preliminary findings were most promising. Thus, according to Cloutier, "The recent jump in joint venture money was the result of two wells which produced useful but expensive information."[160] Here again, then, a Québec state institution set up what could be considered a sophisticated subsidy system or incentive program: It absorbed part of the risks and costs involved in a project but chose to remain a junior partner — leaving the initiative and control of the operation to private companies.

The government went against the wishes of Soquip's management by preventing the company from getting involved in sales and refining. In 1970, for example, Soquip expressed the desire to install a service station outside Québec City. This initiative was blocked by the government. As the *Financial Post* put it: "Soquip got its knuckles rapped by its shareholder last spring when it proposed setting up a service station near Québec City."[161] More recently, Soquip President Cloutier made it clear that the government's unwillingness was the only obstacle to Soquip's involvement in production and distribution: "When the cabinet allows us, we will go on to the second phase: the refining and sale of hydrocarbons . . ."[162]

On November 16, 1972, a governmental white paper on energy policy was made public by Gilles Massé, minister of natural resources. The white paper was critical of the inadequate amounts of exploration and investments made by private oil companies. It suggested that the Québec government should get involved in the refining, by buying an existing refinery or building a new one, and distribution of oil, through service stations. Specifically, the white paper, which was approved by the cabinet, recommended that Soquip be given the mandate to regroup independent distributors of gasoline and heating oil not only to reinforce their market position but also to create a mixed corporation to produce, refine, stock, and distribute oil. The report also suggested the construction of a deep-water port in the St. Lawrence

River for foreign oil tankers in order to reduce Québec's dependence on the Montréal-Portland pipeline and in order to reduce transportation costs.[163]

The objective of the white paper, then, was the creation of a parallel state-controlled oil producing company alongside the existing large private oil companies. This state-controlled sector would participate in all phases of oil exploitation, including purchasing directly from the foreign suppliers, exploration, refining, and sales through service stations. The white paper argued that direct negotiations with the supplying countries and direct competition with the multinational oil companies would serve the long-term needs of the province by keeping prices low and by reducing the province's dependence on the prices fixed by the oil companies.[164]

The governmental white paper was launched with considerable publicity and was heralded by several ministers as a major government move to solve Québec's energy problems. On March 12, 1973, Massé reiterated at a press conference the government's intention to regroup independent distributors and to create, with the help of financial institutions, an integrated state-managed oil sector in Québec. He underlined the urgency of the situation and stated that the project would be started before the end of 1973. He noted that the Québec Deposit and Investment Fund had already been invited to participate in the group and that several meetings had been held with independent distributors and financial institutions.[165]

The government intentions in the oil sector met with considerable opposition in the business community, particularly from the major oil producers.[166] In December 1972, a meeting was held between the oil companies and the department of industry and commerce. The government apparently wanted to consult the companies on its plan to participate directly in the purchasing of oil supplies.[167] As seen earlier, the interviews demonstrated that the General Council of Industry was quite hostile to the government initiative. In May 1973, the GCI presented a brief to St. Pierre and Garneau condemning the projected intervention in the oil field. Further, an interview with an executive of the Québec Chambre de Commerce revealed that this business association was also active in its opposition to the project. He claimed that the Chambre met with Bourassa and several cabinet ministers on May 14, 1973, to tell them that the government was not justified in its decision to intervene in the refining and distribution of oil products. He stated further that the project had its origins in Soquip "wanting to expand its empire."[168]

The recommendations of the white paper seemed to have been dropped, despite their earlier approval by the Québec cabinet. According to a *La Presse* editorial in November 1973, the project was suspended following the highly critical brief presented by the GCI:

> Following the very controversial brief presented to ministers Guy St. Pierre and Raymond Garneau by the General Council of Industry last May, the studies concerning a deep water port and the talks with the eventual partners of a mixed Québec-based refinery were suspended.[169]

Garneau's statement, when he announced a budget increase for Soquip, that the new funds had to be used exclusively for exploration indicated that the project was not simply delayed but dropped.[170]

Thus, Soquip activities have remained exclusively in the area of exploration. Its attempts to get involved in refining and distribution, which were the profitable phases of oil production, were successfully opposed by private companies. As regards exploration, Soquip remained a junior partner to private enterprise; it satisfied itself with financing part of the explorations costs without exercising any control over the projects.

What then can be concluded from this analysis of state enterprises? First, Québec state institutions, with the exception of Hydro-Québec and the Québec Deposit and Investment Fund, were marginal in the overall Québec economy. Because of limited budgets and restricted spheres of operation, they did not have a significant impact on the economic sector in which they operated and they did not contribute to increasing the government's decision-making power in the economic sphere.

Second, the Québec state enterprises conceived their roles in such a way as to make them primarily complements or adjuncts to private enterprise. Soquem and Soquip, for example, subsidized mining and oil companies by paying part of the exploration costs. The Deposit and Investment Fund made capital available to private enterprise without exercising any control on the companies using its capital. The GIC bailed out companies on the verge of bankruptcy. Hydro-Québec made electricity available at a low cost for industrial users and undertook multi-billion dollar projects to increase the supply of electricity. It would be simplistic to dismiss state companies as mere tools of private enterprise, but it would be even more presumptuous to claim that they contributed to making Quebecers "maîtres chez nous."

The interviews with businessmen confirmed the above arguments. Most businessmen dismissed the state economic institutions as marginal. The president of a business association, for example, thought that, apart from the Québec Deposit and Investment Fund, the state enterprises were "insignificant in the Québec economy" and played "supplementive roles to private enterprise."[171] An executive of a bank said: "Governmental interventions do not harm business," and that, "on the contrary, they can be conducive to the development of sectors which can eventually be profitable for private enterprise."[172]

NOTES

(1) Birnbaum, p. 59.

(2) Allan Fenton, "Economic Planning in Free Societies," *Canadian Business*, February 1963, p. 26.

(3) Ibid.

(4) Ibid. Fenton quoted A. J. Little, vice-president of the Canadian Chamber of Commerce, as saying: "An absolute essential prerequisite to economic progress in Canada today is planning — intensive, intelligent planning, both long and short range, at the government level" (p. 28).

(5) Canadian Manufacturers' Association, *An Industrial Policy for Quebec*, p. 3.

(6) Laurent Bélanger, *Evolution du patronat et ses répercussions sur les attitudes et pratiques patronales dans la province de Québec*, study no. 14, Privy Council Office (Ottawa: Queen's Printer, January 1970) (p. 110).

(7) According to Birnbaum, state intervention in the economy has involved the "nationalization of risk" but has not touched corporate profits (p. 85).

(8) Rick Deaton, "The Fiscal Crisis of the State," in Dimitrios Roussopoulos, ed., *The Political Economy of the State* (Montréal: Black Rose Books, 1973), p. 19.

(9) Daniel Johnson, "Les Intentions du gouvernement pour les mois à venir," *Le Devoir*, 2 May 1968.

(10) Guy St. Pierre, "Le Québec en quête d'une politique économique," *Le Devoir*, 1 May 1972. St. Pierre declared he had "faith in private enterprise" and "less faith in public enterprise" (quoted in Ian Rodger, "How Guy St. Pierre Hopes to Save Québec Capitalism").

(11) Guy St. Pierre, "Le Québec en quête d'une politique économique."

(12) Quoted in Claude Beauchamp, "Du Québec doit jaillir . . ." *La Presse*, 23 May 1972.

(13) Quoted in Jacques Keable, "Notre marge de manoeuvre est très mince."

(14) Riopel and Takacsy, p. 62.

(15) La Presse Canadienne, "L'Industrie du textile peut créer 20% des nouveaux emplois nécessaires au Québec," *La Presse*, 12 June 1970.

(16) Interview, May 1973.

(17) *Les Gens du Québec: St-Henri* (Montréal: Éditions Québécoises, 1972), pp. 4-15.

(18) *Financial Post*, 4 February 1961.

(19) According to a Canadian businessman interviewed by the *Montreal Gazette* in 1972, the government has been "getting Bourassa himself on the phone to the larger potential investors recently, asking them what has to be done to get them to move into Québec." An Ontario industrialist confirmed that he received such a call from Bourassa in which he was asked "what could be done to get us to build a plant somewhere in the province" (quoted by David Tafler, "Canadian Businessmen: Everyone is Scared of Québec," 8 June 1972).

(20) Cyrille Felteau, "Québec veut stopper l'exode des épargnes," *La Presse*, 6 February 1973.

(21) Interview, May 1973.

(22) Riopel and Takacsy, in a report prepared for the GCI, warned: "The provincial government must resist the temptation to resort to fiscal gimmickry or outright coercion in its endeavour to ensure that private savings generated in Québec are invested within the province's boundaries" (p. 78).

(23) According to Dominique Clift, "Québec Quizzes Bell," *Montreal Star*, 25 January 1972, "The claims of the Québec government are difficult to prove because of the way in which Bell reports on its operations. The company's financial statement give [sic] few indications of the purpose and nature of its investments nor of their geographical location."

(24) Louis Fournier, "Dossier amiante," *Québec-Presse*, 25 March 1973. See also Louis-Bernard Robitaille, "Dans le secteur de l'amiante, les emplois et les profits vont aux U.S.A.," *La Presse*, 12 June 1972. This severe diagnosis of the industry and of the government's inaction was probably what prompted the government not to publish the report.

(25) Information was from a secret governmental paper on the asbestos industry quoted in Robitaille, "Dans le secteur de l'amiante." The report also noted that much of the profits made by local asbestos producers left the province. Between 1961 and 1966, Québec asbestos mines distributed some $249 million of profits to their shareholders (e.g., American firms), but paid only $193 million in salaries.

(26) Robert Pouliot, "Tessier rassure l'industrie de l'amiante en supprimant des passages d'un rapport," *La Presse*, 26 January 1973. See also Denis Giroux, "Le Scandale de l'amiante," *Magazine Maclean*, January 1975, pp. 30-35.

(27) David Lewis, "Les Cadeaux du régime Trudeau aux grosses compagnies," *Le Devoir*, 19 September 1972.

(28) L. Chisholm, "Bold Plans For Expansion," *Financial Post*, 14 July 1962.

(29) R. E. Powell, unpublished letter to Maurice Duplessis (concerning the needs of Aluminum Company of Canada in electricity), 4 March 1946. The letter was obtained from T. L. Brock, corporate secretary of Aluminum Company of Canada.

(30) Ibid.

(31) Chisholm, "Bold Plans."

(32) Chambre de Commerce de la Province de Québec, *List of Technical and Financial Aids from Federal and Provincial Governments to Commerce and Industry in Québec* Montréal: Chambre de Commerce de la Province de Québec, June 1972).

(33) Ibid.

(34) Ibid.

(35) See annual reports of Industrial Credit Bureau for 1968-1971.

(36) According to article 2, the financial assistance was available for the "construction, improvement or enlargement of a plant," as well as "the purchase of machinery, inventions and patents," or the "improvement of the financial structure of the company." See Québec National Assembly, *Bill 20* (Québec: Editeur Officiel du Québec, 1971).

(37) *Financial Times*, "Perspectives on Quebec."

(38) Canadian Manufacturers' Association, app. G, p. 2.

(39) *La Presse*, 18 August 1972.

(40) Riopel and Takacsy, p. 55.

(41) Ibid., p. 79.

(42) *La Presse*, "La SDI," 17 April 1973.

(43) Two members of the Québec Industrial Development Corporation resigned in July 1972. Robert Gagnon and Jacques Clermont claimed that the corporation was too much of a financial institution and not enough of an industrial development agency. They also complained that the corporation had not been given enough decision-making autonomy by the department of industry and commerce.

(44) Gilbert Athot ("Crise dans l'industrie des pâtes et papier," *Le Soleil*, 29 May 1972) estimated that 12,650 workers were laid off in 1970 and 9,000 in 1971.

(45) Several reasons were given for the economic problems of the industry — including U.S. economic problems, the revaluation of the Canadian dollar, the port strikes in U.S. and Canada, and the fiscal exemptions program of the U.S. government (Disc). J. P. Monge, president of CIP, blamed industry for the problems of the pulp and paper sector. He criticized the industry for "not having been too imaginative," for not spending enough money on research, and for increasing capacity too much after World War II (quoted in *Financial Post*, "Marketing Board No Answer for Paper," 16 October 1971).

(46) Amy Booth, "From Pulp and Paper: Smiles," *Financial Post*, 13 May 1972.

(47) See copy of Robert Bourassa's speech to the American Paper Institute in New York (*Le Devoir*, "Vers une réorientation des priorités québécoises dans l'industrie du papier," 13 March 1974) in which the premier argued that the most effective contribution the government could make to the pulp and paper industry was to help reduce the cost of wood supplies.

(48) It should be noted that ITT, Rayonnier's parent company, had annual sales that were nearly double the Québec budget ($7.3 billion in 1971) and had profits of $353 million in 1970.

(49) Information on ITT — Rayonnier subsidy was from Walter Stewart, "$57 Million Deal Helps ITT Exploit Québec Forests," *Toronto Star*, 8 May 1972.

(50) Ibid. Ian Rodger of the *Financial Post* quoted one pulp and paper industry executive as saying: "The deal looks more to me like a concession with another name, rather than a real domanial forest" (Pulp Firms Surprisingly Willing on Forestry Reform," *Financial Post*, 30 October 1970).

(51) Ibid.

(52) Ibid.

(53) Ibid.

(54) Ibid.

(55) Ibid.

(56) Interview, May 1973.

(57) Interview, May 1973.

(58) Interview, May 1973.

(59) See Louis Sabourin, "Les Bois du Québec sont des cimetières," *Québec-Presse*, 13 August 1972.

(60) Amy Booth, Québec Examines Roots of Woods Tenure Usage," *Financial Post*, 10 August 1963.

(61) Ibid.

(62) Jacques Parizeau, "La Vertu, la maternité et l'exploitation forestière," *Québec-Presse*, 2 April 1972.

(63) Ian Rodger, "Québec to Impose Direct Management of Forest." *Financial Post*, 8 July 1972.

(64) See Gilles Lesage, "Québec abolira progressivement les concessions et les réserves," *Le Devoir*, 29 March 1972.

(65) Roch Desaulnais, "Des Réactions au livre blanc sur la politique forestière," *Québec-Presse*, 9 April 1972.

(66) Parizeau, "La Vertu, la maternité."

(67) See La Presse Canadienne, "Domtar dénonce le réforme forestière projetée au Québec," *La Presse*, 1 September 1972, and "CIP et Consol somment le ministre Drummond de rédiger un nouveau livre blanc sur la forêt," *La Presse*, 8 September 1972. See also Association des Industries Forestières du Québec, *Mémoire sur l'exposé sur la politique forestière* (Québec: Association des Industries Forestières, June 1972).

(68) According to Ian Rodger, "Direct Management," "Depending on how the government juggles the stumpage rates in the future, it could make it even cheaper for the concessionaires simply to give up their concessions without immediate compensation; that is why industry men are reluctant to condemn the principle of a change in the management system before they see the details."

(69) Canadian International Paper, *Brief to the Parliamentary Commission on Natural Resources and Lands and Forests* (Montréal: Canadian International Paper, June 1972), p. 13.

Paul Lachance, president of the Conseil des Producteurs des Pâtes et Papiers, stated that the pulp and paper producers were very open to any modifications in the present system, but they wanted the costs of wood supplies to be reduced and adequate compensation for the concessions (Roch Desaulnais, "Réactions au livre blanc").

(70) Association des Industries Forestières, p. 23.

(71) La Presse Canadienne, "Domtar dénonce le reforme forestière,"

(72) Ian Rodger, "Direct Management."

(73) La Presse Canadienne. "Drummond fustige l'attitude réactionnaire des grandes sociétés de pâtes et papiers," *Le Devoir*, 25 August 1972.

(74) Quoted in *Le Devoir*, "La CIP ne viendra pas nous dire quoi faire!" 11 September 1972.

(75) La Presse Canadienne, "Drummond cède aux pressions et retarde son projet de gestion de la forêt," *La Presse*, 30 October 1972.

(76) La Presse Canadienne, "CIP et Consol somment le ministre."

(77) Idem. "Le projet de loi visant à abolir les concessions forestières sera déposé d'ici l'ajournement," *La Presse*, 23 May 1973.

(78) Interview, May 1973.

(79) Interview, May 1973.

(80) Québec Federation of Labor, *Le Gouvernement de la minorité* (Montréal: Québec Federation of Labor, 1972), p. 14.

(81) Ibid. The FTQ document estimated that government revenues increased fourfold during the 1961 to 1970 period. During the same period, the product of income taxes increased by 1,100% and that of corporate taxes by 150%. See pp. 13-15.

(82) Ibid., p. 28.

(83) The CPQ's budget proposals were published the next day in *Le Devoir*. Acceding to the *Financial Post* ("Input From Market Place, But No Political Fence Mending," 31 March 1973), the proposals, which were prepared with "expert assistance," "were in fact a complete budget for the province," providing "detailed

accounts of expected revenue, how this revenue should be spent and whether the year should end with a deficit or surplus."

(84) Budget information is from Claude Masson and Claude Beauchamp, "Tout sur le budget du Québec," *La Presse*, 19 April 1972.

(85) The budget of the Center was increased from $3.5 million to $4.5 million. The Conseil had asked for a $3 — to $4 — million increase.

(86) The recommendation read as follows: "Le CPQ recommande que la politique salariale du gouvernement tienne vraiment compte des réalités de l'économie québécoise. Toute comparaison avec l'Ontario ou avec les États américains qui ne tient pas compte du fait que le rendement des économies de cette province ou de ces États est bien supérieur au rendement de l'économie du Québec serait inacceptable" (*Le Devoir*, 25 January 1972).

(87) See *La Presse*, "Le Gouvernement démontre qu'il entend vivre selon ses moyens," 20 April 1972, and "Réconfort chez les manufacturiers," 13 April 1972; and Chambre de Commerce de la Province de Montréal, *Mémoire annuel* (Montréal: Chambre de Commerce de la Province de Québec, June 1972), p. 4.

(88) *La Presse*, "Le Gouvernement démontre qu'il entend vivre."

(89) Ibid.

(90) Interview, May 1973.

(91) Interview, May 1973. The same executive quoted Bourassa's reaction towards the Conseil's budget proposals: "C'est excellent votre affaire. Si je ne suis pas plus enthousiaste en publique, si ma réaction est modérée, c'est à cause de l'opinion publique; je ne veux pas qu'il soit dit que c'est le patronat qui nous mène."

(92) *Financial Post*, "Input From Market Place."

(93) Jacques Parizeau, "Au Québec, l'État doit intervenir," *Québec-Presse*, 15 February 1970.

(94) Léon Dion, "L'Entreprise et la société québécoise," p. 15.

(95) Hydro-Québec, *1975 Annual Report* (Montréal: Hydro-Québec, 1973).

(96) Jean-Paul Lefebvre, "État s'abstenir, " *Magazine Maclean*, November 1972, p. 43.

(97) It should be noted that 37.48% of Québec's total electricity was not nationalized. Thus, immunity from nationalization was granted to some 30 private companies, including Aluminum Company of Canada, which produced electricity for their own use. See Carol Jobin, "La Nationalisation de l'électricité au Québec en 1962," MA thesis dissertation, Université du Québec à Montréal, August 1974, pp. 65-68.

(98) *Financial Times*, "Perspectives on Québec."

(99) Alain Batty, "L'Hydro-Québec dix ans après la nationalisation," *Le Jour*, 19 June 1974. The figures are from Statistics Canada, catalogue no. 57-202.

According to Jobin ("La Nationalisation de l'électricité), the domestic rate for electricity increased by 19% from 1960 to 1970, while the commercial rate decreased by 16% and the industrial rate remained stable (pp. 230-33).

(100) Patrick Durrant, "Shareholders Advised to Take Québec Offer," *Financial Post*, 23 March 1963. The *Financial Post* analysis included details of the Québec government's offer and the fluctuation of the market price of the shares for each company. According to Jobin ("La Nationalisation de l'électricité), the Québec government offer was, on the average, 20% higher than the most recent market price for the stock (p. 76).

(101) Jobin ("La Nationalisation de l'électricité) claimed that in 1960, the rate of return on invested capital in the electricity industry was only 4.45% (p. 186).

(102) Ibid. Jobin estimated that Power Corporation obtained $20 million in compensation as a result of the nationalization (p. 187).

(103) The businessmen interviewed also expressed satisfaction with regard to the operations of Hydro-Québec. An executive of a business association did, however, complain that Hydro-Québec had acquired "too much independence," and that "the government should give itself the instruments to control it effectively" (interview, May 1973).

(104) *Financial Post*, "Quebeckers Take No Fliers; Timid with Capital — Filion," 8 February 1964.

(105) Laurie Chisholm, "Bold Plans For Expansion," *Financial Post*, 14 July 1962.

(106) Quoted in Jacques Pigeon, "La SGF mettra en vente au printemps des actions à $10 chacune," *La Presse*, 13 November 1963.

(107) Quoted in *Le Devoir*, "La SGF, première banque d'affaire," 11 July 1962.

(108) René Paré, "Comment Devenir maîtres chez nous," *Revue Commerce*, vol 65, no. 2, March 1963.

(109) In 1971, the government of Québec owned 50.29% of the stock, the caisses populaires 16.58%, other financial institutions 28.38%, and the public 4.75%.

(110) David Lord was bought by the GIC in 1964 for a price of $2.6 million and resold to the original owner in 1972 for $1.1 million,

(111) See Confederation of National Trade Unions, *Qui a mis le cadenas dans Soma* (Montréal: Confederation of National Trade Unions, December 1972).

(112) Gérard Leblanc, "Trois des $25 millions de la SGF serviront à transformer Soma en une usine d'autobus," *Le Devoir*, 19 December 1973.

(113) Gérard Filion quoted in Diane Ethier, "L'Histoire de Sogefor," unpublished paper presented to an MA seminar on Québec politics at the Université du Québec à Montréal.

(114) Jacques Parizeau, "L'État doit intervenir."

(115) Société Générale de Financement: *Rapport Annuel: 1975*, SGF, 1975, 1p. 6.

(116) Quoted in Gérald Godin, "La Caisse de Dépôt permet au gouvernement de se soustraire à l'empire de la haute finance," *Québec-Presse*, 7 December 1969.

(117) Quoted in Claude Prieur, "La Caisse de Dépôt et de Placement," *Forces*, no. 11, 1970.

(118) Quoted in Gérald Godin, "La Caisse de Dépôt."

(119) See the dicussion of the financial syndicate in chapter 5.

(120) Jacques Parizeau, "Claude Prieur, un grand commis de l'Etat," *Québec-Presse*, 15 April 1973.

(121) Alain Pinard, "Your Money at Work for Québec," *Montréal Star*, 11 January 1972.

(122) It should be noted that bonds do not give the investor decision-making power in the company; unlike stocks, they do not represent ownership of a company.

(123) Québec Deposit and Investment Fund, *1973 Annual Report* (Montréal: Québec Deposit and Investment Fund, 1973).

(124) It should be noted that the Fund's stock portfolio was kept secret — contrary to that of mutual funds, trust funds, and other financial institutions. According to Louis Fournier ("SMA + Power + Caisse de Dépôt," *Québec-Presse*, 13 February 1972), the Fund has a 10% interest in Power Corporation and actually helped Power in 1972 to take over control of SMA, a company involved in surveys, cinema production, etc., by purchasing $200,000 of SMA capital stock, while Power was acquiring $400,000 worth.

(125) Claude Prieur, "La Caisse de Dépôt," p. 6.

(126) Ibid., p.7.

(127) Québec Deposit and Investment Fund, *1972 Annual Report* (Montréal: Québec Deposit and Investment Fund, 1972).

(128) Interview, May 1973.

(129) Interview, May 1973.

(130) Interview, May 1973.

(131) See François Taisne, "Sidbec," unpublished paper presented to an MA seminar in Québec politics at the Université du Québec à Montréal, April 1974.

(132) Quoted in Denis Giroux, "Québec Steel Production Far Below Needs," *Montreal Gazette*, 13 December 1973.

Economist Jacques Parizeau defined Sidbec's objective in much the same way as St. Pierre: "L'objectif reste ce qu'il a toujours été: celui de fournir au centre industriel du Québec des produits sidérurgiques et, en particulier, des produits plats à un prix aussi bas et avec des délais de livraison aussi courts que ceux dont dispose le centre industriel de l'Ontario" ("Le Rôle capital des organismes publics et mixtes créés depuis sept ans," *Le Devoir*, 4 December 1969).

(133) Quoted in Denis Giroux, "Steel Production Below Needs."

(134) Quoted in Jean-Paul Lefebvre, "État, s'abstenir."

(135) Ibid.

(136) Denis Giroux, "Steel Production Below Needs."

(137) Québec National Assembly, *National Assembly Debates* (Québec: Editeur Officiel du Québec, May 1965), pp. 2221 and 2622.

(138) Quoted in Québec Mining Exploration Company, *1971 Annual Report* (Québec: Québec Mining Exploration Company, 1971), p. 4.

(139) Côme Carbonneau, "Soquem: bilan de quatre années d'activités," *Le Devoir*, 15 July 1970.

(140) Québec Mining Exploration Company, *1971 Annual Report*, p. 9.

(141) According to Québec Mining Exploration Company, *1968 Annual Report* (Québec: Québec Mining Exploration Company, 1968), p. 10. Soquem contributed $1.5 million to the joint projects, whereas private companies only put in $500,000 in 1967-68.

(142) Québec Mining Exploration Company, *1971 Annual Report*, p. 9.

(143) Ibid., p. 12.

(144) Ibid., p. 22.

(145) Ibid.

(146) Quoted in Candide Charest-Wallot, "La Soquem sert-elle les intérêts de la société québécoise?" unpublished paper presented to an MA seminar in Québec politics at the Université du Québec à Montréal, April 1974.

(147) According to a bank executive, "Soquem is justified because some mining research has not been done by private enterprise. If Soquem discovers a copper deposit, for example, it will probably be transferred to private enterprise; in any case, it will have a good effect on economic development and on private industry" (interview, May 1973).

(148) According to Claude Genest (quoted in Candide Charest — Wallot, "La Soquem"), "Soquem does not get involved in production as a matter of policy, except when the partner prefers it or in order to insure that production is orderly and methodical."

(149) Québec Petroleum Operations Company, *1971 Annual Report* (Québec: Québec Petroleum Operations Company, 1971), p. 4.

(150) Ibid.

(151) Ibid., p. 6.

(152) Ibid.

(153) Ibid., p. 4.

(154) For information, see *Financial Post*, "Québec Still Dreams of Finding the Big Gusher," 30 March 1974.

(155) Québec Petroleum Operations Company, *1971 Annual Report*, p. 4.

(156) David Oancia, "Oil: Give Us Money, We'll Punch Holes," *Montreal Star*, 16 February 1974.

(157) Frederick Rose, "Québec Gets Serious in its Search for Oil," *Financial Post*, 13 April 1974.

(158) Ibid.

(159) *Financial Post*, "Québec Still Dreams of Finding the Big Gusher."

(160) Quoted ibid.

(161) Ian Rodger, "How Soquip Promotes Oil Deals in Québec," *Financial Post*, 6 November 1971.

(162) Quoted in Jacques Forget, "Serons-nous bientôt pétroquébécois?" *Perspectives*, 12 January 1974, p. 3.

(163) Information from *La Presse*, "Québec réduira sa dépendance dans le domaine énergétique," 17 November 1972.

As early as August 16, 1972, Massé had expressed his desire to see a state-controlled oil refinery in Québec. He stated: "Il serait indécent que la prochaine raffinerie soit construite par l'entreprise privée avec les mêmes avantages dont a bénéficié la Golden Eagle à Saint-Romuald près de Québec" (in Denis Giroux, "Un Tribunal de l'énergie pour le Québec," *Le Devoir*, 16 August 1972).

(164) The dependency and helplessness of the Québec government vis-à-vis the oil companies was made evident during the "energy crisis" in 1973-74. Thus, the department of natural resources, despite repeated attemps, did not succeed in finding out from the oil companies the quantity of oil reserves available. Massé told the National Assembly that there was nothing the government could do to force the oil companies to inform the government on the state of their oil reserves (in Bernard Racine, "Le Problème énergétique témoigne de l'impuissance du gouvernement," *Le Devoir*, 18 January 1974).

(165) For more information, see Robert Pouliot, "Québec se hâte de créer une société mixte du pétrole," *La Presse*, 13 March 1973.

(166) Ibid.

(167) Claude Beauchamp, "Québec convoque les 'grands' du pétrole," *La Presse*, 12 December 1972.

(168) Interview, May 1973.

(169) Robert Pouliot, editorial on the energy policy, *La Presse*, 3 November 1973.

(170) See Jacques Parizeau, "Le Torpillage de Soquip," *Québec-Presse*, 7 April 1974.

(171) Interview, May 1973.

(172) Interview, May 1973.

CONCLUSION

THIS STUDY WILL NOT have achieved much if it is perceived simply as yet another episode in the continuing saga of political corruption. Those who gloat smugly over the subservience of the Bourassa government to business interests and who claim that "it could only happen in Québec" have missed the point. It should be emphasized that the source of the political power of the capitalist class is not greedy business leaders or corrupt politicians but results rather from their dominant ownership and control of the means of production, and the ideological hegemony which they exercise over the entire society.

Simply put, the power exercised by the capitalist class over production, investments, technological and scientific innovations, and distribution gives that class a determinant role in the development and welfare of a society. The various case studies of governmental legislation in chapters 8, 9 and 10 demonstrate how business does not hesitate to use raw economic power: threats to relocate, cut down investments or halt production, in order to achieve its political objectives.

Business-government relations in Québec are characterized by an high degree of crudity. The recent events surrounding the Olympic games and dredging contracts, as well as the declarations of Québec cabinet ministers in favour of "good patronage," draw attention to this province. It is also likely however that some French-Canadian entrepreneurs and politicians have adopted a get-rich-quick-no-matter-what-the-consequences attitude reminiscent of the early stages of the industrial revolution. In a way, they are less conscious of the long-term interests of their class.

It is dangerous, however, to overemphasize the unsavoury behaviour of individual members of the capitalist class or the political directorate. It can too easily lay the groundwork for the coming to power of an alternate ruling class or the acceptance of a different programme for governing the same economic system. The experience of social-democratic parties in Europe and Canada is sobering in that respect. Their relatively innocuous behaviour once in office and their constant efforts to maintain "the confidence of business" are proof that the functions of the state are primarily determined by the structures of capitalist society rather than by the individuals who occupy positions of state power.

It should be kept· in mind that we live in a class society, and that the patterns of exploitation and domination cannot be eliminated by simply taking over control of the state apparatus. Social-democratic parties and European communist parties misjudge the negative effects of seizing state power. They forget not only that the means of production must be taken over and reorganized, but also that they must be controlled by the working class and the population as a whole.

While it serves the interests of the capitalist class, the state is not simply an instrument in the hands of business or private enterprise. As Gramsci has argued, the state is relatively autonomous; it sustains the long term interests of the capitalist class as a whole, and it is also capable of transcending the parochial, individual interests of specific capitalists and capitalist class fractions. It is obvious that not all state policies can be explained by direct corporate initiatives. In the analysis of Québec, it is clear that there are some cases where business is not totally satisfied with governmental policy. In the field of language and education, for example, business would prefer the status quo or no legislation at all. The same can be said of consumer protection legislation. Business did however succeed in making these pieces of legislation innocuous by either defusing or amending some of the provisions which it judged detrimental to its interests. Thus, state policies are often the result of a dialogue or compromise between the business sector and the government. Also, the state, at least to some extent, has the function of ensuring the political survival and credibility of the capitalist system, and this is done in part by what have been called "timely concessions" to opponents of the capitalist class.

Much of the data presented in this study constitute an indictment of the "quiet revolution" in Québec. The growth of the state and the flood of so-called reforms since 1960 have not had a major impact on the distribution of power in Québec. The working class and other social groups have been unable to improve their relative economic position and their political power vis-à-vis the capitalist class. The relationship between the Québec state and large capital has remained largely the same as during the Duplessis years. The overall effect of the quiet revolution has been to modernize Québec economic structures and infrastructures, and to strenghten capitalism.

It is also clear from this study that the ruling class in Québec possesses a solid unity of interest and purpose at the political level. This unity binds the English, French and foreign elements of the ruling class firmly together, and is reflected in the actions and priorities of the state, irrespective of the government or political party in power. The ruling class, particularly at the upper levels, has a stong degree of organization and a capacity to understand its self-interest which contributes to the effectiveness of its power. This is in sharp contrast with the working class or unorganized majority which is constantly hampered by its internal divisions and organizational shortcomings. These weaknesses must be remedied as an essential first step to overthrowing the ruling class.

Notwithstanding the general argument presented above, this study makes no claim at having analysed the overall role of the state in Québec society. I pursued the more limited objective of examining the links between the ruling class and the state. I hope to have shed some light on the rapidly developing links between the capitalist class and the state apparatus. The data presented indicates that business has not only been able to dominate key institutional structures but has also enjoyed remarkable success in determining the general orientation and specific contents of Québec governmental policy.

A fuller understanding of the role of the state would require, at the very least, a detailed study of the dynamics of the Québec economy and a more profound analysis of what Gramsci calls "civil society." The role of ideology and of the civil society is obviously crucial in maintaining the hegemony of the capitalist class. To the extent that the capitalist class succeeds in having its own interests and ideology accepted by the society as a whole, the state will be able to avoid using overt or repressive means to ensure the domination by the ruling class.

APPENDIX A

NOTES ON METHODOLOGY

This section will include a brief and critical evaluation of the two major approaches which have been used to study influence and power: the institutional approach and the decision-making approach. It will also show how this study has attempted to integrate the more useful elements of each into a workable methodology.

The Institutional or Positional Approach

The majority of studies dealing with the power and influence of elites, groups, or classes fall into the category of an institutional or positional approach. This approach focusses either on the individuals or elites who control important societal institutions such as the state, media, business corporations, and labour unions, or on the groups and institutions themselves. Many analysts have put particular emphasis on the background and social characteristics of the individuals occupying senior positions in the social, economic, and political systems.[1]

These studies have usually assumed social origins to be crucial determinants of political attitudes and behaviour.[2] If, for example, it is found that the leaders at the top of the economic and political systems have similar upper or upper-middle-class origins, it is usually assumed that the autonomy of the two systems has broken down and that these leaders will cooperate, if not conspire, to foster their "class interests."[3] Speaking of the British political elites, W.L. Guttsman claimed these men "cannot easily be seen in isolation and apart from the character and power of a wider upper class from which so many of its members are recruited."[4]

Other analysts have focussed on the position of individuals and groups in the institutional hierarchy. Mills contended in *the Power Elite*: "No one can be truly powerful unless he has access to the command of major institutions, for it is over these institutional means of power that the truly powerful are, in the first instance, powerful."[5] Although Porter's *The Vertical Mosaic* dwelled extensively on the social characteristics of the Canadian elites, the book placed considerable emphasis on the numerous formal contacts, such as overlapping directorships, and informal contacts, as in membership in social clubs, among leaders of business, politics, media, and other power structures. Porter also analysed the amount of penetration of one system of power by another and the power differentials between institutional systems in terms of resources, means of access to decision-making structures, and pressure groups. More generally, he attempted to determine the relative power and independence of the various elite groups in society. He concluded that Canadian society is dominated by self-perpetuating and homogeneous elite groups, and that the corporate elite is the most important element in the power structure.

The main limitation of positional and institutional studies, including Porter's *The Vertical Mosaic,* Mills's *The Power Elite,* and Miliband's *The State in Capitalist Society,* is that they rely too heavily on class background and institutional factors as determinants of power.[6]. Nonetheless, institutional and positional factors are often crucial sources of power, and they frequently give the researcher some important clues as to why, how, and for whom power is exercised.

Another weakness of most institutional studies is that they tend to ignore the role of ideology in the exercise of power. Thus, an analysis of the political influence of business should include an appreciation of the "effort business makes to persuade society not merely to accept the policies it advocates but also the ethos, values and the goals which are its own, the economic system of which if forms the central part . . . [7] It is clear then that to the extent business succeeds in having its ideology pervade the whole of society and establishes a consensus based on its values, it is able to refrain from using its institutional sources of power. As the next sub-section tries to clarify, the importance of analysing the ideology of business is particularly obvious with respect to decision-making and with respect to a proper understanding of the role of government in the power structure.

Decision-making

The decision-making approach has come into use only recently, and there are still relatively few major studies which have used it. Theoretically, decision-making is quite simple. It involves isolating a decision and determining which individuals or groups were instrumental not only in bringing it about but also in influencing its content. In practice, however, there are major difficulties in this approach.

The first and most obvious difficulty is the secrecy which usually surrounds the decision-making process. The numerous informal contacts and pressures relating to a specific decision are rarely public knowledge. This difficulty can be overcome to some extent by avoiding the study of the process of influence, that is, specific pressures, and by comparing instead the desires or needs expressed by individuals or groups in their briefs and public statements with what they eventually obtained through the decision-making process.

In any case, the results of a pressure campaign in terms of success or failure are more important than its specific mechanics. Inevitably, this method tends to orient decision-making analysis towards group behaviour for in most cases it is easier to document the position of the Canadian Manufacturers' Association, the Board of Trade, or a specific corporation than it is to determine the personal influences which were involved in the process.

A second major difficulty in decision-making analysis is the classification of decisions. Many studies of influence and power have been rejected because of their alleged focus on secondary issues. Robert Dahl's study of community power in New Haven, for example, has been criticized by some observers for analysing decisions which they claimed were not crucial to the interests of business. Specifically, it has been argued that most decisions of importance to the corporate elite are taken at the national level, not at the community level.[8] The important question, then, is to define what is a key political issue. It would be pointless to analyse business influence in Quebec if the decisions were of marginal importance to the corporate elite. In order for a study to be significant, the decision has to be important to the group studied.[9] Peter Bachrach and Morton Baratz defined a key political issue as "one that involves a genuine challenge to the resources of power or authority of those who currently dominate the process by which policy outputs in the system are determined" and also as "one that involves a demand for enduring transformations in the polity in question and the value-allocation itself."[10]

According to the above definition, then, the focus should be on the issues or decisions which threaten or challenge the existing distribution of power and, more specifically, the power position of big business. This method is not entirely satisfactory, however, in that it is difficult to develop objective criteria regarding what represents challenges to the power of business. In fact, this study relies to a great extent on the subjective evaluations by business elites and groups as to what constitutes a threat to their position. It had to be assumed, too, that "when economic elites appear to be disinterested in a political decision, it is more than likely that it is because it is not threatening to their interests."[11]

The example of separatism in Québec sheds some light on the difficulty of distinguishing between subjective and objective interests. Even a superficial analysis of business reactions towards separatism suggests that the corporate elite in Québec considers separatism could undermine its power. But it could easily be argued that separatism, at least the Parti Québécois version of it, would objectively have very little effect on the distribution of power and would not threaten the survival of the economic system. There could also be significant subjective differences of perception between foreign owners, English managers, and French managers. It is likely, for example, that a U.S.-based owner would not feel threatened by separatism as long as the environment remained stable. English-Canadian managers, however, could feel their jobs would be in jeopardy, while some French-Canadian managers might be under the impression that separatism could help them reach the higher echelons of management more quickly.

The relevance of the traditional decision-making approach to the study of power is further jeopardized by the concept of non-decisions. Bachrach and Baratz have argued that a policy must overcome many barriers before it becomes a decision or an effective policy change; thus, community values and ideology as well as institutional factors can prevent a policy from ever entering the decision-making arena. In fact, Bachrach and Baratz chose to broaden the traditional concept of power by adding non-decisions:

> Power is exercised when A participates in the making of a decision which affects B . . . [But] power is also exercised when A devotes his energies to creating or reinforcing social and political values and institutional practices that limit the scope of the political process to public consideration of only those issues which are comparatively innocuous to A.[12]

More than that, they argued: "The primary method for sustaining a given mobilization of bias is non-decision-making"[13] and "there is a possibility that an individual or group in a community [will] participate more vigorously in supporting the non-decision-making process than in participating in actual decisions within the process."[14]

A related difficulty is the possibility of a decision or policy being blocked at the administrative stage. For example, much of the government legislation dealing with pollution, automobile safety standards, consumer protection, and monopoly practices has either not been enforced or been given limited application.[15] Hence, "the mere passage of an 'anti-business' bill may have a negligible effect if the standards and enforcement provisions of the bill are weak."[16]

Finally, a problem with the study of individual decisions is that the approach tends to be ahistorical. Decision-making analysis should include many decisions over a long period of time and also attempt to assess the cumulative effect of these decisions. To quote Miliband: "The important questions about government have to do . . . with the net impact of their tenure of office upon the economic and social order and upon the configuration of privilege and power in their societies."[17]

In addition to analysing the impact of a series of decisions on an issue-area, it is important to study more than one issue-area. Only in this way is it possible to make generalizations concerning the influence of a group within the power structure.

To conclude, a decision favourable to business can take many forms: the passage of legislation advantageous to business or other direct benefits such as protective tariffs, tax cuts, or subsidies; indirect benefits, such as laws or other government measures to limit the power of unions; the prevention of the implementation of legislation which could be detrimental to business; decisions which are not made because of business power or pressure (non-decisions); and, of course, the defeat of legislation unfavourable to business.

An Integrated Approach to the Study of Business Influence in Québec

The above analysis of the two major approaches to the study of influence and power makes it clear that it is not an easy task to develop a wholly satisfactory methodology. It should be obvious that neither of the approaches taken individually presents an adequate picture of the process of influence. An optimal methodology requires using both approaches to counterbalance the shortcomings and drawbacks of each. Such a combination is justified not only on theoretical grounds, i.e., because the approaches complement each other well, but also on the grounds of the difficulty of access to information about business influence.

The institutional or positional approach is vital because it yields some data on the decision-making environment and institutions. If the extent to which business shapes or dominates the decision-making environment can be determined, then a major advance can be made in evaluating business influence.

At a more concrete level, part I focusses on the institutional and strategic advantages of business in Québec. First, the strength and cohesion of the business system of power is examined, because operational and ideological unity are an essential prerequisite if a group is to be effective in the decision-making arena. A clear perception of business ideology is particularly useful in that it sheds light on the political objectives which business seeks to accomplish in the various issue-areas analysed in part II. Of course, a study of the political ideology of business also results in a clearer perception of what issues business considers important.

Two other important components of business power are the financial and organizational resources which it can use to exercise influence and its access to political decision-makers. These two components are the *sine qua non* of influence since, without them, a group cannot possibly be effective. In the study of access in chapter 5, the focus is not only on the degree of accessibility but also on who is involved in the process. The chapter examines, for example, the role of business associations as opposed to business elites, and the channels such as political parties, ministers, and civil servants used by business in its attempts to influence government.

Another important component of business power is its ability to penetrate and control other systems of power. An examination of the links between business and the media are particularly significant at this level. Finally business power is derived, albeit indirectly, from the comparative power positions of other socio-economic groups. If the groups potentially opposed to business, labour, for example, are weak, the result will be to facilitate the exercise of power by the economic elite. As Henry Ehrmann said in *La Politique du patronat en France*: "The weaknesses and the divisions within the forces which oppose capitalism have multiplied the possibilities for the success of initiatives coming from the business elite or its organizations."[18]

Thus, as the foregoing explanation has indicated, part I to some extent follows the methlogy used by Porter. There are important differences, however. Porter chose to emphasize the class origins, recruitment patterns, and socio-economic characteristics of the holders of institutional power in Canada. This study concentrates instead on the various structural factors which are conducive to business influence, including the access of business to government and the dependence of government on business. It also stresses the political ideology of business with the intention of determining, in the study of issue-areas, what decisions are important to business and how responsive the government is to the goals of business.

Rather than concentrating exclusively on decisions, part II examines business behaviour and political involvement with respect to issue-areas. Because of the difficulties and weaknesses involved in traditional decision-making analysis, which were mentioned previously, the approach was modified and broadened substantially.

In each of three issue-areas — economic development, labour and social policy, and language and education — the overall impact of governmental activity is examined, and an attempt is made to determine if the actions of government have conformed to the general expectations of business. Then, the degree of business satisfaction with general and specific policies in the issue-area is measured, and an evaluation is made of the extent of government control over business activities in each area. In addition, the pressure techniques used by the corporate elite in its attempts to influence government and the degree of success obtained by business with respect to specific legislation, are examined.

Hence, although a number of case studies of legislation are included — language legislation (Bills 63 and 22), education reform (Bill 71), the forest reform white paper, consumer legislation (Bill 45), and others — a wider framework is adopted, using issue areas as units of analysis.[19]

Moreover, in evaluating business power, both subjective and objective criteria are included. Business ideology and satisfaction towards governmental policy are without question subjective evaluations. On the other hand, in the study of the role of state economic institutions in Québec, more objective criteria are used. An attempt is made, for example, to determine if these institutions were created to give the state an independent power base in the economy or, rather, to play an exclusively supportive or complementary role to the private sector. Similarly, in the case of social and labour policy, governmental attitudes and reactions towards groups such as consumers and others who seek to challenge business power are analysed.

It should be re-emphasized at this point that the institutional or structural analysis contained in part I is an essential prerequisite to the study of issue-areas. The links between the two approaches are established not only in that specific governmental outputs are compared to business ideology and expectations, but also in that institutions which are dominated by corporations (the Conseil du Patronat and the General Council of Industry, for example) play a role in the policy-making process.

NOTES

(1) See, for example, W. L. Guttsman, *The British Political Elite* (New York: Basic Books, 1963), Porter, and Domhoff, *Who Rules America?* (Englewood Cliffs, Prentice-Hall, 1967).

(2) Porter, for example, maintained: "The definition of reality which provides the framework for making political decisions depends much on the social background and life experiences of politicians" (p. 391).

(3) Such interlocks are, of course, not limited to the economic and political systems. Media, education, labour, and other power systems are also frequently linked at the leadership level.

(4) Guttsman, p. 319.

(5) Mills, p. 9.

(6) Miliband stressed the class background of decision makers and policy makers".

(7) Miliband, p. 211.

(8) Indeed, Epstein claimed: "Today, the corporate leaders — particularly in the case of the managers of absentee-owned corporations — have largely withdrawn from local political affairs" (p. 237). Peter Bachrach and Morton Baratz, *Power and Poverty* (New York: Oxford University Press, 1970), further criticized Dahl's study by contending: "It is evident from Dahl's own account that the notables [economic] are in fact uninterested in two of the three key decisions he has chosen" (p. 12).

(9) Léon Dion, for example, in his study of educational reform in Quebec in the early sixties entitled *Le Bill 60 et la société québécoise* (Montreal: Editions HMH, 1967), concluded that the issue was a secondary one for business and that it had not attempted to wield any influence on the governmental legislation in that area.

(10) Bachrach and Baratz, pp. 47-48.

(11) Mankoff, p. 20.

(12) Bachrach and Baratz, p. 7.

(13) Ibid., p. 44.

(14) Ibid., pp. 8-9.

(15) Among others, see Jerry Cohen and Morton Mintz, *America Inc.* (New York: Dial Press, 1971).

(16) Epstein, p. 127.

(17) Miliband, p. 102.

(18) Henry Ehrmann, *La Politique du patronat en France* (Paris: Armand Colin, 1959), p. 398.

(19) Many policies were chosen for this study deliberately because they are generally believed to have been implemented against the interests of business. These include the creation since 1960 of a network of state economic institutions and the introduction of various social schemes, such as the Québec pension plan.

APPENDIX B

LIST OF 100 QUEBEC COMPANIES TO WHICH QUESTIONNAIRES WERE SENT, BY INDUSTRIAL SECTOR[a]

Mining

Iron Ore Co. of Canada
Asbestos Corp.
Sullivan Mining Group
Canadian Salt Co.

*Noranda Mines Ltd.
*Canadian Johns-Manville Co.
*Gaspé Copper Mines

Pulp and Paper, Wood Products

Canadian International Paper Co.
Consolidated-Bathurst Ltd.
Domtar Ltd.
Price Co. Ltd.

Anglo-Canadian Pulp and
  Paper Mills Ltd.
Rolland Paper Co.
MacLaren Power and Paper Co.

Transport Equipment

United Aircraft of Canada Ltd.
Canadair Ltd.
Bombardier Ltd.
Canadian Vickers Ltd.

Marine Industries Ltd.
M.L.W. Worthington Ltd.
*General Motors of Canada Ltd.
CAE Industries Ltd.

Chemical Products

Canadian Industries Ltd.
Du Pont of Canada Ltd.
National Drug and Chemical
Co. of Canada
Petrofina Canada Ltd.
Sherwin-Williams Co. of
Canada Ltd.

Genstar Ltd.
Monsanto Canada Ltd.
*Gulf Oil Canada Ltd.
*Shell Canada Ltd.
*Imperial Oil Ltd.
*Union Carbide Canada Ltd.

Metals and Mineral Products

Dominion Glass Co. Ltd.
Aluminum Co. of Canada
Reynolds Aluminum Co.
*Steel Co. of Canada

*Atlas Steel Co.
*Quebec Iron and Titanium Corp.
*Canadian Copper Refiners Ltd.

Food, Beverages, Tobacco

Ogilvie Flour Mills Ltd.
Distiller's Corporation
Seagram's Ltd.
Imasco of Canada Ltd.

*Molson Industries Ltd.
*Canada Packers Ltd.
*John Labatt Ltd.
Macdonald Tobacco Ltd.

(a) * indicates companies which have important operations in Québec but no head offices. All the other companies on the list have their head offices in Québec. The classification of industrial sectors is based on Statistics Canada. *Canada Year Book 1973* (Ottawa: Queen's Printer, 1973), p. 720.

Coopérative Agricole de Granby
Coopérative Fédérée du Québec
Atlantic Sugar Refineries Co. Ltd.

*Canada Dominion Sugar Ltd.
*Weston Bakeries Ltd.

Electrical Equipment

Northern Electric Co.
RCA Victor Co. Ltd.
Canadian Marconi Ltd.
Brinco Ltd.

Fleetwood Corp.
Robert Morse Corp.
*Canadian General Electric Co.
*Canadian Westinghouse Co.

Textiles

Dominion Textile Co. Ltd.
Celanese Canada Ltd.

Bruck Mills Ltd.
Wabasso Ltd.

Services (Utilities)

Bell Canada Ltd.
Canadian Pacific Ltd.
Canada Steamship Lines Ltd.

Québec Téléphone Ltée.
Anglo-Canadian Telephone Co.
Gaz Métropolitain Inc.

Other Manufacturing

Canron Ltd.
Dominion Bridge Co. Ltd.
Canada Cement Lafarge Ltd.
Miron Co. Ltd.

St. Lawrence Cement Co.
Domco Industries Ltd.
*Continental Can Co. of
    Canada Ltd.

Merchandising

Steinberg's Ltd.
Zeller's Ltd.

Dupuis Frères Ltd.

Financial: Banks, Trust Companies, Insurance Companies, Holding Companies

Bank of Montreal
Royal Bank of Canada
Banque Canadienne Nationale
Banque Provinciale du Canada
Montreal District and Savings Bank
Mercantile Bank of Canada
L'Assurance-Vie
Unions Régionales des Caisses
    Populaires Desjardins
Royal Trust Co.
Sun Life Assurance Co. of Canada

Trust Général du Canada
Montreal Trust Co.
Société Nationale de Fiducie
Prudential Assurance Co.
Guardian Trust Co.
Crédit Foncier Franco-Canadien
Industrial Life Insurance Co.
Power Corp. of Canada Ltd.
Warnock-Hersey International Ltd.
Canadian International Power Co.

APPENDIX C

QUESTIONNAIRE FOR BUSINESS LEADERS
IN THE PROVINCE OF QUEBEC

Note: The multiple-choice format will allow you to complete the questionnaire in a few minutes. If you wish to explain or qualify some of your responses, use the space provided below the question or the other side of the page.

IA Does the company with which you are involved operate mainly in
( ) Québec   ( ) Canada as a whole
( ) North America and/or internationally

B What is your position with the company?
( ) President or Vice-President ( ) Member of the board of
( ) Manager (division, plant,   directors
    sales, etc.)   ( ) Other (specify)

C Which industry group does your company belong to?
( ) Mining   ( ) Food, beverages, tobacco
( ) Pulp and paper, wood   ( ) Electrical equipment
    products   ( ) Chemical products
( ) Transport equipment   ( ) Textiles, leather, rubber,
( ) Metals and mineral products   clothing
( ) Merchandising (retail)   ( ) Banking, insurance, trusts,
( ) Service (gas, telephone,   holdings
    power companies, etc.)   ( ) Other (specify)

IIA By and large, do you think business associations (the Board of Trade, the Conseil du Patronat, the various trade associations, etc.) reflect the views of the business community?
( ) yes   ( ) no

B In your opinion, which business association has been most effective in dealing with the *Québec* government? [Choose one or rank numerically.]
( ) Board of Trade   ( ) Canadian Manufacturers
( ) Chamber of Commerce   Association
( ) Conseil du Patronat   ( ) Trade Association
                   ( ) Centre des Dirigeants
                     d'Entreprise

C Which business association(s) does your company belong to?
( ) Board of Trade   ( ) Canadian Manufacturers
( ) Chamber of Commerce   Association
( ) Conseil du Patronat   ( ) Trade Associations
                     ( ) Centre des Dirigeants
                     d'Entreprise

D When you confer with the Québec government, with whom do you usually deal? [Choose one or rank numerically.]
( ) Individual MP's ( ) Cabinet minister or PM
( ) Deputy ministers ( ) Committees of the National
( ) Party officials Assembly
( ) Other civil servants

E Who do you feel usually plays the most important role in molding a government decision? [Choose one or rank numerically.]
( ) Individual MP's ( ) Cabinet minister or PM
( ) Deputy ministers ( ) Committees of the National
( ) Party officials Assembly
( ) Other civil servants

F When an important business problem involving the government arises, do you have reasonably quick access to
top civil servants? ( ) yes ( ) no
cabinet ministers? ( ) yes ( ) no

G In most cases, what do you find is the most effective method of influencing the government? [Choose one.]
( ) Personal contact ( ) Acting through business
( ) Initiating public opinion associations
campaign ( ) Other (specify)

H How do you (or your company) usually approach the government? [Choose one.]
( ) Personal contact ( ) Acting through business
( ) Initiating public opinion associations
campaign ( ) Other (specify)

I Does your company* maintain a section or department (public relations, government relations, etc.) whose function it is to deal with the government?
( ) yes ( ) no

J Over the last two years, has your company* made oral or written representations to the Québec government concerning legislative issues?
( ) yes ( ) no

K By and large, were you satisfied with the reaction of the government?
( ) yes ( ) no

L In the last two years, has your (or your company's) opinion been solicited by a government official concerning policy questions?
( ) yes ( ) no

M By and large, do you think that there is agreement within the business community regarding the major social and political problems of the day?
( ) yes ( ) no

---

* Plant and other managers should interpret this to include the plant or divisional office, as well as the head office.

N   By and large, do you feel that business (and its associations) is effective in its attempts to influence government policy?
( ) yes   ( ) no

IIIA What is the most important problem facing business in Québec at present?
( ) Social unrest and labour   ( ) Unemployment and infla-
    problems   tion in North America
( ) The language question   ( ) Weakness of Québec
( ) Separatism   economic structure

B   Rank numerically what you think the most important objectives of business should be.
( ) Economic efficiency and   ( ) Growth of the economy
    profitability
( ) Social objectives   ( ) Other (specify)

C   What should be the main economic function of government? [Rank numerically.]
( ) Welfare and redistribution ( ) Creating the economic
    of income   conditions (tarifs, incen-
( ) Protecting the environment   tives, building of roads, etc.
    and controlling pollution   for the growth of the indus-
( ) Developing and operating   trial sector
    some public enterprises   ( ) Other (specify)

D   Who should take the initiative in resolving social problems in Québec?
( ) Business   ( ) Government

E   Who should take the initiative in making key economic choices for the society?
( ) Business   ( ) Government

F   Which group do you feel has the most influence on government policy in Québec? [Choose one or rank numerically.]
( ) Intellectuals   ( ) Labour groups
( ) Religious groups   ( ) Communications media
( ) Nationalist groups   ( ) Business groups
( ) Other (specify)

G   On the basis of your experience, do you feel that in recent years the boards of directors have lost some of their power and influence to the managers or executives?
( ) yes   ( ) no

H   Some critics have claimed that there are often serious differences of opinion between executive officers and the directors in a company. Do you think this criticism is founded?
( ) yes   ( ) no

I   Some companies have American directors. To your knowledge, are there significant differences of opinion between them and their Canadian colleagues?

( ) yes   ( ) no   ( ) Do not know

J   If Québec's political and social climate were more stable, would your company be likely to increase its investments?
( ) yes   ( ) no

K   Some companies have been criticized for advertising in newspapers opposed to the present political and economic system. Do you feel companies should refrain from advertising in such newspapers?
( ) yes   ( ) no

IVA   By and large, do you think the economic policies of the Bourassa government have been satisfactory?
( ) yes   ( ) no

B   By and large, which provincial party in Québec do you feel is most favourable to business?
( ) Liberal   ( ) Social Credit
( ) Unite Québec   ( ) Parti Québécois

C   Despite certain abuses in recent years, are you generally favourable to the principle of unemployment insurance?
( ) yes   ( ) no

D   Similarly, do you support the Québec pension plan?
( ) yes   ( ) no

E   Do you feel the government should give financial support to projects which involve management by workers? The latest "production cooperative" to receive support from the government was in Cabano.
( ) yes   ( ) no

F   In general, do you feel production cooperatives could be a threat to the smooth functioning of the economic system in Québec?
( ) yes   ( ) no

G   Do you think that the government should move to eliminate strikes in public and essential services?
( ) yes   ( ) no

H   Do you think the government was wise to put an end to the Common Front strike through Bill 19 (May 1972)?
( ) yes   ( ) no

I   Do you support the principle of freedom of linguistic choice as incorporated in Bill 63?
( ) yes   ( ) no

J   By and large, do you feel the present government's attitude towards the language question is satisfactory?
( ) yes   ( ) no

K   Do you agree with Bill 71 (legislation reorganizing school boards in Montréal)?
( ) yes   ( ) no

L Do you support separatism?
( ) yes   ( ) no

M Do you think the government was wise in deferring the forest reform legislation (abolition of the concession system of forest land tenure)?
( ) yes   ( ) no

N In retrospect, do you feel the "nationalization" of Hydro in Québec was a sound move, especially considering the large amounts of capital needed for developments like James Bay, for example?
( ) yes   ( ) no

O Generally speaking, do you feel that the recent economic initiatives of the Québec government (such as the incentives program and the Industrial Development Bank) have been beneficial to business?
( ) yes   ( ) no

P Do you approve the attitude of the Québec government during the FLQ crisis?
( ) yes   ( ) no

Q Some union leaders have suggested that government should fix prices in order to counteract the alleged power of monopolies in Canada. Do you agree?
( ) yes   ( ) no

R Some have also suggested that governments should intervene to regulate profits. Do you agree?
( ) yes   ( ) no

APPENDIX D

SOURCES
THE QUESTIONNAIRE

On January 19, 1973, 250 questionnaires were sent to business leaders in the province of Québec. The persons chosen were not intended to represent a random sample of Québec businessmen. The main target of the questionnaire was the senior level of major corporations and financial institutions. Thus 200 questionnaires were sent to the senior executives (i.e., presidents, vice-presidents, and plant managers) and directors of the 100 largest corporations operating in Québec. For reasons explained later, an additional 50 were sent to the senior executives of less important companies.

The first problem, of course, was to draw up a list of the 100 major companies in Québec. The information is not available to the public and indirect means had to be used to achieve reasonably satisfactory results.

In the case of manufacturing, resource, and utility companies, names for the list were chosen from three different sources. The first source was a list prepared by *Canadian Business* in 1970 which included the largest 200 corporations in Canada.[1]. It actually contained 260 corporations, since the companies were ranked separately by assets, sales, and net income. Fifty-seven of these companies were found to have head offices in Québec, mainly in Montréal. Then a list devised by the research department of the Parti Québécois was used[2]; it comprised 62 industrial corporations responsible for over 50% of industrial production in Québec and five companies in the service and transportation sectors. This list largely duplicated the *Canadian Business* list, but it did, however, contain the names of companies which, although without head offices in Québec, have substantial operations there. Thus 20 companies were added to the list, for a total of 77 in the manufacturing, resources, and utility sectors. As an added precaution, a check was made with the *Financial Post's* list of the 100 largest manufacturing companies in Canada — ranked on the basis of sales.[3] Thirty-nine of the 77 Québec companies were also on the *Financial Post* list. It is noteworthy that 51 companies were on at least two lists.

To complete the list, 20 financial institutions and three large Québec-based merchandisers were added. Seven of the 20 financial institutions, including five banks, were included in the *Financial Post's* "25 Biggest in Finance" ranked on the basis of assets.[4] The remainder were found in the *Financial Post's Financial Institutions Index*. By and large, the list is a reasonable approximation of the 100 major companies operating in Québec.[5] The overall importance of these companies in the economy of Québec is beyond question. In the case of manufacturing, resource, and utility companies, the 77 companies on the list are responsible for well over 50% of industrial production. In the case of financial institutions, the degree of concentration is even higher, considering the relatively small number of banks and trust companies operating in Canada.[6]

Once the list of companies was established, a list was prepared of 200 businessmen on a two-per-company basis. Senior executives, including the president and vice-presidents, were favoured as respondents because they were most likely to be in contact with the highest echelons of government and because, as will be argued later, they are the main decision-makers within the corporations. In the case of companies whose head offices are not located in Québec, questionnaires were sent to the plant or divisional managers since, as mentioned earlier, the focus is on the executives working in Québec. Also, although a complete view of business-government relations would have to include some information from those head offices elsewhere (in Canada, the United States, or Europe), there is evidence to suggest that these companies deal with the Québec government mainly from their offices or plants located in Québec. This point is examined in chapter 5.

In addition to the senior executives, a sample of 40 company directors was sent questionnaires. This group did not exhibit any significant behavioural differences from the senior executives. It is interesting to note, however, that it was difficult to find persons who were exclusively directors. Indeed, a large number of directors were also senior executives of the company or of other corporations. Moreover, since the primary activity of these directors is their executive function, the sample of 40 directors mainly comprised lawyers, retired senior executives, and large stockholders.

Some of the director's replies suggest that the role of the board of directors in company affairs is marginal. Even though most of the questions were of a non-technical and general nature, many directors did not feel they had a sufficient knowledge of company operations to deal with them.

In addition to sending 200 questionnaires to the major 100 companies, 50 questionnaires were sent to the senior executives of 50 Québec-based medium-sized companies.[7] As is shown in chapter 3, there were reasons to believe that significant behavioural differences between executives of large and medium-sized companies would appear. In fact, some interesting differences were found, particularly regarding access to governmental decision-makers. In view of the small size of this sample and the unsystematic sampling procedure, conclusions must remain tentative and hypothetical. Most of the questionnaire data used in the main body of this study come from respondents in the 100 major companies.

Another factor considered when the list of respondents was drawn up was the distinction between the French and English elements in the business elite in Québec. A proportion of two-thirds businessmen of English mother tongue to one-third of French mother tongue was chosen. Although reliable data do not exist, there is evidence to suggest that this overestimates somewhat the representation of Francophones in the top echelons of business. According to the research director of the Commission of Inquiry on the Status of the French Language in Québec, only 15% of the individuals working in Québec head offices in 1971 and earning $22,000 or more were of French mother tongue.[8] However, the over-representation of Francophones in the sample was necessary to give significance to any behavioural differences that might be found between the two language groups. Some significant differences in the overall responses of the French and English business leaders were found, but, the homogeneity of the business elite was the most striking characteristic.

When the 250 questionnaires were mailed, a covering letter was enclosed promising anonymity to the respondents and stating the purpose of the study as "an analysis of the channels of communication between business and government." Also included was a plain stamped envelope in which the questionnaire could be returned. To the extent possible, that is, as far as could be determined by their surnames, businessmen were sent questionnaires and accompanying letters in their mother tongue. A week later, all recipients were sent a reminder enjoining them to reply to the questionnaire if they had not already done so.

Table A indicates that the rate of return was quite satisfactory. Since 143 completed questionnaires were received, the return rate was 57.2%, which is considered to be high for this type of survey. Table A also indicates that the rate of return for each of several subgroups, French and English, large and secondary companies, senior executives and directors, was almost the same.

Interviews

Interviews were the most useful technique to examine some of the hypotheses and to verify some of the conclusions drawn from the questionnaire data. They also enabled me to delve deeper into the intricacies of business-government relations, specifically, the nature and extent of business access to government, the role of business associations, and the degree of business satisfaction with governmental policies. Unlike the questionnaire, the interviews were conducted without a statement that they would be anonymous.

During April and May 1973, 21 personal interviews were held with senior Québec businessmen.[9] Given that most of the major head offices are located in Montréal, the interviews were restricted to persons in this area. In general, businessmen were found to be accessible.

The interviews were aimed at three different groups of businessmen. The first and most important group was composed of senior executives of industrial or financial corporations. With two exceptions, among the 13 interviewed, I talked to someone at least at the vice-presidential level; and with one exception, I spoke to executives from among the 100 major companies. This group provided by far the most useful and productive set of interviews. The six interviews held at the levels of president and chairman of the board[10] were particularly informative and revealing for it became apparent that it is at these levels that most of the key contacts between government and industry take place.

Business associations constituted the second group of interviews.[11] Seven interviews were held at this level. The main objective

TABLE A
RATE OF RETURN OF QUESTIONNAIRES
BY QUÉBEC BUSINESS LEADERS

	Sent	Returned	Percentage rate of return
Total N	250	143	57.2
Large companies: Senior executives[a]	160	94	58.7
Directors	40	22	55.0
Secondary companies: Senior executives[a]	50	27	54.0
English	167	93	55.7
French	83	50	60.2

(a) Includes presidents, vice-presidents, and managers.

was to determine the role of business associations in governmental policy-formation. With the exception of the Conseil du Patronat, the associations appeared less informed than the senior executives, and their access to top governmental decision-makers seemed somewhat more limited. However, contacts with the associations produced some information concerning their activities as well as copies of various briefs they submitted to the Quebec government.

The third group consisted of two former senior executives now in retirement. They provided some comparative information on business-government relations in the nineteen-forties and fifties; specifically, if government relations had been significantly different during the Duplessis era from 1936 to 1959.

Business Publications

Business publications were another useful source of information. The *Financial Post*, a business weekly published in Toronto, and *Canadian Business*, a monthly published in Montréal by the Canadian Chamber of Commerce, were found to be particularly relevant, and their issues from 1960 to 1973 were scrutinized. In addition, selected issues of *Revue Commerce*, *Les Affaires*, and the *Canadian Investor*, all published in Montréal, were perused. Finally, a survey was made of the regular and occasional publications of the business associations.

Other Sources

Especially for the 1968 to 1973 period, I relied heavily on four daily Montreal-area newspapers: *Le Devoir*, *La Presse*, the *Montreal Gazette*, and the *Montreal Star*. For a viewpoint critical of business and the economic system, the writer relied on publications from the three major Quebec unions: the Confederation of National Trade Unions, Québec Federation of Labor, and the Québec Teachers Corporation. In addition, I consulted the weekly newspaper *Québec-Presse*, the monthly magazine *Last Post*, and selected issues of the magazines *Canadian Dimension*, *Socialisme*, and *Point de Mire*, all of which tended to be critical of corporations. Studies were also made of some publications put out by more or less permanent groups, including several studies by the Parti Québécois and by the Groupe de Recherche Économique.

NOTES

(1) *Canadian Business, Canada's 200 Largest Industrial Companies* (Montréal: *Canadian Business*, 1971).

(2) Parti Québécois, *Qui contrôle l'économie du Québec?* (Montréal: Éditions du Parti Québécois, 1972).

(3) Phyllis Morgan, "Canada's Top 100 Club Gets a Lot of New Members," *Financial Post*, 5 August 1972.

(4) *Financial Post*, "25 Biggest in Finance," 5 August 1972.

(5) The relative accuracy of the list was later confirmed by La Chambre de Commerce du District de Montréal. A study entitled *La Chambre de Commerce de Montréal and the Gendron Report* (Montréal: La Chambre de Commerce du District de Montréal, 1973) included a list of the top 100 Québec companies according to the number of employees (pp. 15-18). Seventy-one of the 100 companies appearing on this study's list were also on the Chambre de Commerce's list. The discrepancy can be explained in part by the fact that the Chambre's list contained eight state-owned companies. As further indication of the difficulty of preparing such a list, it should be noted that the Chambre described its own list as "tentative."

(6) See chapter 2 for a discussion of the financial importance of the major Canadian banks. Since no data on the local or provincial operations of financial institutions are available, it is impossible to compute precisely the assets of these institutions.

(7) It should be noted that it was not possible to use a systematic sampling procedure in this case. Any attempt would have been futile since many thousand companies exist and since no financial information is available for many of them, such as family-owned businesses and subsidiaries of foreign companies. Thus, the only criterion used for the definition and selection of medium-sized companies was that they not be part of the major 100 company group; the list included such well-known companies as Kruger Pulp and Paper Co., Uniroyal Ltd., Standard Brands Ltd., Sylvania Electric Ltd., and Allied Chemical Ltd.

(8) Pierre E. Laporte, "Les Dossiers économiques de la Commission Gendron," *Le Devoir*, 14 May 1974. The 15% French representation in senior executive posts in head offices is low if one considers that the persons of French mother tongue constitute approximately 80% of the total Québec population.

(9) See the bibliography for a list of the names and positions of the individuals interviewed.

(10) The chairman of the board seems a useful target for the interviewer. He has more time available, since he is less caught up in the day-to-day routine of the company; but, in many cases, he also appears to play on overall coordinative role in business-government relations.

(11) I interviewed representatives of the Conseil du Patronat; the Board of Trade, the Canadian Manufacturers' Association (Québec), the Centre des Dirigeants d'Entreprises, the Chambre de Commerce (Québec), and of two of the larger vertical associations — the Canadian Pulp and Paper Association and the Canadian Bankers' Association — which limit their membership to a single industrial sector.

BIBLIOGRAPHY

Books

Almond, Gabriel, and Powell, G. Bingham. *Comparative Politics: A Developmental Approach.* Boston: Little, Brown and Company, 1966.

Bachrach, Peter, and Baratz, Morton. *Power and Poverty.* New York: Oxford University Press, 1970.

Baltzell, E. Digby. *An American Business Aristocracy.* New York: Crowell-Collier Publishing Company, 1962.

Baran, Paul, and Sweezy, Paul. *Monopoly Capital.* New York: Monthly Review Press, 1966.

Bell, Roderick; Edwards, David; and Wagner, R. Harrison, eds. *Political Power: A Reader in Theory and Research.* New York: Free Press, 1968.

Bendix, Reinhard, and Lipset, Seymour M., eds. *Class, Status and Power: A Reader in Social Stratification.* Glencoe, Illinois: Free Press, 1953.

Berg, Ivar, ed. *The Business of America.* New York: Harcourt, Brace and World, 1960.

Berle, Adolf, and Means, G. *The Modern Corporation and Private Property.* New York: Macmillan Company, 1933.

Berle, Adolf. *Power.* Harcourt, Brace and World, 1967.

_____. *Power Without Property: A New Development in American Political Economy.* New York: Harcourt, Brace and World, 1959.

_____. *The Twentieth Century Capitalist Revolution.* New York: Harcourt, Brace and World, 1954.

Birnbaum, Norman. *The Crisis of Industrial Society.* New York: Oxford University Press, 1969.

Bottomore, T. B. *Elites and Society.* New York: Basic Books, 1965.

Braunthal, Gerard. *The Federation of German Industry in Politics.* Ithaca: Cornell University Press, 1965.

Brayman, Harold. *Corporate Management in a World of Politics.* New York: McGraw-Hill Book Company, 1967.

Broadbent, Edward. *The Liberal Rip-Off.* Toronto: New Press, 1970.

Burnham, James. *The Managerial Revolution.* New York and London: Putnam Press, 1942.

Campbell, Angus; Converse, Philip; Miller, Warren; and Stokes, Donald. *The American Voter.* New York: John Wiley and Sons, 1960.

Campbell, Angus; Gurin, Gerald; and Miller, Warren. *The Voter Decides.* Evanston, Illinois: Row, Peterson and Company, 1954.

Chambre de Commerce de la Province de Québec. *Québec: le coût de l'indépendance.* Montréal: Éditions du Jour, 1969.

_____. *Politiques d'action 73.* Montréal: Chambre de Commerce de la Province de Québec, 1973.

Champlin, John R., ed. *Power.* New York: Atheneum Press, 1971.

Cheit, Earl, ed. *The Business Establishment.* New York: John Wiley and Sons, 1964.

Child, John. *British Management Thought: A Critical Analysis.* London: Allen and Unwin, 1969.

_____. *The Business Enterprise in Modern Industrial Society.* London: Collier-MacMillan, 1968.

Confédération des Syndicats Nationaux. *L'Avenir des travailleurs de la forêt et du papier.* Montréal: Confédération des Syndicats Nationaux, 1972.

_____. *La Grande Tricherie.* Montréal: Confédération des Syndicats Nationaux, 1973.

_____. *Ne Comptons que sur nos propres moyens.* Montréal: Confédération des Syndicats Nationaux, 1972.

_____. *Qui a mis le cadenas dans Soma?* Montréal: Confédération des Syndicats Nationaux, 1972.

_____. *Aide-mémoire au document "Ne Comptons que sur nos propres moyens."* Montréal: Confédération des Syndicats Nationaux, 1972.

Conseil du Patronat du Québec. *Détruire le système actuel? C'est à y penser.* Montréal: Publications Les Affaires, 1972.

Dahl, Robert. *Pluralist Democracy in the United States: Conflict and Consent.* Chicago: Rand McNally and Company, 1967.

_____. *Who Governs?* New Haven: Yale University Press, 1961.

Devirieux, Claude Jean. *Manifeste pour la liberté de l'information.* Montréal: Éditions du Jour, 1971.

Dion, Léon. *Le Bill 60 et la société québécoise.* Montréal: Éditions HMH, 1967.

Domhoff, G. William. *The Higher Circles.* New York: Vintage Books, 1971.

_____. *Who Rules America?* Englewood Cliffs, New Jersey: Prentice-Hall, 1967.

Edinger, Lewis. *Political Leadership in Industrialized Societies.* New York: John Wiley and Sons, 1967.

_____. *Politics in Germany.* Boston: Little, Brown and Company, 1968.

Ehrmann, Henri W. *La Politique du patronat en France.* Paris: Armand Colin, 1959.

Epstein, Edwin M. *The Corporation in American Politics.* Englewood Cliffs, New Jersey: Prentice-Hall, 1969.

Favreau, Louis. *Les Travailleurs face au pouvoir.* Montréal: Centre de Formation Populaire, 1972.

Finer, S. E. *Private Industry and Political Power.* London: Pall Mall Company, 1958.

Florence, P. Sargent. *Ownership, Control and Success of Large Companies.* London: Sweet and Maxwell, 1962.

Fox, Paul and. *Politics: Canada.* 3rd ed. Toronto: McGraw-Hill of Canada, 1970.

Gagnon, Henri. *C'est quoi l'état?* Montréal: Caucus Ouvrier, 1972.

Galbraith, John K. *American Capitalism.* Boston: Houghton Mifflin Company, 1952.

_____. *The New Industrial State.* Boston: Houghton Mifflin Company, 1967.

Godin, Pierre. *L'Information-opium.* Montréal: Parti Pris, 1973.

Gordon, Robert. *Business Leadership in the Large Corporation.* Berkeley and Los Angeles: University of California Press, 1966.

Groupe de Recherche Économique. *Coopératives de production, usines populaires et pouvoir ouvrier.* Montréal: Éditions Québécoises, 1973.

223

Guttsman, W. L. *The British Political Elite.* New York: Basic Books, 1963.
Hacker, Andrew, ed. *The Corporation Take-Over.* New York: Anchor Books, 1965.
Heilbroner, Robert, ed. *In the Name of Profits.* New York: Warner Paperbacks, 1973.
Hunter, Floyd. *Community Power Structure.* Garden City: Anchor Books, 1963.
Kaplan, Abraham, and Lasswell, Harold D. *Power and Society.* New Haven: Yale University Press, 1950.
Kariel, H. S. *The Decline of American Pluralism.* Stanford: Stanford University Press, 1961.
Keller, Suzanne. *Beyond the Ruling Class.* New York: Random House, 1963.
Kelley, Stanley. *Professional Public Relations and Political Power.* Baltimore: Johns Hopkins Press, 1956.
Key, V.O. *Politics, Parties and Pressure Groups.* 5th ed. New York: Thomas Y. Crowell Company, 1964.
Kitzinger, U. W. *German Electoral Politics.* Oxford: Clarendon Press, 1960.
Kolko, Gabriel. *The Roots of American Foreign Policy: An Analysis of Power and Purpose.* Boston: Beacon Press, 1969.
—————. *Wealth and Power in America: An Analysis of Social Class and Income Distribution.* New York: Praeger Books, 1962.
La Palombara, Joseph. *Interest Groups in Italian Politics.* Princeton: Princeton University Press, 1964.
Laxer, James. *The Politics of the Continental Resources Deal.* Toronto: New Press, 1970.
Les Gens du Québec: St-Henri. Montréal: Éditions Québécoises, 1972.
Le Père Noël des capitalistes jérômiens. St. Jérôme: Presses du Cirque, 1972.
Levitt, Kari. *Silent Surrender.* Toronto: MacMillan Company of Canada, 1970.
Lipset, S. M., and Bendix, R. *Social Mobility in Industrial Society.* Berkeley and Los Angeles: University of California Press, 1966.
Lundberg, Ferdinand. *The Rich and the Super-Rich.* New York: Bantam Books, 1969.
Magdoff, Harry. *The Age of Imperialism.* New York: Monthly Review Press, 1969.
Mandel, Ernest. *Marxist Economic Theory.* London: Merlin Press 1962.
Marvick, Dwaine. *Political Decision-Makers.* New York: Free Press, 1961.
Mason, Edward. *The Corporation in Modern Society.* New York: Atheneum Press, 1970.
Mc Leod, J.T., and Rea, K.J., eds. *Business and Government in Canada.* Toronto: Methuen Publications Company, 1969.
McDougall, W. J., and Fogelberg. *Corporate Boards in Canada.* London, Ontario: University of Western Ontario, 1968.
Menshikov, S. *Millionaires and Managers.* Moscow: Progress Publishers, 1969.
Meynaud, Jean. *Les Groupes de pression en France.* Paris: Armand Colin, 1958.
—————. *Technocracy.* New York: Free Press, 1969.
Michels, R. *Political Parties.* Glencoe, Illinois: Free Press, 1958.
Miliband, Ralph. *The State in Capitalist Society.* London: Camelot Press, 1969.
Miller, D. C. *International Community Power Structures.* Bloomington: Indiana University Press, 1970.
Mills, C. Wright. *The Power Elite.* New York: Oxford University Press, 1956.
Mintz, Morton, and Cohen, Jerry. *America Inc.* New York: Dial Press, 1971.
Moore, W. E. *The Conduct of the Corporation.* New York: Random House, 1962.
—————. *The Impact of Industry.* Englewood Cliffs, New Jersey: Prentice-Hall, 1965.
Paltiel, K. Z. *Political Party Financing in Canada.* Toronto: McGraw-Hill of Canada, 1970.
Paquet, Gilles, ed. *The Multinational Firm and the Nation State.* Don Mills, Ontario: Collier-MacMillan Company, 1972.
Parti Québécois. *L'Affaire de la Baie James.* Montréal: Éditions du Parti Québécois, 1972.
—————. *La Question économique n'est pas un problème.* Montréal: Éditions du Parti Québécois, 1970.
—————. *Qui finance le Parti Québécois?* Montréal: Éditions du Parti Québécois, 1972.
Park, Frank, and Park, Libbie, *Anatomy of Big Business.* Toronto: James Lewis and Samuel, 1973.
Pelletier, Michel, and Vaillancourt, Yves. *Du Chômage à la libération.* Montréal: Éditions Québécoises, 1972.
Piotte, Jean-Marc, ed. *Québec occupé.* Montréal: Éditions Parti Pris, 1971.
Polsby, Nelson. *Community Power and Political Theory.* New Haven: Yale University Press, 1963.
Porter, John. *The Vertical Mosaic.* Toronto: University of Toronto Press, 1965.
Presthus, R. *Men at the Top.* New York: Oxford University Press, 1964.
Proulx, Jerôme. *Le Panier de crabes.* Montréal: Éditions Parti Pris, 1971.
Fédération des Travailleurs du Québec. *L'État, rouage de notre exploitation.* Montréal: Fédération des Travailleurs du Québec, 1971.
—————. *Un Seul front.* Montréal: Fédération des Travailleurs du Québec, 1971.
Quinn, Herbert. *The Union Nationale.* Toronto: University of Toronto Press, 1963.
Raynauld, André. *La Propriété des entreprises au Québec.* Montréal: Les Presses de l'Université de Montréal, 1974.
Reagan, M. D. *The Managerial Economy.* New York: Oxford University Press, 1963.
Richardson, Boyce. *Baie James: sans mobile légitime.* Montmagny, Québec: Éditions l'Étincelle, 1972.
Rose, Arnold. *The Power Structure.* New York: Oxford University Press, 1967.
Rose, Richard. *Politics in England.* Boston: Little, Brown and Company, 1964.
Rothschild, K. W. *Power in Economics.* Middlesex: Penguin Books, 1971.
Roussopoulos, Dimitrios, ed. *The Political Economy of the State.* Montréal: Black Rose Books, 1973.
Safarian, A. E. *Foreign Ownership of Canadian Industry.* Toronto: McGraw-Hill Company of Canada, 1966.
St-Germain, Maurice. *Une Économie à libérer.* Montréal: Les Presses de l'Université de Montréal, 1973.
Schonfield, Andrew. *Modern Capitalism.* London: Oxford University Press, 1965.
Schriftgiesser, Karl. *Business and Public Policy.* Englewood Cliffs, New Jersey: Prentice-Hall, 1967.
Société Pour Vaincre la Pollution: *La Baie James c'est grave, grave, grave.* Montréal: Éditions Québecoise, 1973.
Taylor, George, and Pierson, Frank, eds. *New Concepts in Wage Determination.* New York: McGraw-Hill, 1957.
Thorburn, Hugh G. *Party Politics in Canada.* Toronto: Prentice-Hall, 1963.
Tugendhat, Christopher. *The Multinationals.* New York: Random House, 1972.
Warner, W. L., and Abegglen, J. C. *Big Business Leaders in America.* New York: Harper and Row, 1955.

Weiner, Alex. *Pointe St. Charles: Preliminary Economic Report.* Montréal: Parallel Institute, 1970.
Weinstein, James. *The Corporate Ideal in the Liberal State: 1900 - 1918.* Boston: Beacon Press, 1969.

Academic Journals and Periodicals

Auf der Maur, Nick. "The May Revolt." *Last Post,* September 1970.
Bachrach, Peter. "Elite Consensus and Democracy." *Journal of Politics,* no. 24, 1962.
Brunelle, Richard, and Papineau, Pierre. "Le Gouvernement du capital." *Socialisme Québécois,* no. 23, 1972.
Byleveld, H. C. "The Fourth Circle." *Canadian Banker,* vol 79, July/August 1972.
Canadian Business. "Faribault on Federalism." February 1968.
_____. "Creative Tensions for Business." November 1970.
Centre des Dirigeants d'Entreprise. "Elements of a Strategy for Business." *Industrial Relations,* vol 26, December 1971.
Deaton, Rick. "The Fiscal Crisis of the State." *Our Generation,* vol 8, October 1972.
Diment, Paul. "How Your Trade Association Can Help You." *Canadian Business,* May 1963.
Fenton, Allan. "Economic Planning in Free Societies." *Canadian Business,* February 1963.
Giroux, Denis. "Le Scandale de l'amiante." *Magazine Maclean,* Janvier, 1975.
Goodman, Eileen. "How Boards of Directors Keep Abreast of the Changing Times in Which They Must Operate." *Canadian Business,* September 1960.
Greater Montreal Anti-Poverty Coordinating Commitee. "Statement of Principles: Mass Media." *Poor People's Paper,* vol 2, February 1973.
Greyser, Stephen A. "Business and Politics, 1964." *Harvard Business Review,* vol 42, September/October 1964.
_____. "Business and Politics, 1968." *Harvard Business Review,* vol. 46, November/December 1968.
Guay, Jacques. "Une Presse asservie." *Socialisme Québécois,* Juin 1969.
Gulf Oil Corporation. Advertisement in *Newswwek,* 25 June 1973.
Industrial Canada. Untitled article on language in Québec, February 1971.
Kowaluk, Lucia, and Rosenberg, Dorothy. "The James Bay Development Project: A Trojan Horse." *Our Generation,* vol. 9, January 1973.
Lefebvre, Jean-Paul. "État, s'abstenir." *Magazine Maclean,* November 1972.
Levin, A. E. "Social Responsibility is Everybody's Business." *Canadian Banker,* vol. 79, July/August 1972.
Mace, Myles L. "The President and the Board of Directors." *Harvard Business Review,* March/April 1972.
Mankoff, Milton. "Power in Advanced Capitalist Society: A Review Essay on Recent Elitist and Marxist Criticism of Pluralist Theory." *Social Problems,* vol. 17, 1970.
McLaughlin, W. Earle. "Pitfalls of Economic Planning." *Canadian Business,* June 1965.
Nelson, Louis B. "Les Monopoles de l'information." *Point de Mire,* 2 Avril 1971.
Nettl, J. P. "Consensus or Elite Domination: The Case of Business." *Political Studies,* vol. 13, February 1965.
Newman, Peter. "The Bankers." *Maclean's Magazine,* February and March 1972.
Newsweek. "Maurice Stans, the Moneyman," 4 June 1973.
Morris, Desmond. "Advertisers Don't Use Pressure." *Canadian Forum,* July 1969.
Paré, René. "Comment devenir maîtres chez nous." *Revue Commerce,* vol. 65, Mars 1963.
Prieur, Claude. "La Caisse de Dépôt et de Placement." *Forces,* no. 11, 1970.
Rajan, Vithal. "The Challenge of Youth." *Canadian Business,* September 1969.
Reboud, Louis. "Les Petites et moyennes entreprises." *Relations,* no. 309, Octobre 1966.
Research McGill. "The Conservative Independent Businessman — A Myth?" April 1973.
Resnick, Philip. "The Dynamics of Power in Canada." *Our Generation,* June 1968.
Ritchie, Ronald S. "Analysing Competitive Enterprise." *Canadian Business,* November 1972.
Ross, Marvin. "The Universities and Big Business." *Canadian Dimension,* March 1968.
Sinclair, Sonja. "Domtar: Case History of a Corporate Trend." *Canadian Business,* September 1964.
_____ Untitled article on the press. *Canadian Business,* January 1969.
Surette, Ralph; David, Robert; and Zannis, Mark. "The International Wolf Pack Moves in on the North." *Last Post,* vol. 3, May 1973.
Taylor, E. P. "A Canadian Industrialist's Four-Point Formula For Expansion." *Canadian Business,* November 1961.
Time. "The Disgrace of Campaign Financing." 23 October 1972.
Villarejo, Dan. "Stock Ownership and the Control of Corporations." *New University Thought,* vol. 2, Autumn 1961.
Vastel, Michel. "Mobilisation générale dans les ministères." *Les Affaires,* 23 Novembre 1970.
Watkins, Melville. "The Multinational Corporation in Canada." *Our Generation,* vol. 6, June 1969.

Briefs and Pamphlets

Association des Industries Forestières du Québec. *Mémoire sur l'exposé sur la politique forestière.* Québec: Juin 1972.
Canadian International Paper. *Brief to the Parliamentary Commission on Natural Resources and Lands and Forests.* Montréal: June 1972.
Canadian Manufacturers' Association. *An Industrial Policy for Quebec,* Montréal: 1 August 1972.
_____. *CMA in Quebec.* Montréal: 1972.

——————. *Pre-Budget Submission to the Government of Canada.* Circular no. 4262. Toronto: 30 March 1972.

——————. *The First Hundred Years.* Montréal: 1971.

——————. *What It Is and What It Does.* Montréal: 1972.

Centre des Dirigeants d'Entreprise. *Fonction de l'entreprise et regroupement des cadres.* Montréal: Novembre 1970.

——————. *Structures et fonctionnement.* Montréal: 1972.

Chambre de Commerce de la Province de Québec. *Bulletin on Provincial Legislation,* vol. 10, no. 1. Montréal: 7 April 1972.

——————. *Bulletin on Provincial Legislation,* vol. 10, no. 4. Montréal: 10 July 1972.

——————. *Faits et tendances,* vol. 25, no. 4. Montréal: Mars 1973.

——————. *La Législation provinciale,* vol. 10, no. 2. Montréal: 17 avril 1972.

——————. *La Législation provinciale,* vol. 10, no. 3. Montréal: 1 Mai 1972.

——————. *La Législation provinciale,* vol. 10, no. 5. Montréal: 3 Août 1972.

——————. *La Législation provinciale,* vol. 11, nos. 1-4. Montréal: 1973.

——————. *List of Technical and Financial Aids from Federal and Provincial Governments to Commerce and Industry in Quebec.* Montréal: June 1972.

——————. *Mémoire annuel,* (soumis au Conseil des Ministres du Gouvernement du Québec). Montréal: Juin 1972.

Chambre de Commerce du Canada. *Le Profit: C'est quoi?* Montréal: 1972.

——————. *L'Économie et vous.* Montréal: 1969.

Chambre de Commerce du District de Montréal. *La Chambre de Commerce and the Gendron Report.* Montréal: 1973.

Conseil des Producteurs des Pâtes et Papiers du Québec. *La Capacité de concurrence de l'Industrie des Pâtes et Papiers du Québec.* Montréal: 1972.

Conseil du Patronat du Québec. *Bulletin d'information.* Montréal: Septembre 1974.

General Council of Industry. *The General Council of Industry.* Montréal: February 1971.

James Bay Development Corporation. Press release. Montréal: 16 July 1972.

Montreal Board of Trade. *Memoir to the Standing Parliamentary Committee on Education.* Montréal: 26 January 1970.

Centrale de l'Enseignement du Québec. *Mémoire sur le projet de loi de code des loyers présenté à la commission parlementaire permanente de la justice.* Montréal: Août 1972.

Reports and Public Documents

Bélanger, Laurent. *Évolution du patronat et ses répercussions sur les attitudes et pratiques patronales dans la province de Québec.* Ottawa: Conseil Privé: Janvier 1970.

Bureau de la Statistique du Québec. *Coopérative du Québec: statistiques financières.* Québec: Éditeur Officiel du Québec, 1970.

Canadian Business. Canada's 200 Largest Industrial Companies. Montréal: 1971.

Chambre de Commerce du District de Montréal. *Rapport de son 84e exercice annuel 1970 - 1971.* Montréal: 1971.

Committee On Election Expenses. *Studies in Canadian Party Finance.* Ottawa: Queen's Printer, 1966.

Conseil du Patronat du Québec. *Rapport annuel: 1971 - 1972.* Montréal: 1972.

Department of Consumer and Corporate Affairs. *Bulletin: Canada Corporations Act,* vol. 1. Ottawa: Queen's Printer, November 1971.

Dominion Bureau of Statistics. *Income Distribution 1951 - 1965,* no. 13-529. Ottawa: Queen's Printer, June 1969.

Executive Council of Quebec. *Order in Council,* no. 609. Québec: Éditeur Officiel du Québec, 17 February 1971.

Girard, Jacques. *Géographie de l'industrie manufacturière au Québec.* Québec: Éditeur Officiel du Québec, 1970.

Goldenberg, H. Carl. *Report of the Royal Commission on Metropolitan Toronto.* Toronto: Queen's Printer, June 1965.

Government of Quebec Statutes. *Bill 50.* Éditeur Officiel du Québec, 14 July 1971.

Heidrick and Struggles Inc. *Profile of a Canadian President.* Chicago: 1973.

Hydro-Québec. *Annual Report: 1973.* Montréal: 1973.

Industrial Documentation. Montréal: Gaby Productions, November 1971.

James Bay Development Corporation. *Development of the James Bay: Initial Phase.* Montréal: 1971.

March, R. R. *Public Opinion and Industrial Relations.* Ottawa: Privy Council Office, July 1968.

Montreal Board of Trade. *Annual Report: 1970 - 1971.* Montréal: 1971.

Power Corporation of Canada. *Annual Report: 1971.* Montréal: 1972.

Québec Department of Industry and Commerce. *1972 Annual Report.* Québec: Éditeur Officiel du Québec, 1973.

Québec Deposit and Investment Fund. *Annual Report: 1970 - 1971.* Québec: Éditeur Officiel du Québec, 1971.

——————. *Annual Report: 1971 - 1972.* Québec: Éditeur Officiel du Québec, 1972.

——————. *Annual Report: 1972 - 1973.* Québec: Éditeur Officiel du Québec, 1973.

Québec Mining Exploration Company. *Annual Report 1970 - 1971.* Québec: 1971.

Québec National Assembly. *National Assembly Debates,* ch. 14. Québec: Éditeur Officiel du Québec, 1968.

——————. *National Assembly Debates.* Québec: Éditeur Officiel du Québec, May 1965.

——————. *Bill 20.* Québec: Éditeur Officiel du Québec, 1971.

——————. *Bill 2: An Act Respecting the Lease of Things.* Québec: Éditeur Officiel du Québec, 1973.

Québec Petroleum Operations Company. *Annual Report: 1970 - 1971.* Québec: 1971.

Québecor Inc. *1972 Annual Report.* Montréal: 1973.

Government of Québec. *Rapport de la Commission d'Enquête sur la Santé et le Bien-être social.* Québec: Éditeur Officiel du Québec.

Riopel, Louis, and Takacsy, Nicolas. *Towards Economic Objectives and a Development Strategy for Quebec.* Montréal: General Council of Industry, 19 May 1970.

Senate Committee on Mass Media. *Report on Mass Media.* Ottawa: Queen's Printer, 1970.

Statistics Canada. *Canada Year Book 1973.* Ottawa: Queen's Printer, 1973.

Task Force on the Structure of Canadian Industry. *Foreign Ownership and the Structure of Canadian Industry.* Ottawa: Queen's Printer, 1968.

Newspapers
All Issues

Financial Post: 1960 — September 1974.
Le Devoir: 1968 — Septembre 1974.
Québec-Presse: 1968 — Septembre 1974.

Selected Issues

Le Devoir: 1960 — 1968.
Le Jour: Février 1974 — Septembre 1974.
Le Soleil: 1960 — Septembre 1974.
Montreal Gazette: 1960 — 1974.
Montréal-Matin: 1960 — Septembre 1974.
Montreal Star: 1960 — September 1974.
La Presse: 1960 — Septembre 1974.

Miscellaneous

Bennet, Arnold. "Daoust Says Labor is Now Militant." *McGill Daily,* 3 February 1972.

Delaney, Paul. "Cox Tells Papers to Endorse Nixon." *New York Times,* 29 October 1972.

Financial Times. "Perspectives on Québec," 19 November 1973.

Hains, E. Untitled editorial on Bill 63. *Le Progrès de Magog,* 12 November 1969.

Le Nouvelliste. "Le Bill 63," 29 Octobre 1969.

Shepherd, Harvey. "Montréal Chamber Undergoes Fundamental Changes in Role." *Toronto Globe and Mail,* 28 June 1972.

Stewart, Walter. "$75 Million Deal Helps ITT Exploit Québec Forests." *Toronto Star,* 8 May 1972.

Tremblay, L. Untitled editorial on Bill 63. *La Voix d'Alma,* 5 November 1969.

Newman, Roger. "Flight of Capital, Company Exodus, Project Changes Point to Québec Separatism Fear," *Toronto Globe and Mail,* 6 October 1967.

Unpublished Material

Bélanger, Laurent. "Occupational Mobility of French- and English- Canadian Business Leaders in the Province of Québec." Ph. D. dissertation, Michigan State University, 1967.

Bougie, Yves. "La Presse écrite au Québec: objet et agent de pression." Paper presented to Professor Jean Meynaud's course on pressure groups at the Université de Montréal, 15 December 1969.

Brunelle, Jean. "Business in Québec: Bystander or Partner in Development." Speech given at a meeting of the Centre des Dirigeants d'Entreprise, 7 December 1972.

Charest-Wallot, Candide. "La Soquem sert-elle les intérêts de la société québécoise?" Paper presented to Professor Pierre Fournier's M.A. seminar on Québec politics, Université du Québec à Montréal, April 1974.

Counsell, K. W, manager of public relations of the Canadian Manufacturers' Association. Letter to the author, 14 April 1972.

Dion, Léon. "L'Entreprise et la société québécoise." Speech given at a meeting of the Conseil du Patronat du Québec, Montreal, 26 May 1972.

Ethier, Diane. "L'Histoire de Sogefor." Paper presented to Professor Pierre Fournier's M.A. seminar on Québec politics at the Université du Québec à Montréal, April 1974.

Fantus Company. "Industrial Development in Québec." Report prepared for the department of industry and commerce, government of Québec, May 1972.

Finlayson, S. K. "Social Responsibilities of International Business." Speech given at meeting of the Canada/United Kingdom Chamber of Commerce, London, 2 May 1973.

Fournier, Pierre, "The Politics of School Reorganization in Montreal." M.A. dissertation, McGill University, Montreal, May 1971.

Hart, G. Arnold. Speech at Emanu-El Temple, Montreal, 25 January 1971.

Jobin, Carol. "La Nationalisation de l'électricité au Québec en 1962." M.A. dissertation, Université du Québec à Montréal, August 1974.

Mhun, H. "L'Entreprise au service de la société." Speech given at conference organized by the Conseil du Patronat du Québec, 26 May 1972.

Monière, Denis. "Analyse de l'idéologie de la Chambre de Commerce du Québec." Paper presented to Professor André Vachet's course on modern political thought, University of Ottawa, 15 January 1969.

Perrault, Charles. "The Business-Bureaucracy Interface." Speech to the 17th annual business conference, University of Western Ontario, London, Ontario, 1 June 1973.

Powell, R. E. Letter to Maurice Duplessis. 4 March 1946.

Raynauld, André. "La Propriété et la performance des entreprises au Québec." Report prepared for the Royal Commission on Bilingualism and Biculturalism, May 1967.

Reynolds, Jean. "La Société de Développement Industriel du Québec." Paper presented to Professor Pierre Fournier's M.A. seminar on Quebec politics, Université du Québec à Montréal, April 1974.

Taisne, François. "Sidbec." Paper presented to Professor Pierre Fournier's M.A. seminar on Québec politics, Université du Québec à Montréal, April 1974.

Tétrault, Paul. Interview with Paul Paré, president of Imasco. 13 May 1970.

Tremblay, Arthur. "Arrangements administratifs relatifs aux objets et modalités de communications entre l'Office de Planification et Développement du Québec et le Conseil de Planification et du Développement du Québec." Letter to Pierre Côté, president of the Québec Planning and Development Council, 14 May 1971.

List of Interviews with Businessmen Residing in Québec and Dates of Interviews

J. Brunelle, President, Centre des Dirigeants d'Entreprise, 7 May 1973.

T. L. Brock, Corporate Secretary, Aluminum Company of Canada, 16 May 1973.

N. A. Dann, Vice-President (Public Relations), Imasco, 4 May 1973.

J. M. Ethier, Director of Labour Relations, Canadian Manufacturers' Association, 14 May 1973.

W. L. Forster, Former President, Genstar, 1 May 1973.

E.L. Hamilton; President, Canadian Industries Limited, member of the General Council of Industry, 25 May 1973.

C. F. Harrington, Chairman of the Board and Chief Executive Officer, Royal Trust, member of the General Council of Industry, 18 May 1973.

G. M. Hobart, Former President, Consolidated Paper Company (now Consolidated-Bathurst), 10 May 1973.

G. W. Hodgson, Deputy Chairman and Former President, Montreal Trust, 10 May 1973.

R. A. Irwin, Chairman of the Board and Chief Executive Officer, Consolidated-Bathurst, 4 May 1973.

T. Kennedy, President, Canada Cement Lafarge, member of the General Council of Industry and the Board of Governors of the Conseil du Patronat, 30 May 1973.

S. A. Kerr, Vice-President (Corporate Development), Domtar, 17 May 1973.

G. Lachance, General Manager (Personnel and Development), Mercantile Bank of Canada, 15 May 1973.

J.-P. Létourneau, Executive Vice-President, La Chambre de Commerce de la Province de Québec, 16 May 1973.

V. O. Marquez, Chairman of the Board and Chief Executive Officer, Northern Electric, 30 April 1973.

M. Massé, Executive Vice-President, Bank of Montreal, 2 May 1973.

W. E. McLaughlin, Chairman of the Board and President, Royal Bank of Canada, member of the General Council of Industry, 9 May 1973.

G. Minnes, Executive Secretary, Canadian Pulp and Paper Association, 9 May 1973.

C. Perrault, President, Conseil du Patronat du Québec, 22 May 1973.

J. H. Perry, Executive Director, Canadian Bankers' Association, 9 May 1973.

E. L. Tracey, General Manager, Montreal Board of Trade, 18 May 1973.

THINGS WHICH
ARE DONE
IN SECRET

by Marlene Dixon

**more
books
from**

**BLACK
ROSE
BOOKS**

**write for a
free
catalogue**

This explosive book deals with the attempts to purge Dr. Pauline Vaillancourt from the Political Science Department, and Dr. Marlene Dixon from the Sociology Department of McGill University in Montréal. Both efforts failed "technically". Filled with confidential documents to support the thesis proposed by Prof. Dixon on how department and administrative politics function, this book is a case history.

At the same time the book is a critical study of mainstream sociology, and the university. It is also a handbook for those academics and students who want to understand how power politics operate inside the academy.

"...Many of the professional sociologists are rather defensive about their work, often because they are not sure of its validity or relevance. This has lead to expectations of conformity and a disinclination to take risks. Add to this the political and budgetary pressures a university faces, one can easily understand this predilection of conformity. But sociologists continue to insist they really would welcome true intellectual excellence. But they must recognize that such excellence comes from the turbulence of involvement refined by thought."

Prof. Franz Schurmann to Profs. Wallerstein and Ehrensaft, November. 10, 1971, quoted from *Things Which Are Done In Secret.*

280 pages / Hardcover $12.95
ISBN: 0-919618-68-5
Contains: Canadian Shared Cataloguing in Publication Data

BLACK ROSE BOOKS, No. E 24

ESSAYS ON MARX'S THEORY OF VALUE
by Isaak Illich Rubin

According to the prevailing theories of economists, economics has replaced political economy, and economics deals with scarcity, prices, and resource allocation. In the definition of Paul Samuelson, "economics — or political economy, as it used to be called... is the study of how men and society *choose,* with or without the use of money, to employ *scarce* productive resources, which could have alternative uses, to produce various commodities over time and distribute them for consumption, now and in the future, among various people and groups in society."

If economics is indeed merely a new name for political economy, and if the subject matter which was once covered under the heading of political economy is now covered by economics, then economics has replaced political economy. However, if the subject matter of political economy is not the same as that of economics, then the "replacement" of political economy is actually an omission of a field of knowledge. If economics answers different questions from those raised by political economy, and if the omitted questions refer to the form and the quality of human life within the dominant social-economic system, then this omission can be called a "great evasion".

Economic theorist and historian I. I. Rubin suggested a definition of political economy which has nothing in common with the definition of economics quoted above. According to Rubin, "Political economy deals with human working activity, not from the standpoint of its technical methods and instruments of labor, but from the standpoint of its social form. It deals with *production relations* which are established among people in the process of production." In terms of this definition, political economy is not the study of prices or of scarce resources; it is a study of social relations, a study of culture.

Rubin's book was first published in the Soviet Union, and was never re-issued after 1928. This is the first and only English edition. The translators are Milos Samardzija and Fredy Perlman.

275 pages / Hardcover $10.95 / Paperback $3.95
ISBN: 0-919618-11-1 / ISBN: 0-919618-18-9

BLACK ROSE BOOKS No. D 13

THE BITTER THIRTIES IN QUEBEC

by Evelyn Dumas
translated by
Arnold Bennett

Evelyn Dumas is one of Québec's best known journalists. She pioneered reporting on the labour movement while working for *Le Devoir*, was an Associate Editor with the *Montreal Star* and now works with *Le Jour*.

With this her first book, she has undertaken to prove incorrect the notion previously held widely that the labour movement militancy associated with modern Québec was a feature born in the post-World War 11 period. By examining, through the tradition of oral history, several strikes in the thirties and forties in transportation, textiles and other important industries, and by recording the impressions and feelings of some of the surviving strikers whether leaders or rank-in-file militants, she captures the mood of the period. The book is a fine example of social history, and in fact rewrites the history of a whole period.

"The publisher... (has) done (us) a service by providing... this version of Evelyn Dumas' history. ... (The author), in bridging this... gag has provided an easy... introduction to a period of Quebec labour history... (which) is helpful background for... the equally bitter, seventies."

The Labour Gazette

"...The Bitter Thirties... can be as enjoyable reading as a good adventure story, albeit with far more substance.

...Thoroughly factual, yet written in lively journalistic style."

The Globe and Mail

175 pages / Hardcover $10.95 / Paperback $3.95
ISBN: 0-919618-53-7 / ISBN: 0-919618-54-5

Contains: Canadian Shared Cataloguing in Publication Data

BLACK ROSE BOOKS No. E 19

THE POLITICAL ECONOMY OF THE STATE
Canada/Québec/USA

edited by
Dimitrios
Roussopoulos

The book contains a series of major essays examining the State. These include *"The Fiscal Crisis of the State in Canada"* by Rick Deaton, *"The Growth of the State in Québec"* by B. Roy Lemoine, *"Authority and the State"* by Graeme Nicholson, *"Revolution in the Metropolis"* by Margaret and John Rowntree, and *"The State as socializer"* by Lorne Huston.

The Political Economy of the State begins an important new approach to the study of government and society which political science has ignored for a very long time.

"This book should be mandatory reading... it is a valuable contribution to literature on the modern state... *The Political Economy of the State* does a workmanlike and effective job in its demolition of the myth of the state as a benevolent force in society..."
— Bob Bettson, *The Varsity*

200 pages with charts | Hardcover $10.95 | Paperback $2.95
    ISBN: 0-919618-02 | ISBN: 0-919618-01-4

Chosen for *Canadian Basic Books*

BLACK ROSE BOOKS No. D 8

DURRUTI:
THE PEOPLE
ARMED

by *Abel Paz*

translated by
Nancy MacDonald

Forty years of fighting, of exile, of jailings, of
living underground, of strikes, and of insurrection,
Buenaventura Durruti, the legendary Spanish revolutionary (1896-1936) lived many lives.

Uncompromising anarchist, intransigent revolutionary, he travelled a long road from rebellious
young worker to the man who refused all bureau-
cratic positions, honours, awards, and who at death
was mourned by millions of women and men. Durruti
believed and lived his belief that revolution and
freedom were inseparable.

This book is the story of Durruti and also a history
of the Spanish revolution. It is more than theoretical,
it is a rich and passionate documentary, of a man
and an epoch.

551 pages | Hardcover $12.95 | Paperback $4.95
ISBN: 0-919618-73-1 / ISBN: 0-919618-74-X

Contains: Canadian Shared Cataloguing in Publication Data

BLACK ROSE BOOKS No. F 28

WORKING IN CANADA

edited by
Walter Johnson

Walter Johnson has been working since he was seventeen years of age. During the last seven years he
was working on the assembly-line at General Motors,
in St. Therese. He came to certain conclusions about
the workplace and Canadian society. Having received
a Canada Council to put together a book of his experience, he sought out other young workers to see
whether there was some commonality to his feelings
and thoughts.

Working in Canada is a collection of experiences
written or interviews of young working people about
what they do and feel on a day to day basis and what
they think needs to be done to change their condition
and that of other working people.

Walter Johnson has had articles published in
Canadian Forum, and *Our Generation.*

225 pages | Hardcover $10.95 | Paperback $3.95
ISBN: 0-919618-64-2 / ISBN: 0-919618-63-4

Contains: Canadian Shared Cataloguing in Publication Data

BLACK ROSE BOOKS No E 25

THE STATE

by Franz Oppenheimer

Introduction by C. Hamilton

"Oppenheimer took the best insights from the conflict school in Europe in his time and applied them, with much imagination and learning, to his study of the political state. I have long regarded it as a classic and welcome its fresh publication. I hope it will be read widely by the generation of social scientists, too many of whom have become nurtured by consensus theories of the state."

— Robert Nisbet

"Oppenheimer's *The State* merits the status of a classic of sociology and political science. Although his theory was linked to rather naive proposals for reform, and although some historical details may be inexact, its broad thesis remains true: namely that large-scale systems of power have originated from conquest and functioned as means of exploitation. The book helps us to realize how recent, precious and fragile are the ideas and institutions of democracy and welfare state."

— Stanislav Andreski

122 pages / Paperback $3.95
ISBN: 0-919618-59-6

BLACK ROSE BOOKS No. E 21

THE STATE: Its Historic Role
BY PETER KROPOTKIN

This anarchist classic, long out of print and still in great demand was first to be delivered as a lecture in Paris in March 1896. Kropotkin however, when he landed in France on his way from London was refused entry. The book develops the thesis of how the State grew over decades into its modern form. It deals in particular with the conflict between the free cities in the Middle Ages and the growing power of central states.

014 / 56 pages **Paperback $1.75**

ESSAYS ON IMPERIALISM
BY MICHAEL BARRAT BROWN

There are four major essays, "A Critique of Marxist Theories of Imperialism", "The Stages of Imperialism", "Imperialism and Working Class Interests in the Developed Countries", and "The E.E.C. and Neo-Colonialism in Africa". The essays are a major intervention into the debate between Sweezy, Jalee, Magdoff and Mandel, among others, as to whether capitalist countries will remain united in their joint efforts to exploit the Third World, or split into warring competitive factions. Barrat Brown argues that both views have limitations.

011 / 163 pages **SBN 85124 024 0**
Hardcover $9.95

Printed by
the workers of
Éditions Marquis, Montmagny, Québec,
for
Black Rose Books LTd.